IMMIGRATION IN NEW YORK

IMMIGRANT CLASSIFICATIONS FOR QUICK REFERENCE

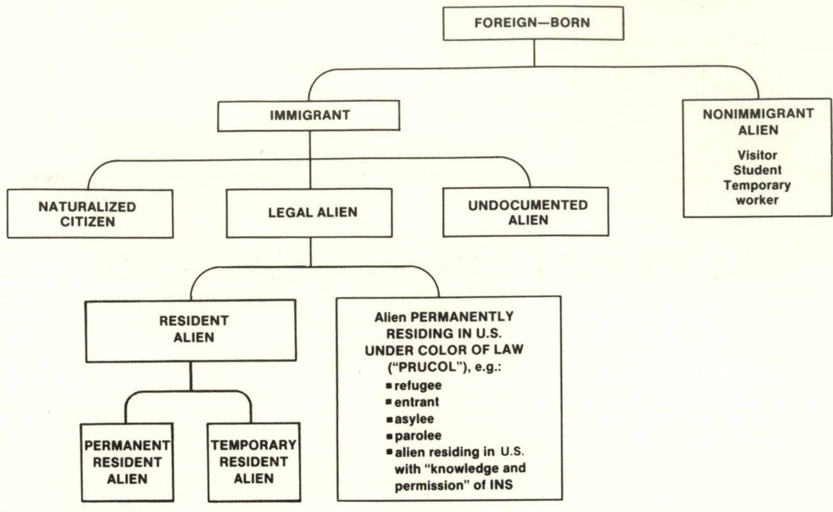

DEFINITIONS

Alien: A person present in this country who is not a U.S. citizen.

Asylee: An alien who has received permission to remain in the United States because of a "well-founded fear" of persecution should he or she return home. Differs from refugee in that asylee applies from U.S. soil rather than from abroad.

Entrant: A unique immigration status created for the Cubans and Haitians who entered the United States illegally in a massive boat lift to Florida in 1980.

Foreign-Born: Born abroad of parents who are not U.S. citizens.

Green Card Holder: Colloquial term for permanent resident alien.

Immigrant: A foreign-born person who intends to live permanently in the United States. Under immigration law, only foreign-born persons with authorization to live here can be considered immigrants, but in this book we use the term to cover anyone who intends to stay.

Legal Alien: An alien with authorization to live in the United States.

Naturalized Citizen: An immigrant who has become a U.S. citizen.

Nonimmigrant Alien: An alien who is authorized to be in the United States only temporarily, for a specific purpose and a fixed length of time.

Parolee: An alien who is authorized to live in the United States temporarily, until the conditions supporting his or her parole no longer exist.

Permanent Resident Alien: An immigrant who is authorized to live and work in the United States, and eventually to apply for citizenship.

PRUCOL: An alien who is viewed as "permanently residing in the United States under color of law," such as a refugee or asylee, and who is therefore eligible for certain public benefits.

Refugee: An alien who has received permission to enter the United States because of a "well-founded fear" of persecution should he or she return home. Differs from an asylee in that a refugee applies for admission from abroad, an asylee from U.S. soil.

Student: An alien authorized to study in the United States for a limited period of time, after which he or she must return home.

Temporary Resident Alien: An alien who is authorized to live and work temporarily in the United States; a classification created by the Simpson-Rodino Act of 1986.

Temporary Worker: An alien who is authorized to enter the United States to perform a temporary job.

Undocumented Alien: A foreign national who entered the United States without authorization, or whose visa has expired.

Visitor: An alien who has authorization to be in the United States temporarily, on business or for pleasure.

Source: New York City Department of City Planning

IMMIGRATION IN NEW YORK

ELIZABETH BOGEN

PRAEGER

New York
Westport, Connecticut
London

Library of Congress Cataloging-in-Publication Data

Bogen, Elizabeth.
Immigration in New York.

Bibliography: p.
Includes index.
1. New York (N.Y.)—Emigration and immigration.
2. Immigrants—New York (N.Y.) I. Title.
JV7048.B63 1987 325.747'1 87–15073
ISBN 0–275–92199–9 (alk. paper)

Library of Congress Catalog Card Number: 87–15073
ISBN: 0–275–92199–9

First Published in 1987

September 6, 1989

Praeger Publishers, One Madison Avenue, New York, NY 10010
A division of Greenwood Press, Inc.

Printed in the United States of America

The paper used in this book complies with the Permanent Paper Standard issued by the National Information Standards Organization (Z39.48–1984).

10 9 8 7 6 5 4 3 2

Contents

List of Tables

List of Figures

Preface

New York is the quintessential city of immigrants. It takes its unique character from the millions of people who have come, are coming, and will continue to come to our city in order to make their homes here. New York welcomes its newcomers and their infusions of new life, new ideas, and new energy.

It made good sense to me when the Department of City Planning undertook the research that was to become this book. I wanted the city to learn as much as it could about its new residents: who they are, how they live, what they give us, and what we give them.

It also made good sense to establish an office that would devote itself full-time to thinking and writing about immigrant issues, and pulling together the efforts of all the city agencies whose clients include immigrants. I set up such an office at the City Planning Department in July 1984, building on the expertise that department had been developing in immigration data and research.

It is a source of satisfaction to me that in its three years of operation, the Office of Immigrant Affairs has been able not only to complete this book but also to produce a directory of immigrant service agencies and a pamphlet explaining the complexities of public entitlement criteria for immigrant applicants. Furthermore, this office has served the city well as a source of information and policy analysis on legislation and service issues, and it has been a coordinating body for agencies serving immigrants, both inside and outside city government.

As far as I know, New York City is the only jurisdiction in the country that has established an office to deal with the needs of *all* its immigrants, not just refugees, naturalized citizens, permanent resident aliens, or undocumented aliens. We look at the spectrum of immigrants and the spectrum of their needs.

Also as far as I know, New York City is the only jurisdiction that has undertaken an analysis of its services to immigrants, as we have done in this book. We weren't happy with everything we learned about ourselves as service providers, and we hadn't expected to be. Instead we were enlightened, sensitized, and reinforced in our desire to provide the best possible service to our foreign-born. I believe we have succeeded in bringing a larger view to immigration issues than they generally get in the national debate.

Last year the nation celebrated the hundredth birthday of our most loved and respected symbol—Lady Liberty, who keeps a welcoming watch in New York Harbor. Her torch is the light of knowledge, and knowledge is the world's greatest protector of freedom. What we learn about our immigrants contributes to fairness and justice for all our residents, no matter where they were born. To learn about immigrants is to learn our own story.

Edward I. Koch
Mayor of the City of New York

Acknowledgments

It comes as a surprise to many people that the City Planning Department is interested in anything other than land use. Planning, of course, takes in a lot more than structures. To plan for New York City is to look at who lives here, to project who will live here 10 or 20 years from now, and to design systems capable of meeting their physical and social needs.

New York City has enjoyed such a remarkable influx of immigrants since the 1960s that City Planning wanted to learn as much as possible about our new residents. In 1983, working out of the Human Resources Division headed by Marvin Roth, we put together a team of City Planning staff members with expertise in such diverse fields as demographics, economics, history, health, and education to work on a study of the city's newer immigrants. Elizabeth Bogen conceived and directed the project. Thanks to some seed money from the New York Community Trust, we were able to create several temporary staff positions. Counting permanent and temporary staff, volunteers, and interns, nearly 50 people worked on the study during its four years of preparation.

The senior writer/researchers were Bruce Cory and Marcia Ruff. Substantial sections were produced by Judith Glassman, Richard Satkin, Rita Barrish and Stephen Levine. Frank Vardy was the chief data analyst, working under the direction of Evelyn Mann and with the assistance of Joseph Salvo.

Other researchers, writers and consultants were Marcelyn Anhouse, Lucia Capodilupo, Catherine Christen, Leo Egand, John Feinblatt, Marvin Greisman, Hailu Kebede, Nancy Harvey, Joseph Lorenzo, Jane Margolies, Catherine Marshall, Arthur Ong, Eva Ostrum-Grunstein, Catherine Revici, Jean Sadowsky, Morris Sweet, and Andres Torres.

Volunteers and interns were Annecy Baez, Ethan Corrigan, Robert Fasano, Raul Fuentes, Sheryl Goldberg, Peggy Levitt, Michele Ryan, Monica Schurtman, Jean Steingasser, Susan Tanenbaum and Thomas Willadsen.

The artwork was designed by Henry Nicholas and executed by Walter Boll, Michael Greene, Eustace Pilgrim, and Edward Whitman. Computer maps were produced by Robert Taszymowicz, under the direction of Robert Amsterdam.

Many agencies and their staff contributed to the project—too many to list each staff member individually. The book could not have been written without the cooperation of the staffs of the Office of the Mayor; the Human Resources Administration, the Law Department, the Office of Management and Budget, the Department of Health, the Health and Hospitals Corporation, the Police Department, and the Board of Education; the U.S. Immigration and Naturalization Service; the New York State Refugee/Entrant Assistance Program; the U.S. Catholic Conference; the Archdiocese of New York; the Diocese of Brooklyn; Conservation of Human Resources at Columbia University; and the Center for Latin American and Caribbean Studies at New York University.

Individual acknowledgement must be made to Thomas Muller, author of *The Fourth Wave*; Samuel Bogen; Charles Palella of Scherzer and Palella, attorneys at law; Rev. Joseph Fitzpatrick of Fordham University; Mary McCorry, formerly of the Law Department; Anne Whalen, formerly of the First Deputy Mayor's Office; Arthur and Prudence Ceppos; Joyce Weinstein, formerly of the Office of Management and Budget; Lt. Robert Mealia of the Police Department; Ellen Rautenberg of the Department of Health; John Dereszewski and Glauco Perez of the Human Resources Administration; Robert Kaye of the Criminal Justice Coordinator's Office; Muzaffar Chishti of the International Ladies Garment Workers Union; Sandra Garrett, former district director of the U.S. Office of Refugee Resettlement; David Reimers of New York University; Charles Keely of the Population Council; Michael Teitelbaum of the Sloan Foundation; Lucy Friedman of the Victim Services Agency; Henry Dogin, former district director of the Immigration and Naturalization Service; and Susan Sheehan, author of *Is There No Place on Earth for Me*?

And, of course, acknowledgement and appreciation must be given to Mayor Edward I. Koch, who created the Office of Immigrant Affairs in response to the study's early findings. By creating the office, the mayor guaranteed that the work would continue beyond publication of this book.

Herbert Sturz, Chairman, 1980–1986
City Planning Commission

PART I

The Background

1 Introduction

SETTING THE STAGE

On a sunny day in October 1965, at a ceremony in New York Harbor, President Lyndon Johnson signed a piece of legislation that radically revised U.S. immigration policy. With the shadow of the Statue of Liberty slanting behind him, Johnson declared that the new law would correct "a cruel and enduring wrong in the conduct of the American nation."

That new law, the Hart-Celler Act, repealed a system of national origins quotas that had, in effect, discriminated against immigrants from almost all of Asia, Africa, and southern and eastern Europe. By eliminating the prejudicial quota system, Hart-Celler opened America's doors to immigrants from many nations until then only minimally represented on our shores.

The signing ceremony on Liberty Island was an affirmation of the words of welcome inscribed at the base of the Statue of Liberty in 1903. Although the fanfare of her centennial was still 21 years away, and although Kennedy Airport had replaced New York Harbor as the principal gateway for New York area immigration, the statue continued to preside spiritually over immigration, not just to New York City but to the entire nation. She continues to do so today.

In the two decades since Johnson signed the Hart-Celler Act, the surge in immigration from continents other than Europe has brought other states into prominence as ports of entry, especially California and Texas, whose airports and border cities have become beacons for immigrants from Latin America and Asia. Today New York City shares its role as refuge for the oppressed, the ambitious, the seekers of the world. With the publication of this book, New York also shares what it has learned as the nation's oldest and largest continuing port of entry for persons from abroad. New York is both unique and typical among immigrant-receiving cities, and the ways in which its public and private institutions have responded to the "new" immigration are both unique and typical. This book explores New York's singularities of history, size, and composition, as well as its approaches to problem resolution, many of which may be applicable in other cities and states.

Nationwide, immigration statistics are in a sorry state. Very few data are collected on immigrants except by the U.S. Census Bureau, and few studies have been done on the issues of primary import in policy making: immigrant employment patterns, immigrants' impact on local business and the native-born workforce, their use of public services, and their overall fiscal and economic impact on American society.

The immigration "reform" discussions of the 1970s and 1980s were held in the virtual absence of statistical information. The Simpson-Rodino Act, signed into law on November 6, 1986, was crafted without benefit of any hard data on the question of greatest concern to its crafters: do undocumented aliens working in the United States hurt the job prospects or wage levels of native-born Americans?

Furthermore, the discussions focused on conditions in two states, California and Texas, but those two states don't constitute the nation any more than New York does. This book invites other states and cities to study and record their immigration histories, and to make those histories known. No single set of facts and figures can suffice in setting sound national immigration policy, nor in dealing effectively with local issues of policy and procedure.

IMMIGRATION IN NEW YORK CITY

In 1980, the U.S. Census Bureau counted 14 million foreign-born persons living in the United States, of whom 1.7 million, or 11.9 percent, were living in New York City. New York had more immigrants than any other city in the nation. If all undocumented aliens had been counted, the numbers for New York, as for many cities, would have been higher.

In 1984, the most recent year for which published statistics were available in early 1987, the U.S. Immigration and Naturalization Service (INS) admitted 543,903 aliens as legal permanent residents of the United States, of whom 92,079, or 16.9 percent, said they intended to live in the New York metropolitan area. The city proper has received an ascending number of legal immigrants each year since 1965, with an average of about 75,000 a year. It has received a probably ascending number of undocumented aliens as well.

This huge influx of immigrant newcomers has been offset somewhat by deaths among the large remnant of immigrants who arrived in New York in the early decades of the century, and by some secondary migration of newer immigrants to other parts of the country. The city's net increase in foreign-born residents was about 24,000 a year between 1970 and 1980, by census count. During that decade the foreign-born population rose from just over 1.4 million (17.9 percent of the city's total population) to just under 1.7 million (23.6 percent). If all undocumented aliens had been counted in the 1980 census, the number of foreign-born would almost certainly have exceeded 2 million.

STREET SCENES

In the P.S. 89 schoolyard in Elmhurst, Queens, Chinese children wearing quilted blue jackets run and laugh beside playmates from South America—Quechua Indian children who are bundled against the cold in earth-tone sweaters of Andean wool.

The latest *disques créoles* from Haiti blare from record shops on Flatbush Avenue in Brooklyn as weekend shoppers throng the sidewalks. Newsstand owners rack the latest issues of Caribbean-published newspapers beside copies of New York dailies. Sandwich shops serve spicy Jamaican meat patties and deep-fried codfish balls.

On a summer day in the Washington Heights area of northern Manhattan, the windows of the second-story garment lofts above the storefronts on St. Nicholas Avenue are thrown open to catch the breeze; the Dominican women who work there do not look up from their sewing machines. At street level, posters and handbills exhorting allegiance to various Dominican political parties plaster the lamp posts and subway entrances.

Immigration is changing New York in a thousand subtle or startling ways. Even the New Yorker who rarely ventures into an immigrant neighborhood sees its effects. Korean greengrocers, Indian newsstand owners, Jamaican nurses, Greek coffee shop owners, Russian cab drivers—in today's New York, close encounters with immigrants of all kinds are a daily occurrence.

A population of various nationalities is hardly a novelty in New York. In 1660 the Dutch governor of Nieuw Amsterdam noted that 18 different languages were spoken by inhabitants of his colony. In 1980 the number of languages spoken in New York was 121. The immigrant waves of the 19th and early 20th centuries helped to shape the city's political system, neighborhoods, and social and economic institutions. The influence of immigration can still be detected in matters as mundane as the foods

New Yorkers eat, and as elevated as the succession of archbishops in the Archdiocese of New York.

What *is* new about the new immigration is the countries from which immigrants are coming. Traditionally New York City has been a city of European immigrants—first the Dutch and the English, later the Irish and the Germans, and finally the Italians and the peoples of eastern Europe. But in 1980 only two European nations—Italy and the Soviet Union—were among the top ten nations whose immigrants were arriving in New York. The Dominican Republic was first on the list, followed by Jamaica, China, and Haiti. In all, about three-quarters of the immigrants who arrived in New York between 1965, the year of Hart-Celler, and 1980, the year of the census, were from the nations of the Caribbean, Latin America, and Asia.

These new immigrants have replenished many of the city's neighborhoods with young families and children. They have started new businesses, inherited old ones, and become the predominant work force in others. They confront the city's service system—schools and hospitals, for example—with new issues in service delivery, starting with the availability of interpreters.

Contrary to a popular image, immigrant households are not made up of just immigrants. The 1980 census shows that of the 2 million New Yorkers who were living in households headed by someone of foreign birth, 27.7 percent were born in the United States. More than half the children in households headed by a foreign-born person were born in the United States, which made them U.S. citizens by birth.

AIMS OF THIS STUDY

This book attempts to gauge the effects of immigration in New York City today, with particular attention to those newcomers who arrived after 1965. In 1980 these more recent immigrants made up 56.5 percent of the city's foreign-born population. Particular attention is paid to the ways immigrants interact with the city's service system. The book looks at the demographic characteristics of the city's foreign-born: their countries of origin, their distribution in the city's residential neighborhoods, and their patterns of employment. It reviews the history of U.S. immigration law and its effects on immigration in New York City. It describes the use that immigrants make of the city's service system, and the adaptations that service agencies have made to these new clients. Finally, it explores the question of what immigrants cost the city in services and what they contribute in taxes.

The book attempts to bring some balance to the question of illegal immigration. So sore is the subject in 1987 that some Americans have come to view *all* immigration as somehow illicit or harmful to the United

States. The unauthorized immigration since the mid–1960s deserves attention, but not to the exclusion or denigration of legal immigration. The vast majority of this country's foreign-born residents entered the United States with authorization.

Aside from their mode of entry, today's undocumented immigrants differ little from the documented. They arrive from the same countries, they work at the same jobs, and they live in the same neighborhoods, often in the same households. Frequently they are the unmarried brothers, sisters, or cousins of the legal immigrants whose households they share. From a demographic standpoint, undocumented immigrants are not remarkable, in New York at any rate.

It is an irony of U.S. immigration history that the Hart-Celler Act, that corrector of "cruel and enduring wrongs," played a role in creating today's unauthorized immigration. Hart-Celler expanded the opportunities for legal immigration from some parts of the world but limited the opportunities for immigrants from others. Among the nations of the Western Hemisphere, for example, it extended a welcome to immigrants from former British colonies of the Caribbean—Jamaica, Barbados, Trinidad and Tobago—that previously had been restricted to minuscule quotas; but for the first time the law set limits on immigration from Latin America. The limits were no more stringent for Latin American nations than for any others, but they were unprecedented and, as it turns out, unenforceable. Latin Americans continued to enter the United States, in numbers even greater than before, but now many of them were "illegal." Soon unauthorized aliens were arriving from many other parts of the globe.

Hart-Celler was not the only cause of increased migration, authorized or unauthorized. Factors that propelled immigrants from their homelands included rapid population expansion in slowly developing economies and the dislocations of war, political oppression, and famine. Factors that drew immigrants to the United States included this country's continuous need for labor and the industrial expansion of the Sunbelt. Both "push" and "pull" factors were felt in the expanding interconnections of the global economy.

IMMIGRANT CLASSIFICATIONS

One of the first tasks confronting anyone who wants to understand U.S. immigration is to sort out the bewildering multiplicity of immigration categories into which the foreign-born can fall. Foreign-born persons can be U.S. citizens, noncitizens, legal aliens, illegal aliens, permanent residents, temporary residents, visitors, and so on. These immigrant statuses are interrelated and fluid; aliens can, and do, pass readily from one to another (see Figure 1.1). A tourist can become an undocumented

Figure 1.1
Possibilities for Movement Among Immigrant Classifications

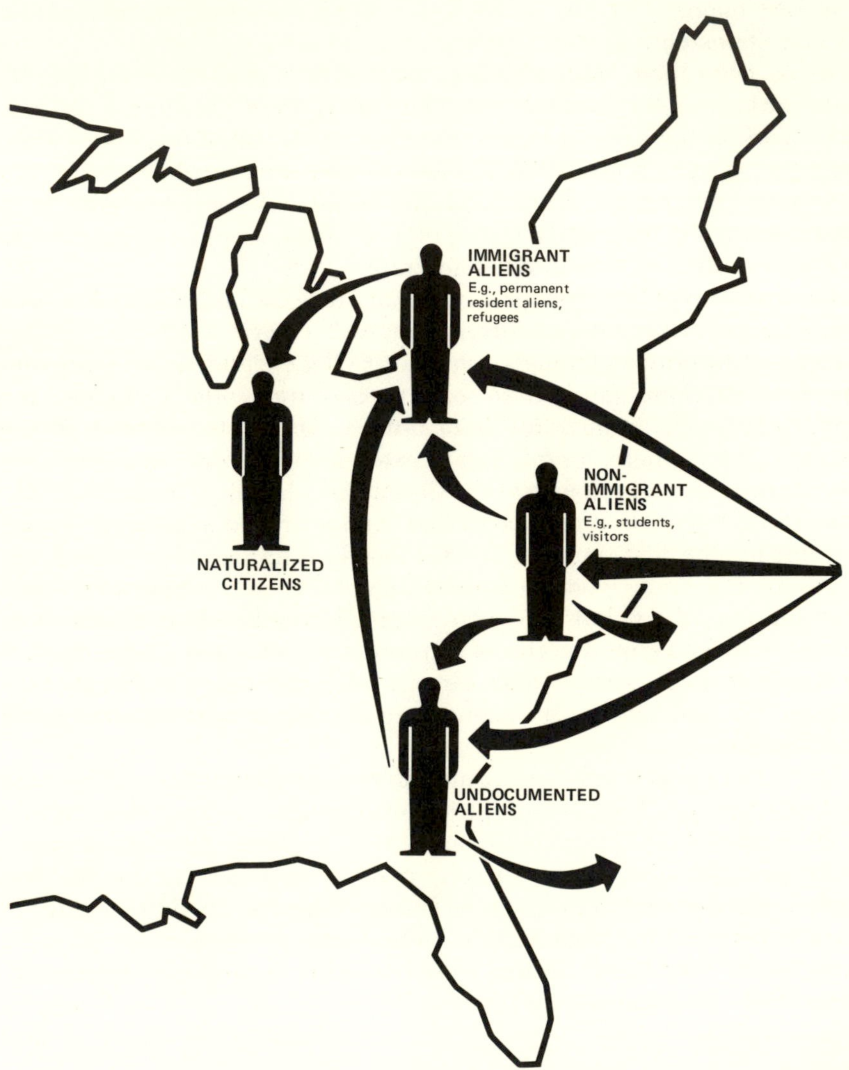

alien if his or her visitor's visa expires. Even before the Simpson-Rodino Act of 1986 created an "amnesty" program for some undocumented aliens, an undocumented alien could become a legal permanent resident alien if his or her application for adjustment of status met INS approval. A permanent resident alien can become a naturalized citizen. In 1980, 53 percent of the city's recorded foreign-born persons were naturalized citizens.

ISSUES IN DATA COLLECTION

This book relies heavily on the 1980 U.S. census for its statistical base. Despite some serious shortcomings, the census provides the most detailed data on the country's immigrants. The Census Bureau has acknowledged that hundreds of thousands of New Yorkers, almost certainly including many thousands of undocumented aliens, were not counted in the 1980 census. If more undocumented aliens had been counted, our findings would be modified, but it is hard to say in what directions or by how much.

Furthermore, the census data were collected seven years ago, in 1980, and were not available for analysis until 1983. In the years since the data were collected, time has not stood still. Immigration to New York has continued to change. The city has seen a large influx of refugees and entrants from Southeast Asia, Haiti and other nations of the Caribbean, and asylum seekers from the Middle East and Central America, in addition to the usual immigration flows. Until the 1990 census, changes in the city's ethnic composition can be studied only from limited INS data, small samples, and anecdotal information.

The census is very nearly the only source of statistical information on immigrants in New York. Published INS data tend to be sketchy and far from current. Data from the public and private agencies that serve immigrants tend to be sketchy or nonexistent. Even statistics on refugees and entrants—the most closely monitored segments of the immigrant population—are difficult to obtain by city. The theme of insufficient data threads throughout this book.

WHAT THIS BOOK IS AND ISN'T

This book is a preliminary assessment of the new immigration in New York City; it is not the last word on the subject. Some questions of obvious importance have not been addressed at all, and in every area there is room for more research. The team of writers, data analysts, and researchers who put the book together hope their work will inspire research on topics not covered and critical examination on topics that are.

From the start the study team members were favorably disposed toward immigrants, believing that immigrants contribute more to the life of the city than they detract from it. Team members sought out new evidence, but few facts emerged to shake their faith. They strove, however, to achieve a balanced presentation so that readers with different points of view would find the book reliable and informative.

Although the book was written primarily for public administrators and policy makers, it is also meant for anyone who is interested in immigration. It is intended to help community leaders who want to know more about their new constituents, social workers serving an immigrant clientele, university researchers, and students writing term papers. It is also intended for the immigrants of New York, many of whom have a great yearning for knowledge about the elaborate patchwork of which they are a part.

2 Social and Legislative History

New York City will take its place in history beside Tyre, Venice, and Hong Kong as one of the great mercantile port cities of the world. In colonial times the gateway for German textiles and British machinery, it was later the port of entry for millions of immigrants who populated the United States in the 18th and 19th centuries.

Between 1820 and 1920 two-thirds of the nation's 34 million immigrants entered through the Port of New York. Although many traveled on to other destinations, nearly half of them settled in the city. Virtually every nationality was represented. The diversity attracted more newcomers, and does so to this day. New York is still the gateway for a third of the country's immigrants, and still the American city with the most ethnically diverse population.

Although New York has seen no truly "new" faces in the last 100 years, the ethnic distribution has shifted several times in ways that have been perceived as revolutionary each time. The last great shift in ethnic mix, both nationally and locally, began in 1965, when the nation's immigration laws were restructured for the third time in the century. Now, skin tones of yellow, brown, and black are seen increasingly on New York City streets as Chinese, Koreans, Haitians, and Dominicans follow the paths laid down by the Irish, Germans, Italians, and eastern European Jews who came before them. Jamaican nurses, Indian news dealers, Chinese garment workers, and Korean greengrocers are New York's "new" immigrants. They invite a look at the "old" immigrants and the role they played in making the city what it is today.

Figure 2.1
Immigration to the United States by Decade, 1820–1980

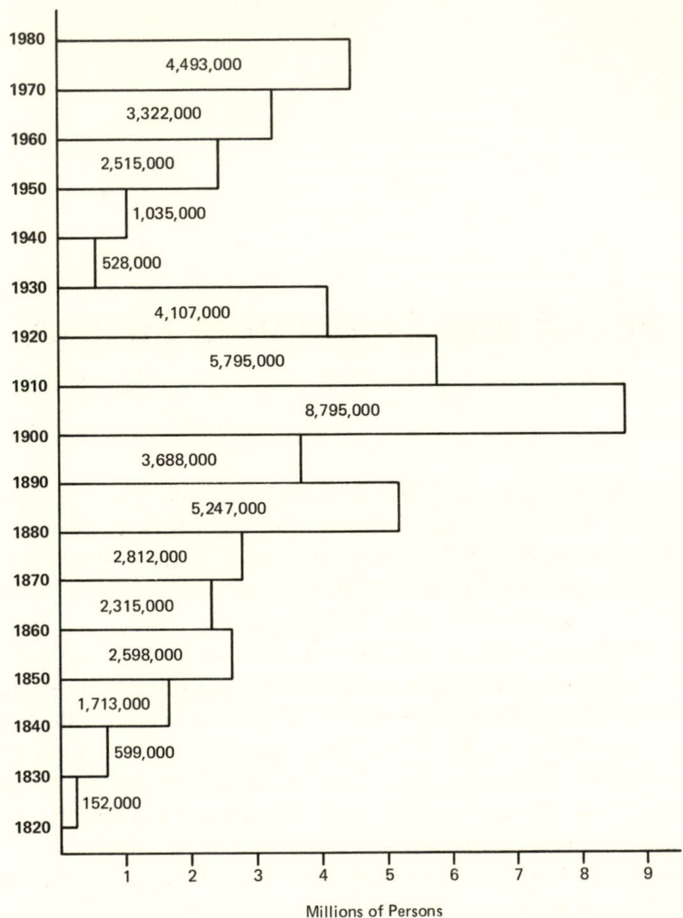

Source: 1981 Statistical Yearbook of the U.S. Immigration and Naturalization Service

THE EBB AND FLOW OF IMMIGRATION

From the late 19th century to the early 20th, immigrants flowed to the United States in a steadily increasing stream, reaching a peak in the decade 1900–10. After that the immigration rate dropped sharply to the lows of the 1930s, then rose again after World War II (see Figure 2.1).

Which ethnic groups came, and in what numbers, changed over time under the influence of two interacting factors: socioeconomic conditions here and abroad, and changes in U.S. immigration law (see Figure 2.2.) The stream of 19th-century immigrants came primarily from Europe,

Figure 2.2
Immigration Flows by Area of the World, 1820–1980

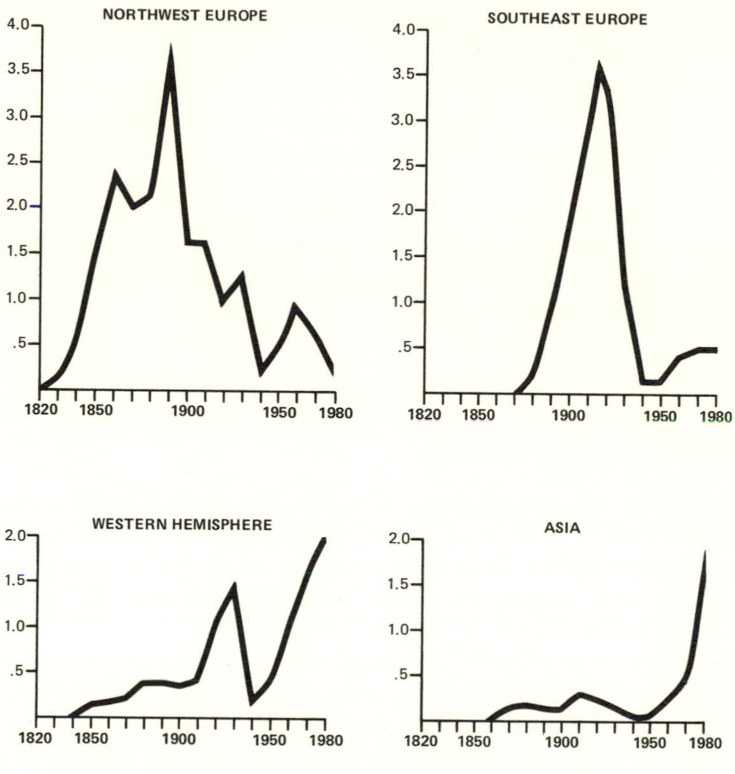

Source: 1981 Statistical Yearbook of the U.S. Immigration and Naturalization Service

first from northern and western Europe, and later from southern and eastern Europe. Enactment of a sharply restrictive immigration law, combined with war abroad and economic hardship in the United States, dammed the stream from the 1920s into the 1940s, after which the eastern European flow resumed. By the 1960s pressure to migrate had built in many nations of the Third World, and the migration flow shifted from southern Europe to Asia and the nations of the Western Hemisphere.

The United States did not attempt to regulate the numbers or national origins of its immigrants until World War I. The country's notion of itself as a haven for Europe's "huddled masses" accorded completely with national need. The empty continent required large numbers of people to settle the frontier, lay the rails, and labor in the factories. Before the

1920s U.S. immigration law focused on personal characteristics that might limit employability. Immigrants should not be sick, criminal, or unskilled. One group alone was excluded on the basis of national origin: the Chinese. Unskilled Chinese workers were banned after 1882, as a result of a strong lobbying effort by West Coast trade unions whose members wanted no competition from Chinese labor. In general, however, the pattern of immigration was an authentic reflection of shifting political and economic opportunities in Europe and America.

Since World War I a succession of complex immigration laws has patterned the flow. Ceilings have been placed on total immigrant admissions, and the nationalities of newcomers have been regulated according to various schemes. The process began in the 1920s with laws designed to freeze the country's ethnic composition. The laws were modified many times afterward as Congress attempted to accommodate global issues and U.S. policy goals.

THE 19TH CENTURY: OVER-POPULATED EUROPE AND LABOR-HUNGRY AMERICA

Immigration was negligible in the early days of the Republic. Between the first census in 1790, when there were 4 million Americans, and the fourth census in 1820, when there were 9.6 million, immigrants accounted for only 4.5 percent of the population increase (250,000 people). The rest of the increase was due to births.

In the first years of the 19th century, economic and political conditions in the United States and Europe altered radically. The Louisiana Purchase of 1803 doubled the size of the country, and the frontier began to draw settlers away from the East Coast just as the demand for labor there was growing. The War of 1812 cut off U.S. access to British supplies, spurring the growth of this nation's infant industries and increasing the need for workers. Construction of the canal and railroad system began with New York's Erie Canal in 1817.

In Europe an improved economy allowed more people to marry and have children, infant mortality declined sharply, and overpopulation became a problem for the first time. Governments lifted laws that restricted emigration; some countries and philanthropists paid people to leave. Between 1840 and 1860, 4.3 million emigrants left Europe for America—a sixfold increase over the previous two decades.

Ninety-five percent of the new arrivals came from three countries: Ireland (1.7 million), Germany (1.4 million), and Great Britain (1 million). Failure of the potato crop drove more than a quarter of Ireland's population to America between 1840 and 1860. German and British craftsmen were displaced by mechanized production as the Industrial Revolution progressed; small farmers sold their farms to larger landowners and used the proceeds to start over in America.

Emigrants made their way first to their own commercial ports: Liverpool in England, Bremen in Germany, and Le Havre in France. Provisions stores sprang up on the wharves; in them emigrants could sell family heirlooms, and buy food for the voyage and ratproof boxes in which to store it. The trip took one to three months, with constant danger of disease and shipwreck. In the worst year—1847—20 percent of Irish emigrants died of "ship fever." In the 1850s more than 40 emigrant ships sank in the North Atlantic.

Some immigrants landed in Boston, Philadelphia, and New Orleans, but most entered through New York. Newcomers were the responsibility of the city; there were no federal administrative regulations, no passports, no visas. On New York's East River docks, hustlers descended on the new arrivals, frequently preying on their own countrymen. Some sold fraudulent train tickets; others snatched up the newcomers' baggage, to be redeemed only for cash. Male immigrants stopped in saloons for a drink and woke up employed on clipper ships to China. Women were directed to "boardinghouses" that were actually brothels.

The New York State Commission of Emigration was organized in 1849 to regulate the chaos. It had no power to control who could enter the country, but it could try to ease abuses against immigrants. In 1849 it took over the Marine Hospital on Staten Island to treat immigrants who had contagious diseases, and it opened another, the New York State Immigrant Refuge, on what is now Roosevelt Island.

In 1855 the commission opened the Castle Garden Emigrant Landing Depot, the nation's first official entry point for immigrants. It was located in abandoned Fort Clinton, a circular stone fort on a rocky island off the southern tip of Manhattan. (The structure still stands, but landfill has made the island part of Battery Park.) A door was carved in the seaward side; passengers disembarked into the fort. Private concessions were set up to exchange money and to sell tickets and food. The commission counted arrivals, recorded their names, and performed cursory medical examinations. Most people spent about six hours on the island. Those who were bound for New York crossed a wooden gangplank to Manhattan.

The Emigration Commission met only a few immediate needs of the newcomers. The larger task of helping them adjust to life in the city was carried on then, as now, by private organizations formed of earlier immigrants. These groups warned newcomers about hustlers, delivered information about friends and relatives, found housing and jobs, lent money, sold train tickets, and helped immigrants send money home.

The largest of these groups were the Irish Emigrant Society of the Roman Catholic Church, the German Society, the Hebrew Benevolent

Society, and the Spanish Benevolent Society begun by Cuban and Puerto Rican merchants. Smaller organizations were established by Welsh, Dutch, Italian, and Polish immigrants.

THE GREAT AGE OF IMMIGRATION

Immigration slowed during the Civil War and the economic turmoil of the 1870s, but rose again as industrialization progressed. More than 20 million immigrants arrived between 1880 and 1914, twice the number of the previous 40 years. The nationalities of the newcomers began to shift. By 1890 German, Irish, and British arrivals were equaled by Italians, Greeks, Czechs, Slovaks, Hungarians, and Russian and Polish Jews. Ten years later these southern and eastern Europeans constituted two-thirds of new arrivals.

Changing conditions in Europe produced the shift. The economy of northern Europe was stabilizing, but southern and eastern Europe began to wrestle with displacement from industrialization, poverty, pogroms, frequent wars, high taxes, and the constant threat of the military draft. A technological advance—the steamship—greatly facilitated emigration from the ports of the Mediterranean. Wind-powered vessels had been dependent on the North Atlantic trade winds and had sailed infrequently to southern ports.

Transatlantic voyages became faster, safer, and cheaper for everyone. The trip took only two weeks, not two months, thereby cutting down dramatically on expense and contagious disease. Steamship companies competed fiercely, and price wars brought a steerage ticket down from $30 to $15. Now migrants could travel to the United States for just a season, a year, or a few years. Single men, many of them Italian or Greek, stayed long enough to earn the money for a farm, a business, or a bride back home.

Meanwhile, Castle Garden, originally intended as a shelter from predations on the wharves, had itself become corrupt. Concessionaires charged exorbitant prices for food and transportation, and cheated immigrants on the exchange of currency. In 1892 the federal government closed Castle Garden and replaced it with the imposing, federally operated Ellis Island Immigration Station. The prize-winning architecture of Ellis Island's Great Hall, built in 1900, said clearly that immigrants were important to the United States. The hall had modern elevators, hot and cold running water, flush toilets, brass chandeliers, magnificent windows overlooking the harbor, and massive pots of hanging plants.

Luxurious as it may have been, the Ellis Island installation was never big enough. In a facility constructed to receive 1,400 immigrants a day, Ellis Island staff handled between 2,000 and 7,000. In the first decade of the 20th century, 90 percent of the country's 9 million immigrants came through Ellis Island—90 percent, that is, of the immigrants who came steerage. Those wealthy enough to travel cabin class disembarked at Hudson River steamship piers, from which they were permitted to enter the country with the most perfunctory inspection and no registration. There is no way of knowing how many immigrants came cabin class, but most steerage passengers are listed in the Ellis Island registry.

NEW YORK: CITY OF IMMIGRANTS

New York City grew 50-fold during the 19th century, principally because of immigrants and their children. On the eve of World War I, as the great age of immigration was drawing to an end, New York had three times as many foreign-born residents as the average city. The foreign-born had made their mark everywhere—in the city's neighborhoods, in its economy, and in its politics. Public works construction had boomed in late–19th-century New York to support the masses of newcomers. By 1880 the city had paved streets, horse-drawn streetcars, and an extensive sewer system; none of these amenities was typical of other U.S. cities at that time. At the turn of the century, immigrant labor—largely Italian, Hungarian, and Russian—built the subway system, the aqueduct, and the Bronx sewer system.

Immigrants made their mark on New York's most prominent industries. The garment trade was dependent on immigrant labor. Immigrant newspapers helped build the publishing trade. The constant flow of money orders back to the homelands sharpened the skills and expanded the networks of New York's international banking community. Immigrant entrepreneurs, from Jewish pushcart peddlers to Italian greengrocers, stimulated the entire economy.

THE DISSENTING VOICES

Some Americans resented the newcomers. There were labor unionists who feared job displacement and wage depression, eugenicists who believed that southern Europeans were racially inferior, and Protestants who believed that Irish and Italian immigrants would be unable to reconcile Catholicism with democracy. Before World War I, however, anti-immigrant sentiment prevailed only in isolated instances—for example, when Chinese laborers were excluded in 1882.

Immigrants stimulated the local economy but also generated costs. New York State paid for the operation of Castle Garden; New York City paid for hospitals, jails, and insane asylums; and private charities paid for orphanages, employment offices, and boardinghouses. To recoup its costs, the state levied entrance taxes on immigrants and collected fees from ship companies, but the U.S. Supreme Court repeatedly struck down these practices. The Court held that such fees restrained immigration, which only the federal government had the right to do.

To replace these impermissible fees, the states urged Congress to levy a federal tax on immigrants. New York State threatened to close down Castle Garden if such a tax was not levied. The threat pushed Congress into action. In 1882 Congress passed legislation giving authority over immigration to the Secretary of the Treasury and imposing a 50-cent head tax on immigrants, to be returned to the states in an early form of revenue sharing. The new law also barred the entry of various undesirables, such as "idiots, lunatics, convicts, and persons likely to become public charges"—restrictions still on the books. Prostitutes and convicts had been barred in 1875. Since that time the list has been enlarged to include, among others, alcoholics, anarchists, Nazis, Communists, and homosexuals.

NATIONAL ORIGINS QUOTAS: THE DOORS CLOSE

The U.S. attitude toward immigrants continued to change in the years before World War I. A coalition of antiwar isolationists urged the government to keep its distance from Europe's problems. Nativist groups capitalized on the anti-European mood to lobby successfully for anti-immigrant legislation.

In 1917 Congress overrode President Wilson's veto to pass a law barring entry of the illiterate—that is, the peasants of southern and eastern Europe. The new law was successful in reducing the immigrant flow. Other events also served to decrease immigration. During the war many European countries prohibited emigration of draft-age men. The Atlantic became increasingly dangerous to cross because of war maneuvers. Only 110,000 immigrants entered the United States in 1918, less than 10 percent of the figure for 1914.

As the numbers rose again after the war, Congress slammed on the brakes with a series of temporary quotas and a ceiling on total immigration. The quotas limited the numbers to a percentage of the foreign-born from each country who were already in the United States. They had the most severe effect on prospective immigrants from southern and eastern Europe, where emigration rates were rising; in northern and western Europe, emigration was declining of its own accord.

With some changes in the formula, the quota system became permanent law in 1924 with the passage of the Johnson-Reed Act, also known as the Permanent National Origins Quota Act. In this reformulation, quotas were assigned as a percentage of each ancestry group in the United States. Every group but the British lost ground. Forty-two percent of the U.S. population claimed British ancestry, so Britain got 42 percent of the visas. Ireland, Germany, and Scandinavia together received 30 percent. The southern and eastern European countries shared 15 percent. The outright ban on the Chinese was extended to almost all Asians.

The independent nations of the Western Hemisphere were not incorporated into the quota system. America's neighbors enjoyed a protected position. Furthermore, U.S. farm interests relied on migrant labor from Latin American nations, and the numbers were not large enough to arouse congressional concern. Colonial possessions like Jamaica, Barbados, and Trinidad were not given preferential treatment, but they were permitted to use their mother countries' unfilled quotas. As European immigration dropped, immigration from the Western Hemisphere became proportionately greater, from 20 percent in the 1910s to 37 percent in the 1920s.

In New York, West Indians constituted the largest group of immigrants from the Western Hemisphere. The West Indian migration had begun around 1900, when the introduction of European beet sugar triggered a depression in the Caribbean sugar industry. The principal sending countries were Jamaica and Barbados.

West Indians were drawn to New York because it had a reputation for being less hostile to blacks than other U.S. cities. In 1930 more than half the West Indians in the United States lived in New York; almost 70 percent of subsequent arrivals settled in the city. One-quarter of Harlem's black population was West Indian. Frequently well-educated and entrepreneurial, West Indians provided most of the city's black doctors, lawyers, and dentists, and became major landholders in the black community, evoking some resentment among native-born blacks that still exists.

NEW YORK IN THE DEPRESSION: A QUIET HARBOR AND A TENSE CITY

The 1924 immigration act brought an end to the Ellis Island era, literally and figuratively. Immigration dropped sharply. Prospective immigrants were screened at consulates in their homelands, not in New York Harbor. Ellis Island became a ghost town, thinly populated with detainees whose papers were not in order, and with deportees waiting for the next steamship home.

The Depression was even more effective than the national origins quotas in lowering immigration rates. The exodus from the United States during the 1930s was virtually equal to the inflow. The largest entering group was the Jews fleeing Nazism in Europe. They made up a quarter of the decade's immigrants. Two-thirds of them were destined for New York State, particularly New York City.

The 1930s was a difficult time for New York's white ethnic communities. In the shrinking economy of the Depression, immigrants and the children of immigrants fought to hold on to what they had. During World War I many "hyphenated" Americans, particularly German-Americans, had been accused of dual loyalty. The restrictive quota laws of the 1920s exacerbated their fears of social rejection. So did the rise in the 1920s of the Ku Klux Klan, with its prejudices against foreigners, Catholics, Jews, and blacks.

Anxiety and frustration led to conflict among ethnic communities. Much of it centered on competition for jobs and housing. Irish-Jewish relations deteriorated when Mayor Fiorello LaGuardia's civil service reforms loosened the Irish hold on hiring and promotion. Jews begin to win competitive positions in teaching and other civil service jobs.

At the same time the two groups competed for housing in Washington Heights and the South Bronx. As Jews began to move out of the Lower East Side, Irish neighborhoods presented the next step up. In northern Manhattan, Broadway became a dividing line, with Jews to the west and Irish to the east. Irish youths made frequent forays to beat up Jewish youths while Irish police looked the other way.

The rise of anti-Semitism in Europe heightened the conflicts between New York's Jews and its Germans and Italians. The Jews, urging early intervention in Europe, met resistance from Germans and Italians who wished the United States to remain neutral so they could avoid the accusations of dual loyalty they had encountered during World War I. Jews also clashed with Irish who opposed U.S. intervention because they opposed alliance with Britain.

Many of these conflicts dissolved in the larger turmoil of World War II. Economic expansion after the war reduced competition among white ethnic groups as jobs became plentiful for all.

THE POSTWAR WORLD

World War II left multitudes of Europeans homeless and stateless. President Truman issued a directive in 1945 giving displaced persons priority within their countries' immigration quotas, but the large numbers from southern and eastern Europe were restricted by small quotas. Hundreds of thousands waited in camps.

Congress dealt with the problem by opening a separate doorway, the Displaced Persons Act of 1948, which permitted refugees to enter the United States outside the national origins quotas. Their numbers were charged against their homelands' future quotas. Over the next four years 400,000 refugees were admitted, along with 200,000 foreign wives, husbands, and children of U.S. military personnel.

The machinations required to meet the demands of the postwar world within the restrictions of the national origins system prompted a full-scale review of the immigration law. The resulting legislation, the McCarran-Walter Act of 1952, took a conservative stance, retaining the national origins quotas "to best preserve the cultural and sociological balance" of the country. But the act also introduced a preference system to determine which applicants would receive visas. The new system reserved half the visas for persons with needed job skills, and half for relatives of U.S. citizens and permanent resident aliens. The preference system remains a cornerstone of today's law, although the priorities have shifted in favor of family reunification.

Anti-Communism permeated the McCarran-Walter Act, which contained tough provisions for screening and deporting suspected Communist immigrants. Western Hemisphere immigration remained largely unrestricted under the act, but Congress did limit immigration from Caribbean colonies by revoking their access to European quotas and restricting them to quotas of 100 per year. West Indians began to migrate to Britain instead of the United States. The outright ban on Asian immigration was lifted, but barriers remained; Asians had a minuscule base in America from which to derive their quotas.

Truman vetoed the McCarran-Walter Act, calling the national origins quotas an insult to Americans of southern and eastern European stock and to NATO allies in southern Europe. Congress overrode the veto, claiming that the anti-Communist provisions were vital to national security, and that national origins quotas were necessary to ensure smooth assimilation of new arrivals.

In the years during and after World War II, native minorities also were making their way to New York, drawn by the labor shortage of the war years and by the expanding economy of the postwar years. The Puerto Rican migration accelerated in 1945 with inauguration of air service between San Juan and New York. The number of island-born Puerto Ricans living in New York more than doubled between 1950 and 1960, from 190,000 to 430,000. A similar phenomenon occurred among blacks moving north from the rural South, as they had done during and after World War I. New York's black population doubled between 1940 and 1960, from 500,000 to 1 million (from 6 percent to 14 percent of the city's population).

THE HART-CELLER ACT

The McCarran-Walter Act maintained the national origins quota system on the presumption that northern Europeans were more assimilable than southern and eastern Europeans, Asians, and Africans. This presumption later came under attack. President Eisenhower four times called upon Congress to repeal the quota system. Rather than repeal, Congress had repeated recourse to "separate doorways"—for refugees from Europe in 1953, for Hungarian freedom fighters in 1957, and for Cuban exiles in 1960. The exceptions eventually eroded the credibility of the act.

Congress revised the immigration law in the Hart-Celler Act of 1965, which produced mixed results. Hart-Celler repealed the national origins quotas and gave all countries in the Eastern Hemisphere equal access to immigration visas, with a maximum of 20,000 visas for any single country and a hemisphere ceiling of 170,000 visas a year. Repeal of the quotas made migration increasingly possible for persons from Asia, southern and eastern Europe, and other parts of the globe that had been constrained by quotas since 1921.

For the first time in U.S. history, however, Congress limited immigration from the Western Hemisphere, which had been averaging 100,000 a year through the 1950s. A group of southern senators, who feared that Latin America's expanding population presaged an increase in immigration, insisted on a total annual ceiling of 120,000. No per-country limits were set.

The new law was a blow for most of Latin America, but it was a boon for former British possessions in the Western Hemisphere, such as Jamaica, and Trinidad and Tobago. The McCarran-Walter Act had limited them to colonial quotas of 100. Hart-Celler gave them parity with other nations of the Western Hemisphere.

The new law increased the emphasis on family reunification. The preference system was amended to reserve three-quarters of all visas for family members, and the remainder for people with scarce job skills and for refugees. (See the section "Preference System.") Emanuel Celler, the Democratic congressman from Brooklyn who was one of the bill's cosponsors, argued that favoring relatives would prevent a rapid shift in the ethnic mix of the new immigrants because their nationalities would match those already here.

In actuality a dramatic change in countries of origin followed passage of the new law. At first there was a flurry of European arrivals as visa waiting lists cleared, but then European immigration declined. Western Europeans were not strongly interested in emigrating, and residents of Soviet bloc nations were held back by their governments. Europeans had made up 53 percent of immigrants in 1960, but they were only 43 percent in 1970, and 17 percent in 1980.

Congress had not been able to predict the strength of the pressure to emigrate that arose in the late 1960s in Asia and the Americas. Asians, Caribbeans, and Latin Americans were 46 percent of all immigrants in 1960; in 1980 they were 80 percent. The legislators had not realized that the preference system, with its emphasis on family reunification, could make possible such a change. In some ways the system encouraged the change. By reserving the majority of visas for immediate family members, it favored immigrants who still had close family abroad, and that meant recent immigrants, not older ones. The process worked like a wedge. A few immigrants from one of the "newer" nations entered the United States on occupational preferences; then they sponsored a wider stream of close family members under the more plentiful relative preferences.

New York City soon began to reflect the new order. Chinatown, which had been a small bachelor town of elderly Chinese men (sons of the laborers of the late 1800s), became a lively community of young immigrants and their children. In 1960 there were 20,000 foreign-born Chinese in New York; in 1970 there were 37,000; in 1980, 95,000.

The number of Jamaican immigrants in New York City increased almost ninefold between 1960 and 1980, from 11,000 to 93,000. Immigration from Trinidad and Tobago increased sevenfold, from 5,500 to 40,000. Hart-Celler created the opportunity for the increased immigration, and a change in British law fostered it; in 1962 Britain closed its door on free migration from nonwhite Commonwealth countries. More than ever, then, West Indians looked to the United States.

Although the Hart-Celler Act set new limits on immigration from the independent nations of the Western Hemisphere, other forces were at work. Dominicans, for example, began to arrive in New York in large numbers after 1961, when the assassination of the Dominican dictator Rafael Trujillo ended restrictive emigration policies. There were 9,000 Dominican-born persons in New York in 1960; by 1980 there were 121,000.

ILLEGAL IMMIGRATION: A NEW DEVELOPMENT

The 1965 law solved some problems but it created others—in particular, new waves of unauthorized immigration into the United States. The limits on Western Hemisphere immigration were put in place at the same time the Latin American baby boom generation of the 1950s was coming of working age. In 1964 Congress ended the bracero program, a guest worker program that permitted Mexicans to work on U.S. farms; but U.S. demand for Mexican labor did not end with the program. The booming economy of the southwest was creating a "pull" for all kinds of workers. When the number of would-be immigrants exceeded the per-country limits, or when prospective migrants did not fit the qualifications of the preference system, illegal immigration resulted.

At one time these prospective workers might have migrated from the countryside to their own cities for jobs, but there weren't enough jobs for all of them. Furthermore, their increasing familiarity with U.S. conditions, obtained from radio, television, and the local activities of multinational corporations, drew them increasingly to the United States. Direct flights became available at moderate cost.

During the 1970s the INS began to apprehend larger and larger numbers of undocumented aliens. At first the increase reflected greater enforcement efforts and the changed status of Mexican guest workers as much as it reflected an increase in immigration. Still, by 1983 apprehensions had reached 1.2 million a year. Immigration experts speculated that 3 to 6 million undocumented aliens might be living in the country, with another million arriving each year.

RECENT LEGISLATIVE EFFORTS

Congress considered the illegal immigration issue at various times throughout the 1970s but did not take legislative action. In 1977 President Carter proposed legislation that would give amnesty to undocumented aliens already living in the country, penalize employers for hiring undocumented aliens, and increase INS border patrols. The concepts of employer sanctions and amnesty had been advanced earlier in the decade by, among others, Congressman Peter Rodino (D.-N.J.), but several administrations and Congresses had let these ideas languish, as they did again in 1977.

In 1978, recognizing that the issue was not going to disappear but eager to postpone legislative consideration until after the 1980 elections, Congress established the Select Commission on Immigration and Refugee Policy to make recommendations for an overhaul of the immigration law. Rev. Theodore M. Hesburgh, president of the University of Notre Dame, accepted the chairmanship.

While the commission was at work, Congress was able to act on one immigration matter: refugee admissions. The country's ad hoc refugee policies had been tested severely by the influx of hundreds of thousands of Vietnamese who fled their country after the fall of Saigon. Refugee admissions were decided crisis by crisis, year by year; government funding for resettlement activities was erratic and inadequate, and local resettlement agencies struggled under the financial burden. Congress passed the Refugee Act of 1980 (discussed further in Chapter 9) to make the admissions and resettlement process more orderly.

The year 1980 was a turning point in the U.S. perception of immigration. The unexpected arrival of 140,000 Cubans and Haitians on the shores of southern Florida attracted the nation's attention. The flow of Indochinese refugees reached a peak of 160,000. The year's admission total for refugees, other legal immigrants, and Cuban and Haitian "boat people" was more than 808,000, the highest since 1921. It was an inflammatory figure in a country already upset about unusually high inflation and unemployment, as well as 52 American hostages held in Teheran.

These events fed a fear that the United States had "lost control" of its borders. Illegal immigration became a target of public anxiety.

The Select Commission on Immigration and Refugee Policy released its recommendations in 1981, shortly after President Reagan took office. Its recommendations were similar to those proposed by Congressman Rodino in the early 1970s and by President Carter in 1977. The commission held that illegal immigration had to be closed off in order to preserve the legal immigration system. Its main recommendations were a system of sanctions against employers who knowingly hired undocumented aliens, and a legalization program for some undocumented aliens who were already in the country. It made many other recommendations, including increased support for the INS, a temporary increase in the immigration ceiling to eliminate the application backlog, a worker identification system, and revisions of the temporary worker program to help growers who would lose their undocumented labor force if employer sanctions were imposed.

The next year legislation following these general lines was introduced in Congress by Sen. Alan K. Simpson (R.-Wyo.) and Rep. Romano L. Mazzoli (D.-Ky.). Their bills paired employer sanctions with amnesty for undocumented aliens who had arrived in the United States before 1980 (in the Senate version) or before 1982 (in the House version). Opposition came from Hispanic leaders and other civil liberties advocates who feared that employer sanctions would lead to the development of a national identification system and to job discrimination against all foreign-seeming persons, and from western farmers who felt that the proposed changes in the temporary worker program were inadequate to compensate for their loss of the undocumented labor pool.

In New York City, Mayor Edward I. Koch supported amnesty and employer sanctions, but insisted on criminal penalties against employers who used employer sanctions as an excuse to discriminate against legal workers. Koch also insisted on full reimbursement to the localities for any public service costs they might incur during the first years of the legalization program.

The House and Senate each passed a version of the bill, but the conference committee could not resolve the differences between them. The committee's work foundered on the questions of how to guarantee the rights of legal aliens in the work force and an equitable reimbursement formula for local public service costs attendant upon the legalization program.

New versions of the bill made their appearance in 1985. Alan Simpson once again was sponsor in the Senate, and Representative Rodino joined Rep. Mazzoli to become chief sponsor in the House. The Senate bill passed in September 1985. The Rodino bill, however, moved slowly because of controversy over its provisions for agricultural guest workers. Temporary agricultural workers proved to be the single most inflammatory debate of 1985 and 1986, although legal workers' rights and reimbursement of local costs attendant upon the amnesty were still important as well.

Western growers advanced a well-organized and powerful campaign for continued use of immigrant day labor—now mostly undocumented. They were fought by U.S. labor interests and activists concerned about exploitation of migrant workers. Agreement seemed impossible.

In the summer of 1986, Representative Charles Schumer of New York proposed a daring compromise on agricultural workers: aliens who had worked in U.S. agriculture for at least 60 days in the previous year would be eligible immediately for legal permanent residence. Reaction to Schumer's proposal was mixed, and in late September of 1986, the House failed to reach agreement on the rule that would govern final debate. The Rodino bill seemed dead.

The bill made a remarkable recovery, however, in the final days of the session, as a result of aggressive behind-the-scenes negotiations undertaken by Rodino and other supporters. The House passed the Rodino bill, with a revised version of the Schumer compromise, and a House-Senate conference committee was able to agree on a unified version of the Simpson and Rodino bills. More than a decade of Congressional debate came to an end on October 17 with passage of the Simpson-Rodino bill, known officially as the Immigration Reform and Control Act of 1986. President Reagan signed it into law on November 6.

The law makes it illegal to hire aliens who lack work authorization, imposes civil and criminal sanctions against employers who do so, and established an office to investigate complaints of discrimination against legal workers in hiring. Under Simpson-Rodino's amnesty program, aliens who can prove illegal presence in the United States since before January 1, 1982, and who meet other standard INS criteria, are eligible for legal temporary residence and later for legal permanent residence. Aliens who can prove they worked in U.S. agriculture for at least 90 days in the period May 1985-May 1986 are similarly eligible for temporary and then permanent residence.

The law also increases INS enforcement appropriations, raises colonial immigration quotas from 600 to 5,000 (a boon especially for Hong Kong), grants Cuban-Haitian entrants and some other Cubans and Haitians who arrived in the United States before January 1, 1982, the opportunity to apply for legal permanent residence, and updates what is known as the "registry" date from 1948 to 1972. Now, aliens who have lived in the United States since 1972 or earlier may apply for legal permanent residence.

Aliens legalized under the amnesty program (not including Cubans and Haitians) are ineligible for most federal benefits for five years. The law permits state and local reimbursements of $1 billion per year for each of four years to offset local service costs for newly legalized aliens.

The law allows the federal government to institute its Systematic Alien Verification for Entitlements program, commonly known as SAVE, through which states are required to verify the immigration status of all aliens applying for benefits that are federally supported. The SAVE program is part of a Reagan Administration effort to cut down on purported high levels of welfare fraud among aliens.

We cannot predict the ultimate effects of the Simpson-Rodino Act with any greater certainty than could lawmakers predict the effects of Hart-Celler. It will be several years before we know whether the law has been effective in discouraging the employment of unauthorized aliens, and discouraging their entry into the United States. It will be years before we know what will happen to industries that have relied heavily on an undocumented labor pool. The numbers of aliens who will qualify for amnesty cannot be predicted, nor can the effects on those many aliens who will remain illegal. If the law is successful in discouraging the employment of unauthorized aliens, we will see whether job prospects improve for our native-born unemployed. That, after all, was the point.

PREFERENCE SYSTEM

The Hart-Celler Act of 1965 made "family reunification" the stated goal of immigrant admissions policy, and established a preference system that favored applicants with close relatives in the United States. In its present, slightly amended form, the preference system has seven tiers, four based on family relationships, two based on job skills that are needed in the United States, and one discretionary tier.

The emphasis on reuniting families at first makes it difficult for new ethnic groups to gain a foothold in the United States because they lack a base of relatives to petition for their entry. But once a few arrive, perhaps on occupational preferences, their numbers can increase rapidly as they petition for a now-favored stream of their close relatives.

In general, immediate relatives are favored over distant relatives, and relatives of U.S. citizens over relatives of resident aliens. The most favored group of relatives—spouses, parents, and minor children of U.S. citizens—is not subject to the preference system. They can enter the United States at any time, exempt from the annual ceiling of 270,000 immigrants. Between 1965 and 1980, 2.5 million immediate relatives of U.S. citizens—one-third of all immigrants—were admitted in this way.

All other prospective immigrants are regulated by the preference system and its hierarchy of justifications for admission. Each country is allotted a maximum of 20,000 immigrant visas a year, apportioned in the following preference categories:

- First preference—unmarried adult sons and daughters of U.S. citizens (20 percent of available visas).
- Second preference—spouses and unmarried sons and daughters of permanent resident aliens (26 percent of available visas).
- Third preference—members of the professions, scientists, and artists of exceptional ability, and their spouses and children (10 percent of available visas).
- Fourth preference—married sons and daughters of U.S. citizens, and their spouses and children (10 percent of available visas).
- Fifth preference—brothers and sisters of U.S. citizens, and their spouses and children (24 percent of available visas).
- Sixth preference—skilled and unskilled workers in occupations for which labor is in short supply in this country, and their spouses and children (10 percent of available visas).
- Seventh (nonpreference)—open to immigrants not entitled to visas under any of the other six preferences; this category was inactive from 1978 through 1986, but 10,000 visas were made available for 1987 and 1988 combined.

CHRONOLOGY OF IMMIGRATION LEGISLATION

1882 Immigration Act

- Authority over immigration given to the Secretary of the Treasury, and a 50-cent head tax imposed on each immigrant.
- Mental defectives, convicts, and paupers barred from entry.

1882 Chinese Exclusion Act

- Immigration of Chinese laborers prohibited, although students, merchants, and professionals could enter.

1917 Language Test

- Immigrants age 17 and over must be literate in at least one language.

1921 Temporary National Origins Quotas

- Eastern Hemisphere immigration limited to 350,000 annually.
- Number of immigrants from each country limited to 3 percent of those born in that country who were already here in 1910.
- Western Hemisphere immigration unlimited, except from European possessions.
- European possessions subsumed under the quotas of their colonial powers.
- Asian immigration prohibited.

1924 Johnson-Reed Act (Permanent National Origins Quota Act)

- Eastern Hemisphere immigration limited to 150,000 annually.
- Quotas assigned as a percentage of U.S. residents of each ancestry group.
- Western Hemisphere immigration still unlimited.
- Asian immigration still prohibited.
- Foreign-born spouses and minor children of U.S. citizens admitted outside of quotas.

1943 Chinese exclusion repealed

1948 Displaced Persons Act

- Wartime refugees admitted outside quotas.

1952 McCarran-Walter Act (Immigration and Nationality Act)

- Eastern Hemisphere immigration still limited to 150,000.
- National origins quotas retained.
- Four-tiered preference system designed to allocate visas. First preference (50 percent of available visas) for workers with scarce skills. Second, third, and fourth preferences for relatives of U.S. citizens and permanent resident aliens.
- Western Hemisphere immigration still largely unlimited.
- Ban on Asian immigration repealed. Asian countries brought under quota system.
- European possessions assigned quotas of 100 visas each.
- Stiff anti-Communist screening and deportation procedures enacted.

1953 Refugee Relief Act

- Refugees admitted outside quotas.

1957 Refugee-Escapee Act

- Refugees and escapees defined as aliens fleeing political or religious persecution in Communist or Middle Eastern countries.

1960 Cuban refugee program established

1965 Hart-Celler Act (Amendments to the Immigration and Nationality Act)

- Eastern Hemisphere immigration limited to 170,000, including refugees. All countries granted equal visa limit of 20,000.
- Seven-tiered preference system adopted. First, second, fourth, and fifth preferences (74 percent of available visas) for relatives of U.S. citizens and permanent resident aliens. Third preference (10 percent) for professionals, scientists, and artists. Sixth preference (10 percent) for workers with scarce skills. Seventh preference (6 percent) for refugees.
- Western Hemisphere immigration limited to 120,000, with no per-country limits and no preference system.
- European colony quotas raised to 200; former colonies get parity with other nations.

1976 Amendment to Immigration and Nationality Act

- Western Hemisphere brought under its own 20,000-per-country visa limit and preference system; rest of world remains covered by separate, parallel system.
- Colony quotas raised to 600.

1978 Amendment to Immigration and Nationality Act

- Hemisphere ceilings combined into single worldwide ceiling of 290,000.

1980 Refugee Act

- Refugees removed from preference system and given a separate quota, set annually by Congress and the president.
- Worldwide immigration ceiling lowered to 270,000.
- Visas formerly reserved for refugees now assigned to second preference, raising visas reserved for relatives to 80 percent of total.
- United Nations definition of refugee adopted, to include persons fleeing non-Communist nations.
- Federal resettlement benefits provided for refugees.

1980 Fascell-Stone Amendment to Refugee Education Assistance Act

- Cuban and Haitian "entrants" awarded same benefits package as refugees, but rights to permanent status not awarded.

1986 Immigration Reform and Control Act (Simpson-Rodino Act)

- Employers prohibited from hiring foreign-born workers who lack work authorization, with penalties against employers who do.
- Aliens living in the United States without authorization since before January 1, 1982, now eligible to apply first for temporary legal residence and later for permanent legal residence ("amnesty" program).
- Cuban-Haitian "entrants" and certain other Cubans and Haitians who arrived before January 1, 1982, now eligible to apply for permanent residence.
- Agricultural workers who worked at least 90 days in U.S. agriculture between May 1985 and May 1986 eligible to apply for temporary and then permanent legal residence.
- Registry date updated from June 30, 1948, to January 1, 1972.
- Colonial quotas increased from 600 to 5,000.
- Seventh preference reopened temporarily for first time since 1978.

1986 Marriage Fraud Amendments to the Immigration and Nationality Act

- Legal permanent residence achieved through marriage to a U.S. citizen or permanent resident alien is made "conditional" for two years, pending verification that the marriage was and is still valid.

PART II

Today's Demographics

3 Recent Statistics on New York City Immigration

INTRODUCTION

In 1969, Salvador Rodriguez, then age 25, left the Dominican Republic for New York. He moved in with his sister in Washington Heights and soon found a job as a truck loader for a downtown Manhattan factory where his brother-in-law was employed.

Immediately after he started work, Salvador petitioned the INS for the admission of his wife Isabel, age 21, and their year-old son Jose. A year later Isabel and Jose were in New York.

Isabel took a job as a sewing machine operator in a garment factory in Washington Heights. While she was at work, Salvador's sister cared for Jose, and later for Maria and Richard, who were born in 1971 and 1973. Together, Salvador and Isabel earned about $10,000 a year. In 1975 they were able to leave Salvador's sister's apartment for one of their own.

By 1978 Salvador was earning $10,000 a year as a truck driver for the company that had hired him in 1969. He was able to help his brother Pedro, who was still in the Dominican Republic, with airfare to New York and a room in the family's home. When Pedro arrived in New York, he went to work as a dishwasher in a local restaurant, where he earned $5,000 a year. Now Isabel no longer needed to work; the family income was $15,000 without her contribution. Salvador was gratified that his finances were secure enough for Isabel to stay at home.

The Rodriguezes are not an actual family, but they are representative of today's immigrant families in New York City. Data from the 1980 U.S. census confirm that the Rodriguezes were typical in many ways:

- They came from the Dominican Republic, which sent more immigrants to New York between 1965 and 1980 than any other nation.
- They were a two-parent family.
- They shared their home with a relative.
- Two of their three children were born in the United States.
- Their family income was considerably lower than the median for native-born New Yorkers when they first began to work, but as time passed, their income moved closer to the native median.
- Isabel Rodriguez worked as a sewing machine operator, the largest single source of employment for Dominican (and Chinese) women.
- Salvador Rodriguez got his first job as a manual laborer at a factory and worked his way into a more skilled and better-paying position.

USING CENSUS DATA

The 1980 census provides the fullest available picture of New York City's immigrant population, in spite of the fact that it was taken seven years before this book was published and did not succeed in counting all New Yorkers, particularly immigrants who were living in the United States without authorization to do so.

Census data can be used to analyze the demographic characteristics of individual immigrants like Salvador, Isabel, Jose, and Pedro Rodriguez, and they can be used to study the characteristics of households headed by immigrants, which often include native-born members like Maria and Richard Rodriguez.

Census data permitted analysis of immigrant characteristics based on the period of immigration. In this study three entry periods were selected for analysis: the period before 1965, the year in which the Hart-Celler Act changed the course of immigration to America; 1965–74, the middle period; and 1975–80, the period of the newest arrivals. All arrivals after 1965 were viewed as "new" immigrants, but the post–1965 period was subdivided in order to distinguish between families like the Rodriguezes, who had had some time to settle into their lives in New York, and the newest families, who were not yet so well established.

The term "immigrant" is used interchangeably with "foreign-born." An immigrant is defined as a U.S. resident who was born abroad of parents who were not U.S. citizens. The immigrant category includes foreign-born persons who are naturalized U.S. citizens and those who are not naturalized. In 1980 just over half of the city's 1.68 million foreign-born were naturalized citizens.

Extensive use was made of the 1980 U.S. Census Public Use Microdata File, which permitted cross-tabulations of data on immigrants that are not available in Census Bureau publications. The Microdata File is a representative 5 percent sample of New York City's population.

NEW YORK CITY IMMIGRATION TRENDS: THE NUMBERS

In the decade between 1970 and 1980, New York City's foreign-born population rose from 1.44 million (17.9 percent of the city's total population) to 1.68 million (23.7 percent), according to census data. If all undocumented aliens had been counted in the 1980 census, the recorded number of foreign-born would probably have exceeded 2 million. The undercount of undocumented aliens, and estimates of their numbers in New York, are discussed in Chapter 4.

The 1910 census was the first in which data on immigrants became available for all five boroughs. The size of the immigrant population for 1910 and each subsequent census year is shown in Table 3.1.

Although immigration to the United States began to be curtailed with the national origins quota legislation of the 1920s, the decline did not show until the 1940 census, when immigrant population figures dropped for the first time in New York City's history.

It was not until the 1970s that the downward trend was reversed, largely as a result of the liberalized immigration legislation of 1965 and growing pressure for emigration in the nations of Asia and Latin America.

Census figures showed a net increase of about 240,000 foreign-born in the decade 1970–80. The trend almost certainly will continue unless new legislation intervenes, perhaps even if it does. If the 1970–80 rate of increase continues, by 1990 New York City will have almost 2 million recorded foreign-born residents. By the turn of the 21st century, the figure will come close to the all-time numerical high of almost 2.4 million, reached in 1930.

COUNTRY OF ORIGIN

New York City's newest faces in 1980 were Latin American, Caribbean, and Asian. Some European nations continued, however, to send significant numbers of immigrants to New York, especially the USSR, Greece, and Italy.

The 1.68 million foreign-born residents of New York in 1980 were the products of many decades of immigration. A large remnant of the century's early immigrants remained in the city and mixed with the post–1965 wave. In 1980 Italians were still more numerous in New York than any other immigrant group because of the magnitude of their earlier

Table 3.1

Foreign-Born Population of New York City, 1910-1980

Census year	Total Population	Foreign-born Population	Foreign-born as percent of total
1910	4,767,000	1,944,000	40.8
1920	5,620,000	2,028,000	36.1
1930	6,930,000	2,359,000	34.0
1940	7,455,000	2,139,000	28.7
1950	7,892,000	1,861,000	23.6
1960	7,782,000	1,559,000	20.0
1970	7,895,000	1,437,000	18.2
1980	7,092,000	1,675,000	23.6

Source: Published Tabulations, U.S. census, 1910-1970. For 1980, unpublished Public Use Microdata File figures were used for consistency with other data in this study.

migration. Of the 156,000 Italian-born persons in the city, almost three-quarters had arrived before 1965 (see Table 3.2).

The Dominican Republic was second on the list of countries of origin in 1980. More than 80 percent of the city's 121,000 recorded Dominicans had arrived in the United States after 1965.

It is worth noting that in the years between 1960 and 1980:

- Italian-born New Yorkers maintained their number-one position despite a 44 percent decrease in their numbers.
- The Dominican-born moved up in rank from 26 to 2, with a percentage increase of 1,200.
- The Korean-born population had the highest percentage increase, moving from a minuscule base of 562 in 1960 to 20,380 in 1980.
- All decreases occurred among European immigrant groups—Italians, Russians, Poles, Germans, Irish, Austrians, English, Hungarians, and Romanians.
- Immigrants were distributed among many more countries of origin in 1980 than in 1960.

The Dominican Republic ranked first among countries of origin for New York City immigrants who entered the United States between 1975 and 1980 (see Table 3.3). For that immigration period five of the top ten sending nations were Caribbean, three were Asian, one was South American, and only one, the USSR, was European. The USSR was high on the list because the Soviet government permitted a large number of Jews to emigrate during 1975–80. After 1981 very few were permitted to leave.

There is good reason to believe that the top-ranked nations of 1975–80 will continue to be major sources of New York City immigration throughout the 1980s, with the possible exception of the USSR. But some notable changes in the immigration flow have occurred since the 1980 census was taken:

- Larger-than-usual numbers of Cubans and Haitians entered the United States in 1980, and migrated northward from Florida, where they had arrived in a massive boatlift that spring.
- The Refugee Act of 1980 resulted in the organized resettlement in New York City of many refugees from Vietnam, Cambodia, Poland, Romania, and Afghanistan.
- Asylum seekers from the strife-torn nations of Central America began to arrive in New York, as in many other American cities.

The 1990 census will show the magnitude of these changes.

Table 3.2

Immigrants in New York City, by Country of Birth, 1980 and 1960

Country of Birth	Rank in 1980	Number in 1980	Rank in 1960	Number in 1960	Percent Change 1960-1980
All countries		1,675,160		1,562,478	+7
Italy	1	156,280	1	281,033	-44
Dominican Republic	2	120,600	26	9,223	+1,208
Jamaica	3	93,100	24	11,160	+734
USSR	4	87,360	2	204,821	-57
China*	5	85,100	15	19,769	+330
Poland	6	77,160	3	168,960	-54
Germany, West and East	7	60,760	4	152,502	-60
Haiti	8	50,160	42	3,002	+1,571
Cuba	9	49,720	11	28,567	+74
Ireland/N. Ireland	10	43,520	5	114,163	-62
Greece	11	41,760	12	28,882	+45
Colombia	12	41,200	34	4,766	+764
Trinidad and Tobago	13	39,160	32	5,495	+613
Ecuador	14	39,000	44	2,796	+1,295
Guyana	15	31,960	**	**	**
Austria	16	26,160	6	84,389	-69
England	17	22,720	8	40,769	-44
Hungary	18	22,660	7	45,602	-50
Yugoslavia	19	22,300	19	12,399	+80
India	20	21,500	54	1,243	+1,630
Philippines	21	21,260	39	3,997	+435
Panama	22	20,840	33	677	+2,978
Korea, North and South	23	20,380	59	562	+3,526
Barbados	24	19,680	**	**	**
Romania	25	17,560	14	24,784	-29
Total countries listed		1,231,900		1,249,541	-1
All other countries		331,620		305,835	+8
Not reported		111,640		7,102	+1,472

*Includes Hong Kong and Taiwan

**These figures are not available for 1960 because Guyana and Barbados were included in the total for the British West Indies.

Source: 1980 U.S. Census Public Use Microdata File; 1960 U.S. Census.

Table 3.3

Foreign-Born in New York City, 1980
Who Entered Between 1975 and 1980

Birthplace	Number
All countries	353,900
Dominican Republic	35,860
U.S.S.R.	29,020
China*	25,520
Jamaica	23,660
Guyana	15,720
Haiti	13,840
Korea	11,660
Colombia	11,420
Trinidad and Tobago	10,640
India	10,500
Ecuador	9,820
Philippines	7,060
Greece	6,680
Italy	6,560
Barbados	5,480
Japan	5,440
Israel	4,660
England	4,640
Panama	4,540
Poland	4,220
Iran	3,560
Vietnam	3,280
Peru	3,080
El Salvador	3,000
Romania	2,860
Total countries listed	262,720
All other countries	68,480
Not reported	22,700

*Includes Hong Kong and Taiwan.

Source: 1980 U.S. Census Public Use Microdata File.

RACE

The racial makeup of New York City's immigrants shifted with their countries of origin (see Table 3.4). In 1980, 45.8 percent of the city's total immigrant population was white non-Hispanic, but of the most recent immigrants—those who arrived between 1975 and 1980—only 25.7 percent were white. The recent arrivals were almost evenly divided among whites, blacks, Hispanics, and Asians. Consistent with the shift in countries of origin, the percentage of immigrants who were Asian increased as dramatically as the percentage who were white decreased.

Table 3.4

Racial Distribution (percent) of New York City's Population, 1980

	Total Population	Native-Born	Foreign-born by period of immigration			
			Total	Pre-1965	1965-74	1975-80
Total	100.0	100.0	100.0	100.0	100.0	100.0
White Non-Hispanic	52.0	53.9	45.8	73.1	24.0	25.7
Black Non-Hispanic	24.0	25.7	18.4	8.4	27.9	23.4
Asian Non-Hispanic	3.6	1.1	11.7	4.3	14.1	22.7
Other Non-Hispanic	0.3	0.2	0.5	0.3	0.6	0.8
Hispanic	20.2	19.1	23.6	13.9	33.4	27.4

Note: Because of rounding off, totals may not equal 100.0 percent.
Source: 1980 U.S. Census Public Use Microdata File.

AGE AND SEX

New York City's immigrant population clusters in two age groups: working-age people and the elderly. There is a large cluster of the former because immigrants tend to migrate during their prime working years; and there is a cluster of the latter because a large remnant of the century's early immigrants remains in New York. The childhood years are underrepresented among immigrants because immigrants by definition are not born here and are less likely than the native-born to spend their childhoods here. These factors pushed the median age of the city's foreign-born to 42.6 in 1980, compared with 29.4 for the native-born (see Table 3.5). The median age of the most recent arrivals was lower, however, than that of the native-born; immigrants arrive young. The percentage of males and females in 1980 was the same for the native- and foreign-born: 46 percent males and 54 percent females.

EDUCATION

Data from the 1980 census showed that New York City's immigrants had less education than the city's native-born residents. (The census does not indicate where the education was obtained—abroad, in the United States, or both; it just tells the highest level achieved.) The gap appeared to be narrowing over time. The most recent immigrants—those who arrived between 1975 and 1980—had more high school graduates than any earlier immigrant group, but not yet as many as the native-born. Interestingly, they had a higher proportion than the native-born of persons who had completed college.

These findings correspond with the fact that the new immigrants include a substantial number of professionally trained persons, especially Asians, who may or may not have the opportunity to practice their professions once they arrive in New York. English-speaking immigrants, such as Asian Indians and British West Indians, are more likely to be working in the professions here than are professionally trained persons from non-English-speaking countries.

Although the relatively high educational achievement of the 1975–80 immigrants was not reflected in their 1980 income, it should be in later censuses.

The percentages of high school and college graduates among the native- and foreign-born show a wider gap between foreign-born men and women than between native-born men and women (see Table 3.6). This gap was greater among the most recent immigrants than among the earlier ones, probably because of the social roles and expectations for men and women in the countries of origin. For many of the recent

Table 3.5

Age Distribution of New York City's Population (percent), 1980

	Total population	Native-born	Foreign-born by period of immigration			
			Total	Before 1965	1965-1974	1975-1980
Total	100.0	100.0	100.0	100.0	100.0	100.0
Under 15	20.7	25.0	7.0	--	7.4	20.6
15 to 29	25.1	26.1	21.7	5.8	30.4	39.6
30 to 64	40.8	38.5	48.3	47.5	57.2	35.7
65 and over	13.4	10.4	23.0	46.7	4.9	4.1
Median age	32.6	29.4	42.6	62.9	34.1	26.5

Note: Because of rounding off, totals may not equal 100.0 percent.
Source: 1980 U. S. Census Public Use Microdata File.

Table 3.6

High School and College Graduates (percent) in New York City's Population, 1980

	Total Population	Native-Born	Foreign-Born by period of immigration			
			Total	Pre-1965	1965-1974	1975-1980
High School						
Total	60.2	64.3	50.8	45.8	55.3	58.7
Male	62.2	65.7	54.1	48.4	58.2	63.8
Female	58.7	63.2	48.1	43.9	52.8	54.1
College						
Total	17.2	18.8	13.8	11.0	14.8	23.1
Male	21.3	22.8	17.8	13.8	17.9	27.5
Female	14.1	15.6	10.6	8.0	12.1	17.2

Source: 1980 U.S. Census Public Use Microdata File.

immigrants, education is regarded in their country of origin as less necessary for women than for men.

EMPLOYMENT

Two standard measures are generally used to describe labor force activity: the labor force participation rate and the unemployment rate. The participation rate indicates the proportion of the total potential work force that was working or looking for work in the calendar week prior to census enumeration. The unemployment rate shows the proportion of active labor force participants who were not able to find work.

To ensure an unambiguous comparison, the analysis of native and immigrant employment patterns in this study was restricted to persons aged 25–44; younger and older persons, with their unique employment problems, were excluded.

In 1980 the overall differences in labor force participation between native- and foreign-born men were statistically insignificant. Native-born men had a participation rate of 87 percent, compared with 90 percent for foreign-born men. Among women the figures were virtually the same for the native- and foreign-born: 61 and 62 percent, respectively.

The unemployment picture was similar—that is, differences between the native- and foreign-born were minimal. The unemployment rates (percent) were 7.0 for native-born men, 6.2 for foreign-born men, 6.6 for native-born women, and 7.6 for foreign-born women.

Despite these overall similarities, important differences emerged when the native- and foreign-born groups were analyzed by race. The labor force participation rates were significantly higher for foreign-born blacks and Hispanics than for native-born blacks and Hispanics. The data are presented in Chapter 7.

HOUSEHOLD AND FAMILY CHARACTERISTICS

In the traditional immigrant story, a young man ventures to his new land alone. He establishes himself geographically and financially, then sends for, or acquires, his family. This pattern prevailed for many immigrants of the 19th and early 20th centuries, and it still holds for many immigrants like the hypothetical Rodriguez family, with whose story this chapter began.

Today, however, there are variations on the theme. Today's immigrants are more likely than before to arrive as family units, especially if they are refugees. If they do arrive alone, it is often the women who come first. If they arrive alone, they are likely to become part of a household of close relatives, such as sisters or brothers, who arrived before them. And it is not long before they send for their own families.

Current immigration law favors families, and that fact shows up in the demographic data; immigrants are more likely than the native-born to live as family members.

Thus far, this chapter has analyzed the characteristics of individual immigrants. Now the analysis moves to households and families. An immigrant household is defined as one whose self-identified head is foreign-born. The terms "immigrant household" and "foreign-headed household" are used synonymously.

Immigrant households can, and do, contain native-born members, much as native-headed households can and do contain members who were born abroad, but the former is much more common than the latter.

A household, whether immigrant or native, is an individual or group of individuals who occupy one housing unit, as opposed to persons who live in nursing homes, dormitories, or other group quarters. Households may contain family members and unrelated persons.

HOUSEHOLD TYPE

In 1980 there were almost 2.8 million households in New York City, of which just over 2 million had native-born heads and 781,000 had foreign-born heads. Immigrant households were more likely than native households to contain a family; 68.6 percent of foreign-headed households were what is known in census terminology as family households, compared with 61.4 percent of native-headed households. Immigrant households were more likely to consist of married couples than were native-headed households, and immigrants were less likely than the native-born to be living alone or with unrelated persons. Immigrants who were living alone were more likely to be widows and less likely to be young singles than were native-born persons living alone (see Table 3.7).

Family households were especially common among post–1965 immigrants, in part because of their age and in part because of today's immigration patterns.

IMMIGRANT HOUSEHOLDS: THE FOREIGN/NATIVE MIX

As the story of Salvador and Isabel Rodriguez demonstrated, immigrant households are not made up solely of immigrants. Many of the children living in immigrant households were born in the United States, and other household members may be U.S.-born as well, though such was not the case in the Rodriguez household. In 1980, more than a quarter of the members of immigrant households were native-born. Of

Table 3.7

Household Type by Nativity of Householder and Period of Immigration (percent)

	Total population	Native-born	Foreign-born by period of immigration			
			Total	Pre-1965	1965-1974	1975-1980
Total households	100.0	100.0	100.0	100.0	100.0	100.0
Family households	63.4	61.4	68.6	61.4	79.5	72.6
Married couple	44.0	40.8	52.3	48.9	57.1	55.5
Male householder, no spouse	3.0	3.0	3.2	2.5	3.8	4.7
Female householder, no spouse	16.4	17.6	13.1	10.0	18.6	12.4
Nonfamily households	36.6	38.6	31.4	38.6	20.5	27.4
Householder living alone	32.6	34.0	28.8	36.6	17.7	22.7
Householder sharing living quarters	4.0	4.6	2.6	2.0	2.8	4.7

Source: 1980 U.S. Census Public Use Microdata File.

Table 3.8

Nativity of Foreign-Headed Household Members

	Total Members		Native-born Members		Foreign-born Members	
	Number	Percent	Number	Percent	Number	Percent
Total members	2,082,500	100.0	576,220	27.7	1,506,280	72.3
Householders	781,000	100.0	--	--	781,000	100.0
Spouses	408,400	100.0	91,160	22.3	317,240	77.7
Children	700,600	100.0	433,820	61.9	266,780	38.1
Other Relatives	141,420	100.0	33,340	23.6	108,080	76.4
Nonrelatives	51,080	100.0	17,900	35.0	33,180	65.0

Source: 1980 U.S. Census Public Use Microdata File.

Table 3.9

Household and Family Size

	Total Population	Native-Headed	Foreign-Headed
Average Household Size	2.50	2.43	2.67
Average Family Size	3.24	3.19	3.34

Source: 1980 U.S. Census Public Use Microdata File.

Table 3.10

Median Household Income by Household Type

	Total households	Native-Born	Foreign-born by period of immigration			
			Total	Pre-1965	1965-1974	1975-1980
Total households	$13,859	$14,325	$12,783	$12,309	$14,139	$11,217
Family households						
Married couple	20,625	21,966	17,601	18,924	17,561	13,460
Male householder, no spouse	16,698	16,900	16,250	17,500	16,117	13,790
Female householder, no spouse	8,516	8,042	10,073	2,329	8,902	7,025
Nonfamily households	9,301	10,188	6,918	6,000	10,206	8,489

Source: 1980 U.S. Census Public Use Microdata File.

the children living in immigrant households, 61.9 percent were born in this country (see Table 3.8).

HOUSEHOLD AND FAMILY SIZE

In 1980 both the average immigrant household and the average immigrant family were larger than the corresponding native-headed units. Households include persons living alone, which brings the average household size below the average family size (see Table 3.9).

Immigrants' larger household and family size results from several factors: the greater economy of larger households; the age concentration in the childbearing years; cultural patterns that favor larger families; and U.S. immigration law, which encourages extended-family members, such as parents and adult siblings, to join their families in the United States.

INCOME

The median household income of foreign-headed households was almost $1,500 lower than that of native-headed households in 1980: $12, 783, compared with $14,325 (see Table 3.10). The lower immigrant median prevailed in most cases regardless of household type, except in family households headed by immigrant women, whose median income was $10,073 compared with $8,042 among family households headed by native-born women. The higher immigrant median was probably due to income contributed by adult, wage-earning children of middle-aged and elderly immigrant women.

The data suggest that immigrant family income increases steadily over time. In all types of immigrant family household, income was lowest among the most recent immigrants and highest among those who arrived before 1965.

4 Undocumented Aliens and the Census Undercount

The national discussion of immigration control has been accompanied by widely varying and often somewhat inflammatory efforts to estimate the number of undocumented aliens in the United States. New York City officials have made efforts to estimate the undocumented in the city, not so much to make a case for immigration control as to guarantee the city its fair share of federal funds and legislative seats. The city estimates its undocumented population at somewhere between 400,000 and 750,000.

Efforts to estimate the undocumented are obstructed by many factors, not the least of which is the lack of a single, commonly accepted definition of what an "undocumented" or "illegal" or "unauthorized" alien is. Nor is there a solid understanding of who these people are that we call "undocumented" or "illegal" and what kind of lives they are living in the United States. In this chapter, we will look at the problem of definition, we will offer some informed speculations about the characteristics of undocumented aliens in the City of New York, we will discuss the efforts that have been made to estimate the numbers of undocumented, and we will examine why the numbers matter.

WHAT IS AN "ILLEGAL" ALIEN?

The term "illegal alien" exists nowhere in immigration law or in any other U.S. law. It is strictly a colloquial term, used to describe aliens who are living or working in the United States without official authorization. It covers a spectrum of aliens whose claims to legal status vary from virtually hopeless to almost certain. The term is misleading in that it suggests a pervasive flouting of the rules, which is far from common practice among the country's aliens. Most "illegal" aliens live law-abiding lives among aliens or citizens whose status is legal. Some are in the process of applying for regularization of their status, with excellent likelihood of achieving it because of the strength of their claims under immigration law. Some have been approved for legal permanent residence and are waiting for a visa to become available. Long before the "amnesty" program offered by the Simpson-Rodino Act of 1986, many undocumented aliens were finding entirely legal ways to obtain legal resident status from the INS.

The term "illegal" is also misleading in that it suggests a criminal immigration status. Technically, unauthorized presence in the United States is a civil offense, not a criminal one. In theory, it is not punishable by the criminal penalties of imprisonment or fine. In actuality, however, aliens under deportation proceedings are often held in detention, sometimes for protracted periods of time. Peter H. Schuck, a legal scholar whose specialty is immigration law, believes that some of the legal consequences of classifying deportation as a civil proceeding are highly injurious to aliens, in particular because certain constitutional rights, such as those protected by the Sixth Amendment, are expressly limited to criminal proceedings.[1]

Schuck contends that immigration law is based on an outmoded concept of the priority of property rights; the United States is like a landowner with absolute authority over trespassers—that is, aliens. The sovereign right of a nation to exclude strangers still takes precedence over the human rights that have come increasingly to take a place in other forms of law.

The inspiration for the term "illegal alien" arises from immigration law although it does not appear there. The technical INS term for a green-card holder is "legal permanent resident." The use of the word "legal" implies that other aliens are not legal. In fact, there are many other categories of aliens whose long-term presence in the United States is authorized by the INS, including refugees, entrants, and asylees. In addition, there are innumerable classifications of legal "nonimmigrants," to use INS terminology, such as foreign students, tourists, and business visitors. Furthermore, the "amnesty" provisions of Simpson-Rodino add a new legal category: temporary resident alien. In broad terms, the INS subdivides aliens as follows:

- *Valid visa holders*. Temporary or permanent aliens who hold valid current visas. They include legal permanent residents, refugees and asylees, students, tourists, temporary workers, and business visitors, as long as they are not violating the conditions set forth in their visas.
- *Aliens out of status*. Persons who were issued valid visas but have violated the

conditions of those visas by, for example, working without authorization or staying beyond the visa expiration date.

- *Entries without inspection (EWIs).* Aliens who entered the country without visas and without making themselves known to immigration authorities.

There is no special terminology for aliens who have applied for regularization of their status, nor for aliens whom the INS permits to stay for humanitarian reasons, such as children, the elderly, and the ill. On paper these aliens have no special rights, although the INS tends not to exercise its authority to deport them.

U.S. social service law takes a somewhat different approach to alien classification, and its definitions coordinate poorly with the language used in immigration law. In making determinations of eligibility for social services, aliens are classified as follows:

- Permanent resident aliens.
- Aliens "permanently residing in the United States under color of law (PRUCOL)" including refugees, asylees, entrants, and persons living in the country with the knowledge and permission of the INS.
- Persons "unlawfully residing" in the United States, a term that appears in New York State social service law but not in federal social service law. Federal law lists eligible categories only.

Now, temporary and permanent resident aliens who achieve their status under the Simpson-Rodino amnesty program will have to be added as separate categories on the list since the law specifies that their entitlements differ from those of PRUCOL aliens or of aliens who achieve permanent resident status through other INS mechanisms.

Immigrant advocates take the position that any alien who is known to the INS, and against whom the INS has not instituted deportation proceedings, is living here with INS "knowledge and permission" and should be considered PRUCOL. That interpretation would include visa overstayers and all aliens who have made application for adjustment of status. In recent years the courts have tended to support more liberal interpretations of legal status, at least for purposes of social service delivery. These matters are discussed further in Chapter 8.

The issue of legality often arises in the context of employment. An alien may be authorized to be in the country as a student, for example, or as the spouse of a student, but that authorization does not automatically confer permission to hold a job. Alien jobholders are supposed to be able to show a "green card" or other immigration documents stamped with the authorization to work. Otherwise, if they are working, they are doing so illegally. The Simpson-Rodino Act specifies the type of documents an employer must see before he or she can hire an alien applicant.

COUNTING UNDOCUMENTED ALIENS

An early estimate of the number of undocumented aliens in New York was made by Maurice F. Kiley, who was then director of the New York district of the INS. He estimated that there were about 1.5 million undocumented aliens in the greater New York INS district, of whom about 1 million were living in the five boroughs.[2] Kiley based his estimate on his knowledge of the numbers of aliens who had entered the Port of New York as tourists and students during the previous ten years but had not left when their visas expired. (The New York INS district no longer keeps records that would make a current estimate possible.)

Subsequently, City Planning Department demographers reanalyzed Kiley's estimates and reduced the city figure to a maximum of 750,000. They began, as Kiley did, with an aggregate of nonimmigrant (temporary) aliens entering the city, then analyzed each major country of origin by its migrants' assumed propensity to overstay.

Nationwide, demographers agree that many undocumented aliens were missed by the 1980 Census, but some were included. Efforts have been made to determine how many undocumented aliens were counted by subtracting the number of aliens who registered with the INS in 1980 from the number of foreign-born non-citizens recorded in the census. Theoretically, the balance is unregistered aliens, most of whom are presumed to have been unauthorized to be in the United States. This type of analysis suggests that about 200,000 unregistered aliens living in New York City were recorded in the 1980 census, a figure that might be viewed as the lowest responsible estimate of the city's undocumented aliens. Various problems in the data have to be taken into account, however, such as some *legal* aliens' failure to register with the INS or with the census, and the tendency of some aliens to misidentify themselves to census takers as naturalized citizens.

Studies of this sort have been made by U.S. Census Bureau demographers Jeffrey Passel and Karen Woodrow.[3] They attempted to correct for the data problems mentioned, and developed estimates of undocumented aliens counted in the census. They estimate that 234,000 undocumented aliens were included in census figures for New York State, of whom 212,000 were in the greater New York City area. Their findings are discussed later in this chapter and in Chapter 5.

CHARACTERISTICS OF NEW YORK CITY'S UNDOCUMENTED ALIENS

By and large, undocumented aliens have evaded the nation's data-collecting mechanisms. Most information about them is anecdotal, although the Passel and Woodrow study cited earlier provides some corroboration of anecdotal information.

Most of New York City's undocumented aliens are visa overstayers—that is, they enter the country on valid temporary visas, usually through John F. Kennedy International Airport, and do not leave when their visas expire. The city has some "border crossers" as well—aliens who enter the country secretly, without visas or passports. Most of the city's border crossers are Haitians who enter the country along the Florida coast and make their way north, and Central Americans who enter over the Texas and California borders. The border crossers also include some aliens who make their way to Canada, and enter secretly at the New York/Canadian border.

New York's undocumented aliens are thought to come from the same nations that are the sources of large numbers of legal aliens, an idea that receives confirmation from Passel and Woodrow. Undocumented aliens often come from nations where there are strong political or economic pressures to leave; from nations that are close to the United States; from nations where there are long waiting lists for legal admission; and from nations whose governments make it difficult to leave legally. New York State has more undocumented aliens from the Caribbean than any other state—especially from the Dominican Republic, Haiti, and the former British West Indies. Undocumented aliens from Central and South America also gravitate to New York, as do aliens from countries much farther away, such as China, Korea, India, and Israel. Although Mexicans are the largest group of undocumented aliens in the United States, few of them migrate to New York.

New York's location doesn't invite the daily border crossing that is typical of the Southwest. Aliens who come to New York come here to live; consequently New York's undocumented aliens form a relatively stable, long-term community. INS statistics show that 60 percent of aliens deported from the New York district in 1980 had been in the United States for more than a year, whereas only 35 percent of deportees nationwide had been in the country that long. Passel and Woodrow found that New York State's undocumented aliens had been in the country longer than those of any other state.

Once inside the United States, New York's undocumented aliens become virtually indistinguishable from the rest of the city's recent immigrant population. Their ethnic backgrounds are the same, they work at many of the same jobs (especially at the lower end of the wage scale), and they live in the same neighborhoods, often in the same households. Many are single relatives—brothers, sisters, cousins—of permanent resident aliens. Passel and Woodrow found that New York State's undocumented aliens tended to be older than those of other states, which accorded with their earlier arrival dates. The ratio of women to men was unusually high, in part, Passel and Woodrow believe, because of women's greater longevity.

The theory that undocumented aliens tend to live in legal immigrant households, not in isolated clusters, gains corroboration from the Census Bureau finding that census undercounting generally results from undercounting within a household rather than failure to reach the household at all. One family member may have been missed, but the household was not.

Of the undocumented aliens who were enumerated in the census, one may speculate that many were married couples with households of their own. There is reason to believe that the census recorded most persons with school-age children, since the city's school enrollment figures for 1980 were very close to the census count of school-enrolled children. Some undocumented aliens may be keeping their children out of school for fear of detection, but it is unlikely that this could be taking place on a large scale without drawing the attention of persons who work with the immigrant community.

Some demographers estimate that undocumented aliens may be entering the city at nearly the same rate as legal aliens—75,000 a year. The undocumented population does not grow at anywhere near that rate, however, since many undocumented aliens achieve legal status, some return to their home countries, and some move elsewhere.

INCENTIVES FOR ILLEGAL IMMIGRATION

The prospects for an alien who wishes to become a legal resident of the United States, generally depend upon whether he or she meets the qualifications for permanent resident status under the preference system that governs immigrant admissions. The preference system favors applicants with close relatives who are U.S. citizens or permanent resident aliens, and applicants who have received offers for skilled jobs that cannot readily be filled by American workers.

Applicants for refugee status and political asylum face a different set of requirements. They must be able to prove that they have a "well-founded fear" of persecution if they return home.

For aliens who do not meet these criteria for legal admission, there are strong motivations to enter the country illegally. Their best hope of achieving permanent legal status is to develop a qualification, and that usually means a U.S. citizen spouse or a skilled job for which there is a shortage of American workers. Such qualifications are more easily developed in the United States than abroad. (Experienced immigration lawyers who know how to build successful cases are also more easily obtained here.) INS statistics show that in 1980, half the aliens who achieved permanent residence by marrying a citizen were already in the country. Many of them were undocumented aliens. Similarly, 44 percent of job-related "admissions" were already in the country.

Legislators who opposed the concept of an amnesty program generally did so because they believed that an amnesty would be seen as an invitation to more illegal immigration. Proponents insisted that the amnesty would be one time only, and therefore not an invitation, and that it would be offset by the new measures prohibiting the employment of unauthorized aliens. Whether or not amnesty brings new waves of hopeful green-card seekers remains to be seen, but we cannot be surprised if it does. Already the immigration system is rife with double messages of invitation and rejection.

To date, experience seems to show that most undocumented aliens who are sure enough of their case to apply eventually receive permanent resident status. The wait for a visa, however, can be many years. While they are waiting, applicants live in a legal limbo, technically deportable but unlikely to be deported. Aliens who qualify for amnesty will be spared these long waits, and the INS claims that they will also be spared the fear of deportation if their applications are turned down.

From an alien's point of view, U.S. immigration law can look so arbitrary that that itself is an invitation to circumvent it. Aliens who have maintained student or temporary worker status cannot see why they should not qualify for amnesty along with or ahead of those who have lived entirely out of status. Aliens from cultures with large extended families cannot understand a family unification system that admits brothers but not cousins. There is a fine art to demonstrating that one's labor is needed in the United States, and it is sometimes hard to understand or accept official definitions and decisions. The United States offers safe harbor to persons fleeing persecution from unfriendly nations like Vietnam, but not from "friendly" nations like El Salvador.

Immigration law is asked to deal with phenomena that are so powerful and complex that total equity is impossible. It is neither surprising nor entirely reprehensible that the world's prospective immigrants do what they can to make the system work to their benefit.

WHY THE NUMBERS MATTER

New York City has good reason to want its entire population counted in each census, no matter what the immigration status of each resident. Federal revenue-sharing grants and many other sources of federal funding are based in whole or in part on population count. So is congressional apportionment. Because New York City provides most major public services to its entire population, city officials contend, the city ought to be proportionately reimbursed and represented.

Using the post-census evaluation conducted by the U.S. Census Bureau itself, experts engaged by the city estimated that the city's population was undercounted by a minimum of 400,000. The Census Bureau contended that the evaluation was inadequate for a formal adjustment of the figures. To force an adjustment of the census figures, in August 1980 the city and state filed suit against the Census Bureau (*Carey v. Klutznick*). The case was tried in U.S. District Court for the Southern District; the city and state won. The Second Circuit Court of Appeals reversed the decision because of a procedural error and ordered a new trial. The case was retried as *Cuomo v. Baldrige*, and a decision is pending.

Besides New York, some 50 other states, cities, counties, and small jurisdictions filed suits against the Census Bureau, complaining of population undercounts.

In New York, the city alleges, the 1980 count was plagued by incomplete and erroneous data collection, bad publicity, and litigation. While the census count was in progress, the Mayor's Census Effort Office received complaints from all over the city that residents had not received census questionnaires, and that other practices were occurring that could lead to an undercount, particularly in minority neighborhoods, both native-and foreign-born.

An undercount of a half million would mean for the city the loss of one congressional seat and millions of dollars annually in revenue-sharing and other federal funds.

The amnesty program may offer an unusual opportunity to reevaluate the 1980 census count, as aliens come forward with evidence showing that they have lived in the United States, and perhaps in New York City, since before January 1, 1982. The number of aliens who come forward cannot be taken, however, as a full count of the undocumented population of the early 1980s. Many other factors countervail: aliens who lived in New York City then may by now have gone home, moved elsewhere, or found a way to adjust their status to permanent residency; prospectively eligible aliens may fear to come forward lest a rejected application result in deportation for self, family or friends. Still, the amnesty registration is an unprecedented opportunity for information on the numbers and characteristics of the aliens we call "undocumented."

NOTES

1. Peter H. Schuck, "The Transformation of Immigration Law," *Columbia Law Review* 84, no. 1 (January 1984):1–90 at 25.

2. See M.A. Farber, "Million Illegal Aliens in Metropolitan Area," *New York Times*, December 29, 1974, pp. 1 and 28.

3. Jeffrey S. Passel and Karen A. Woodrow, "Geographic Distribution of Undocumented Immigrants: Estimates of Undocumented Aliens Counted in the 1980 U.S. Census by State," *International Migration Review* 18, no. 3 (Fall 1984):642–75; Jeffrey S. Passel, "Immigration to the United States," speech delivered at symposium "*The New Immigrants*," Southwestern University, Georgetown, Texas, June 25, 1985.

5 Five-City Comparison

> New York is so enormous that even large population changes affect the proportions slowly. . . . The kind of change that transforms a city the size of Newark is for New York only a neighborhood shift.[1]

With this observation Nathan Glazer and Daniel Patrick Moynihan go a long way toward explaining the relative ease with which New York City is absorbing its latest wave of immigrants, compared with the cities of the American South and West.

New York is so big that ripples here would be tidal waves anywhere else. For example, about 124,000 people of Cuban birth were living in Miami in 1980, almost the number of Dominican-born in New York. But the Cuban-born made up 35.9 percent of central Miami's population, whereas the Dominican-born made up only 1.8 percent of New York's. Similarly, San Francisco is regarded as the center of immigrant Asian life in the United States, but in 1980 New York City had twice as many Asian immigrants as San Francisco.

Besides New York's enormous size, there are other reasons for its receptiveness to immigrants. Its unique history of receiving newcomers over an uninterrupted period of two centuries sets it apart from other American cities. Even during the 1930s, 1940s, and 1950s—decades of low immigration to the United States—New York continued to receive a steady flow of newcomers from abroad, and it also became the main receiving center for native-born migrants from the South and Puerto Rico.

For many of the nation's cities, the flood of Third World immigrants who entered the United States after 1965 produced a culture shock from which the cities have yet to recover. New York was prepared, however, by the internal black and Hispanic migrations before 1965, which readied the city's political, religious, educational, and economic institutions for the subsequent arrival of foreign-born blacks and Hispanics.

Other northern cities received large numbers of black migrants, but only in New York was the black migration matched by an equally dramatic Puerto Rican influx. In 1950 there were about 250,000 people of Puerto Rican birth or parentage in New York City; by 1960 the number was more than 600,000. Between 1920 and 1960 the black population of New York City increased by a factor of seven, from 152,000 to 1.1 million, mostly as a result of migration from the South. Compared with these numbers of Puerto Ricans and native-born blacks who entered New York before 1965, the numbers of Latin American and Afro-Caribbean immigrants who subsequently settled here—the census counted 400,000 in 1980—seem relatively modest.

The key to understanding the differences between immigration in New York and immigration in other large receiving cities, says the economist Thomas Muller, "is not in the numbers or even the characteristics of the immigrants, but in the attitudes of the receiving cities." New York's history of continuous immigration has encouraged a political culture that is "accustomed to making accommodations to newcomers."[2] Muller is at work on a book that will compare the immigration experience in the five major immigrant-receiving cities: New York, Los Angeles, Chicago, San Francisco, and Miami—the five cities discussed in this chapter.

New York City's Department of City Planning did not analyze the immigration histories of each of the five cities; such an analysis will have to wait for Muller's book. Its intent was to analyze 1980 census data on the five cities to obtain insights into New York's particular experience. The variables examined were the size and proportion of the immigrant population in the five cities, the immigrants' period of arrival, and the ethnic mix in each city.

ISSUES IN THE ANALYSIS

There are problems involved in making these comparisons. First, it can be misleading to compare immigrant statistics from city to city because cities differ markedly in structure and population distribution. In Los Angeles, for example, most immigrants (like most native-born residents) live outside the central city, but most of the immigrants in metropolitan New York live within the five boroughs. Comparing central city data for New York and Los Angeles inevitably creates some distortions. To correct for these distortions, two kinds of analysis have been undertaken. The metropolitan regions that are known as standard metropolitan statistical areas (SMSAs) have been analyzed, and so have the central cities. An SMSA consists of a central city and its surrounding counties. By analyzing SMSA figures it is possible to take account of Los Angeles' sprawling residential pattern. It is important to do so because Los Angeles is the city most comparable with New York in size and immigration statistics.

The second major problem in comparing cities is the absence of data on each city's undocumented aliens. Census records are thought to include some undocumented aliens, but not most of them. It is impossible to compare the immigration experience of U.S. cities without taking account of the size and character of their respective undocumented populations.

Although there is no way of ascertaining the number of undocumented aliens in the five cities, comparisons have been made, by state and by SMSA, of undocumented aliens thought to have been included in the 1980 census. Census Bureau analysts Jeffrey Passel and Karen Woodrow concluded that in 1980, 49.8 percent of the nation's census-recorded undocumented aliens lived in California, 11.4 percent in New York State, 9.0 percent in Texas, 6.6 percent in Illinois, 3.9 percent in Florida, 1.8 percent in New Jersey, and the remaining 17.5 percent in other states.[3]

Passel and Woodrow calculated that 658,000 undocumented aliens were recorded in the Los Angeles SMSA, 212,000 in the New York City SMSA, 127,000 in Chicago, 56,000 in San Francisco, and 50,000 in Miami. The Los Angeles figure represented one-third of the national total and two-thirds of California's total. Los Angeles, New York, and Chicago together accounted for almost half the nation's total.

IMMIGRATION AS AN URBAN PHENOMENON

Immigration is overwhelmingly an urban phenomenon. In 1980, 91.8 percent of the foreign-born recorded in the U.S. census lived in metropolitan areas, compared with 73.7 percent of the native population. Nearly 40 percent of the country's recorded immigrants lived in the greater metropolitan areas of the five cities discussed in this chapter. Only 10.9 percent of the native population lived in those same five areas.

Among metropolitan areas or SMSAs, New York had the largest recorded foreign-born population in 1980, in absolute numbers and as a share of the nation's total immigrant population (see Table 5.1).

Shifting focus from SMSAs to central cities, we find that in 1980 there were only eight American cities with recorded immigrant populations of more than 100,000: the five cities listed in Table 5.1 plus Houston, San Diego, and Philadelphia. As Table 5.2 shows, the number of immigrants in New York's central city far exceeded the number in any

Table 5.1

Total and Foreign-Born Population of Five Metropolitan Areas, 1980

	Total population	Percent of U.S. total	Foreign-born population	Percent of U.S. foreign-born
United States	226,545,805	100.0	14,079,906	100.0
Total five SMSAs	28,577,884	12.6	5,443,930	38.7
New York	9,120,346	4.0	1,946,800	13.8
Los Angeles	7,477,503	3.3	1,664,793	11.8
Chicago	7,103,624	3.1	744,930	5.3
San Francisco	3,250,630	1.4	509,352	3.6
Miami	1,625,781	0.7	578,055	4.1

Source: 1980 Census of Population, Vol. 1, Chapter C; General Social and Economic Characteristics.

Table 5.2

Foreign-Born Population of Eight Central Cities, 1980

	Total population	Foreign-born population	Foreign-born as percent of total
New York	7,071,639	1,670,199	23.6
Los Angeles	2,966,850	804,818	27.1
Chicago	3,005,078	435,232	14.5
San Francisco	678,974	192,204	28.3
Miami	346,865	186,280	53.7
Houston	1,595,138	155,577	9.8
San Diego	875,538	130,906	15.0
Philadelphia	1,688,210	107,951	6.4

Source: 1980 Census of Population, Vol. 1, Chapter C; General Social and Economic Characteristics.

other central city but immigrants in New York constituted a smaller proportion of the city's total population than they did in several other cities. Miami had by far the highest percentage of foreign-born in its population: 53.7 percent.

PERCENTAGE INCREASE

Between 1970 and 1980, New York received immigrants in large numbers, but the proportional increase there was nowhere near as great as the increase in several other American cities. It is the growth spurt of recent years that has attracted national attention to cities like Los Angeles and Miami. The immigrant population of Los Angeles, for example, nearly doubled between 1970 and 1980, and Miami's immigrant population increased by a third during that decade (see Table 5.3).

It is possible to get a sense of the immigrant growth rate in the greater metropolitan areas by looking at the proportion of recent immigrants among the total foreign-born population. In this analysis Los Angeles again emerges as the region with the greatest proportionate influx of new immigrants; 70 percent of the foreign-born recorded as living in greater Los Angeles in 1980 had arrived in the United States after 1965 (see Table 5.4).

ETHNIC MIX

Each immigrant-receiving city is characterized by its own ethnic mix, the result largely of history and geography. New York City, with its long immigration history and its eastern location, has a varied mix with a large European base; European immigrants continue to be attracted to a city where there is a well-established European community. Among new immigrants New York draws the preponderance of Caribbean peoples, particularly Dominicans, Jamaicans, and Haitians, and it has more South American immigrants than any other American city.

Chicago is similar to New York in its ethnic diversity and its large European base. In Miami and Los Angeles, immigration is preponderantly Hispanic—Cuban in Miami and Mexican in Los Angeles—but Los Angeles also has a large Asian community. San Francisco's Asian community makes up more than 50 percent of its immigrant population.

Figure 5.1 shows each central city's ethnic mix, by region of origin, at the time of the 1980 census. Europe includes the Soviet Union; the Western Hemisphere includes Latin America and the Caribbean but not Canada. (Canada's figures are included in "Other.")

Language is also a key to a city's ethnic "feel." In New York, Los Angeles, and San Francisco about 35 percent of the residents aged five and over spoke a language other than English at home, according to

Table 5.3

Population Change Between 1970 and 1980
For United States and Five Selected Cities

	Total 1970 population	Foreign-born 1970 population	Total 1980 population	Foreign-born 1980 population	Percent change of total	Percent change of foreign-born
United States	203,210,158	9,619,302	226,545,805	14,079,906	+11.5	+46.4
New York City	7,894,798	1,437,058	7,071,639	1,670,199	-10.4	+16.2
Los Angeles	2,815,998	410,870	2,966,850	804,818	+ 5.4	+95.9
Chicago	3,362,947	373,919	3,005,078	435,232	-10.6	+16.4
San Francisco	715,673	154,507	678,974	192,204	- 5.1	+24.4
Miami	335,062	140,207	346,865	186,280	+ 3.5	+32.9

Source: 1970 and 1980 Censuses of Population, Vol. 1, Chapter C; General Social and and Economic Characteristics.

Table 5.4

Foreign-Born in Metropolitan Areas in 1980, by Period of Arrival

	Total	Pre-1965	Post-1965	Post-1965 as Percent of total
New York	1,946,800	887,017	1,059,783	54.4
Los Angeles	1,664,793	499,981	1,164,812	70.0
Chicago	744,930	340,357	404,573	54.3
San Francisco	509,352	221,440	287,912	56.5
Miami	578,055	232,946	345,109	59.7

Source: 1980 Census of Population, Vol. 1, Chapter C; General Social and Economic Characteristics.

Table 5.5

Foreign-Language Speakers Aged Five and Over, 1980

	Population aged five and over	Speak a language other than English at home		Speak Spanish at home	
		Number	Percent	Number	Percent
New York	6,606,223	2,342,299	35.5	1,202,335	18.2
Los Angeles	2,758,112	969,126	35.1	647,865	23.5
Chicago	2,773,897	667,257	24.1	342,387	12.3
San Francisco	648,106	232,486	35.9	60,556	9.3
Miami	327,586	209,568	64.0	188,270	57.5

Source: 1980 Census of Population, Vol. 1, Chapter C; General Social and Economic Characteristics.

Figure 5.1
Foreign-Born in Central Cities, by Region of Birth, 1980

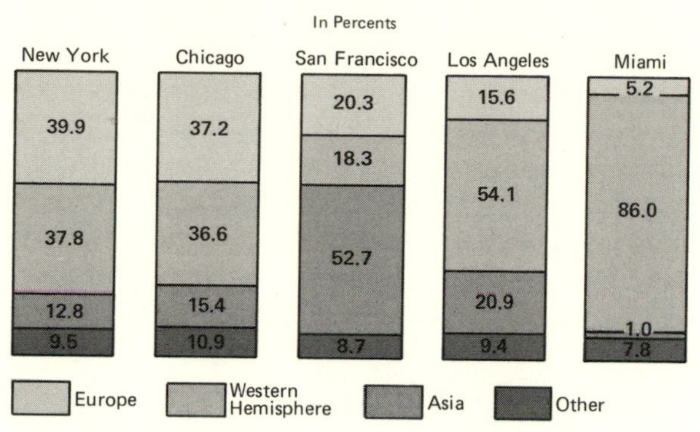

Source: 1980 U.S. Census of Population, Chapter C; General Social and Economic Characteristics

1980 U.S. census data. Twenty-four percent of Chicago residents spoke a foreign language at home, as did 64 percent of central Miami. Spanish was the predominant non-English language spoken in every comparison city but San Francisco, where roughly 60,000 people spoke Spanish at home and 72,000 spoke Chinese (see Table 5.5).

New York's size and variety became clear once more in its language mix. In 1980 New Yorkers spoke a total of 121 languages. Although Spanish was the predominant foreign language, six others were spoken by 50,000 people or more: Italian, Yiddish, Chinese, French, German, and Greek. Of the five comparison cities, only two others had 50,000 or more speakers of any language besides Spanish or English: Chicago, with 88,000 speakers of Polish; and San Francisco, with 72,000 speakers of Chinese.

"To understand our history is to understand our singularity," wrote the philosopher Octavio Paz in *The Labyrinth of Solitude*, his meditation on the Mexican national character. Paz might have been writing about New York. If so, he would have added, "And to know our singularity is to know our multiplicity."

NOTES

1. Nathan Glazer and Daniel Patrick Moynihan, *Beyond the Melting Pot* (Cambridge, MA: MIT Press, 1963), p. 26.
2. Thomas Muller, personal communication.
3. Jeffrey S. Passel and Karen A. Woodrow, "Geographic Distribution of Undocumented Immigrants: Estimates of Undocumented Aliens Counted in the 1980 U.S. Census by State," *International Migration Review* 18, no. 3 (Fall 1984):642–75.

6 Ethnic Geography

In song, story, and folk memory, the Lower East Side of Manhattan is the city's quintessential immigrant neighborhood. In 1890 more than half the city's Italian immigrants and three-quarters of its Jewish immigrants lived in the tenements of lower Manhattan. The celebrated journalist Jacob Riis caught the pathos and squalor of the neighborhood in his pictures of pushcarts, bathhouses, tenement dwellings, and home workshops.

To be sure, not all immigrants lived on the Lower East Side. Some lived in the tenements of downtown Brooklyn and the South Bronx. For many of these inner city settlers, their fondest dream was escape to the middle-class neighborhoods of outer Brooklyn and Queens. Many achieved their goal and moved beyond the perimeters of immigrant tenement life. The tenement neighborhoods were their first stopping places on the way to somewhere else.

Few of today's immigrants stop on the Lower East Side, in downtown Brooklyn, or in the South Bronx. Tenements there have been gentrified, overfilled, abandoned, or burned down. Many of today's immigrants head straight for middle-class neighborhoods like East Flatbush in Brooklyn or Flushing in Queens. They may have difficulty paying the rents, but families may double or triple up to make ends meet, in time-honored immigrant tradition.

The 1980 census captured the new pattern of immigrant settlement. If most immigrants still were starting out in Manhattan, it would have had by far the largest number of immigrants, especially recent immigrants, in the city. But that was not the case. In 1980 Manhattan had almost exactly its "fair share" of immigrants, in proportion to its total population (see Table 6.1). Brooklyn also had its proportionate share; Queens had slightly more than its share, and the Bronx and Staten Island somewhat less.

SETTLEMENT PATTERNS

Two factors appear to have influenced where new immigrants settle: the existing ethnic geography of the city, and the availability of accessible and affordable housing (see Figure 6.1).

Where possible, immigrants settle in ethnically familiar territory. Particularly in Brooklyn, recent European immigrants have moved into traditional ethnic communities. Italian immigrants have settled in Italian-American Carroll Gardens and Bensonhurst, Polish refugees have resettled in Polish-American Greenpoint, and Soviet émigrés have revived the once-flagging Russian Jewish community of Brighton Beach. So, too, the large-scale post–1965 Chinese immigration to New York has filled Manhattan's Chinatown to overflowing. As a result Chinatown's boundaries now extend into parts of Little Italy and the Lower East Side. Chinatown is still so overcrowded that many Chinese immigrants who work in its restaurants and garment factories commute from Brooklyn and Queens.

Sometimes new immigrant groups piggyback onto other, similar population groups in the city. The Puerto Rican and Cuban presence in Manhattan's Washington Heights and Inwood areas, for example, made those neighborhoods attractive to early immigrants from the Dominican Republic in the 1960s. The black West Indian settlement in Crown Heights, Brooklyn, adjoins the native-born black community of Bedford-Stuyvesant; immigrant and native-born black populations commingle in Brooklyn's North Flatbush and East Flatbush.

Many of what are now the city's immigrant neighborhoods were originally developed in the 1920s. That was when subway and elevated train lines were extended to such previously inaccessible areas as Washington Heights, Flatbush, and the Grand Concourse area of the Bronx. Block after block of elevator apartment buildings sprang up in these neighborhoods. The apartments were filled by the children and grandchildren of immigrants fleeing the Lower East Side.

Because these communities were settled en masse, they aged en masse. By the 1960s many of the original residents were old or dead, and their children had likely joined the exodus to the suburbs. When the new immigrants began arriving in New York, neighborhoods like Washington Heights and North Flatbush were slightly rundown, but still attractive to aggressive, upwardly mobile newcomers from the West Indies, Latin America, and Asia.

One reason the Bronx has fewer post–1965 immigrants than Brooklyn,

Table 6.1

Immigrant Population by Borough, 1980

	Total population	Percent of City population	Total immigrants	Percent of total immigrants	Post-1965 immigrants	Percent of post-65 immigrants
New York City	7,071,639	100.0	1,670,269	100.0	946,845	100.0
Bronx	1,168,972	16.5	215,348	12.9	106,652	11.3
Brooklyn	2,230,936	31.5	530,989	31.8	313,380	33.1
Manhattan	1,428,936	20.2	348,589	20.9	208,871	22.1
Queens	1,891,325	26.8	540,829	32.4	304,483	32.2
Staten Island	352,121	5.0	34,514	2.1	13,469	1.4

Source: 1980 U.S. Census Summary Tape File 3.
Note: Figures have been rounded off; totals may not equal 100.0%

Figure 6.1
"New" Immigrant Concentrations in New York City

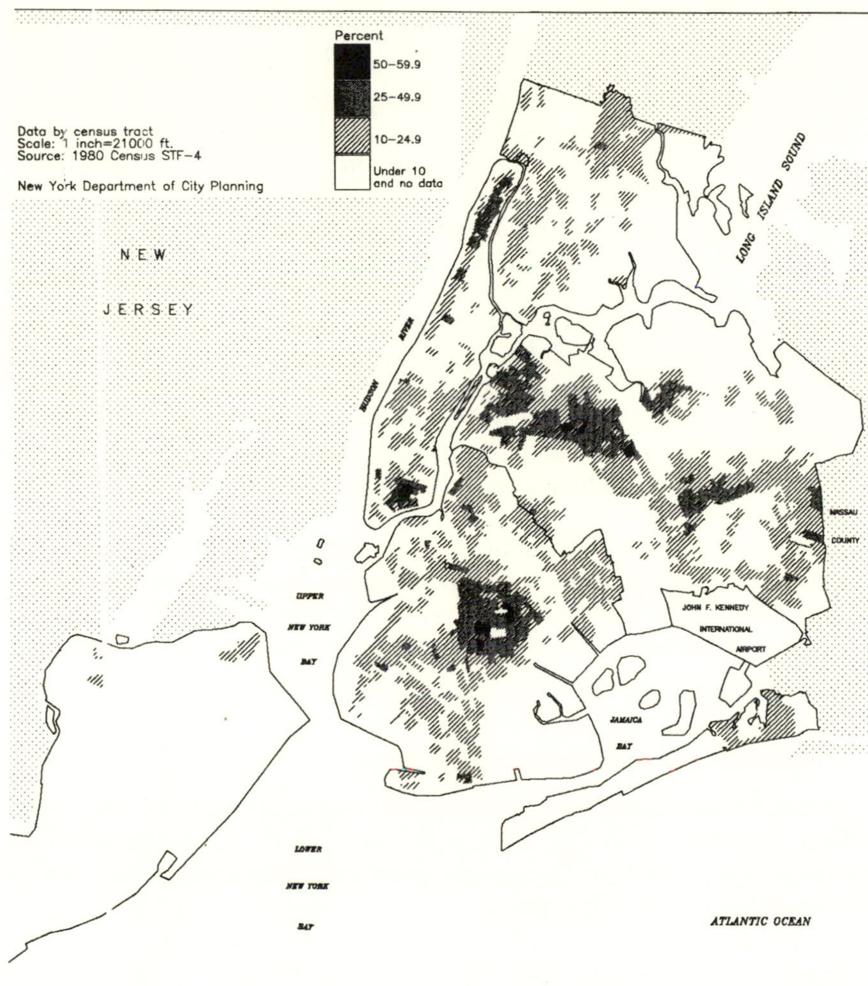

Queens, and Manhattan is that Puerto Rican migrants to New York had already occupied much of the housing. Like Italian and Jewish immigrants before them, Puerto Rican migrants followed the East Side IRT subway out of the Lower East Side and East Harlem to the Bronx. There are, nevertheless, significant immigrant communities in the Bronx. West Indians have settled in Kingsbridge, for example, and there is an Albanian immigrant population of 4,000 to 5,000, concentrated principally in East Tremont and the Fordham University area. Some Dominican immigrants have moved into Hunt's Point. As housing in the South Bronx is restored, the area may well become attractive to the city's continuing influx of newcomers.

Staten Island, the most suburban of the city's boroughs, has the smallest population of new immigrants; the borough presents proof by reverse example of the factors that create immigrant neighborhoods. The population of Staten Island is largely of white, European extraction; there are few nonwhite communities for nonwhite immigrants to blend into. Staten Island is also the newest of the boroughs; until the Verrazano Narrows Bridge was opened in 1964, it was largely undeveloped. With the opening of the bridge, a large Italian community relocated from Brooklyn, looking for a less urban environment.

Few portions of Staten Island have gone through the cycle of decline and rejuvenation that characterizes immigrant neighborhoods. One exception is the North Shore, which has seen a marked regrowth since the mid–1970s and an influx of new immigrants since the early 1980s.

The Staten Island life-style depends heavily on the automobile, another factor that tends to discourage new immigrants, who rely on public transportation.

Immigration's most dramatic effects on the city's ethnic geography have occurred in neighborhoods of Brooklyn, Queens, and Manhattan. The sketches that follow map some of the broader contours of these changes in central Brooklyn, northwest Queens, and northwest Manhattan.

Brooklyn: The Afro-Caribbean Tide

West Indian immigration to Brooklyn began about 1940. The writer Paule Marshall, whose parents were immigrants from Barbados, describes its beginnings in her autobiographical novel about coming of age in Brooklyn's Crown Heights:

> First there had been the Dutch-English and Scotch-Irish who had built the houses. There had been tea in the afternoon then, and skirts rustling across the parquet floors and mild voices. For a long time it had been only the whites, each generation unraveling in a quiet skein of years behind the green shades.
>
> But now, in 1939, the last of them were discreetly dying off behind those shades, or selling the houses and moving away. And as they left, the West Indians slowly edged their way in.[1]

World War II and the postwar restrictions on immigration into the United States held this tide in check for 25 years. But since 1965, Afro-Caribbean immigrants have spread from Crown Heights into East Flatbush and parts of Flatbush.

The 1980 census found that about 161,000 people of West Indian birth—English-, French-, and Spanish-speaking—lived in Brooklyn. About 90,000 (56 percent) lived in Crown Heights, East Flatbush, and Flatbush, but these numbers only begin to tell the story. A large number of undocumented immigrants who were not included in the 1980 census are believed to be West Indians living in Brooklyn. The West Indian population has continued to expand rapidly since 1980; this is especially true of the Haitian community, which is concentrated along Flatbush Avenue south of Prospect Park and was swelled by an estimated 10,000 entrants from the 1980 Haiti-to-Florida open boat flotilla. Finally, although they are not technically considered West Indians, there were some 37,000 Guyanese immigrants and 21,000 Panamanian immigrants in New York in 1980. Most are descendants of West Indian migrants to those lands; culturally they are Afro-Caribbean, and they have put down roots in central Brooklyn.

This West Indian immigrant population explosion has produced dramatic and rapid changes. One noticeable change has been in the elevator apartment buildings in Flatbush and East Flatbush. They were built in the 1920s and were filled by the children of Jewish immigrants from the Lower East Side. By the mid–1960s upwardly mobile blacks—immigrants and American-born—began to look on them as desirable housing.

From 1970 to 1980 the population in those census tracts where apartment buildings are located changed from about 85 percent white to about 80 percent black, and became much more dense in the process, as young families replaced elderly singles and couples (see Figure 6.2). The neighborhood sustained some deterioration during this transition. Commercial rents on Flatbush Avenue, for example, dropped from about $1,500 a month in the late 1960s to $600 a month by 1977.[2] New York's West Indian immigrant population has long been renowned for its thrift, industry, and skillful property management, however, and some observers believe that, as a result, the deterioration along Flatbush Avenue has already bottomed out. They point to Dubin's bakery on Church Avenue, for example, which was long a thriving Jewish-owned business and neighborhood institution. Now it is a thriving West Indian-owned business and neighborhood institution. And they point to the successful tenant management of a 79-unit apartment building on Newkirk Avenue, in which West Indian tenants have played a leading role.

Queens: "I Don't Know Where I Am"

In an assembly room on the second floor of a manufacturing plant in Long Island City, Queens, about 200 men and women sit at workbenches linked by conveyor belts, joining, testing, and packaging staplers. The tapping of their hammers and the steady whir of industrial-size floor

Figure 6.2
Foreign-Born Blacks Living in Brooklyn

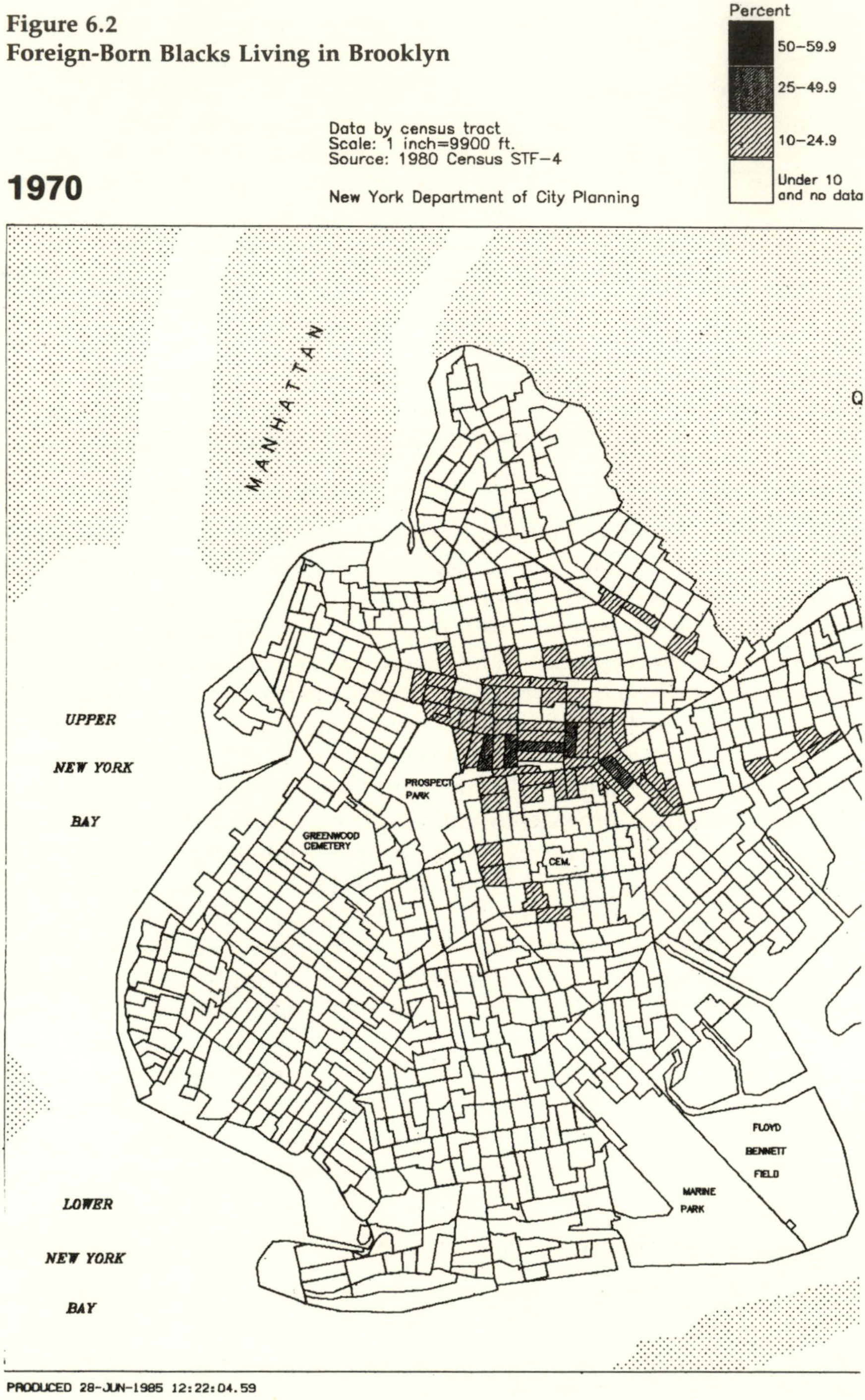

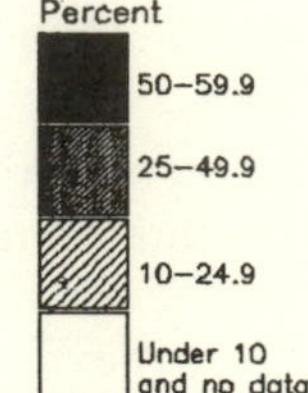

Percent
50–59.9
25–49.9
10–24.9
Under 10
and no data
Data by census tract
Scale: 1 inch=9900 ft.
Source: 1980 Census STF–4
1970
New York Department of City Planning
MANHATTAN
Q
UPPER
NEW YORK
BAY
PROSPECT
PARK
GREENWOOD
CEMETERY
CEM.
FLOYD
BENNETT
FIELD
MARINE
PARK
LOWER
NEW YORK
BAY
PRODUCED 28-JUN-1985 12:22:04.59

Figure 6.2 (continued)

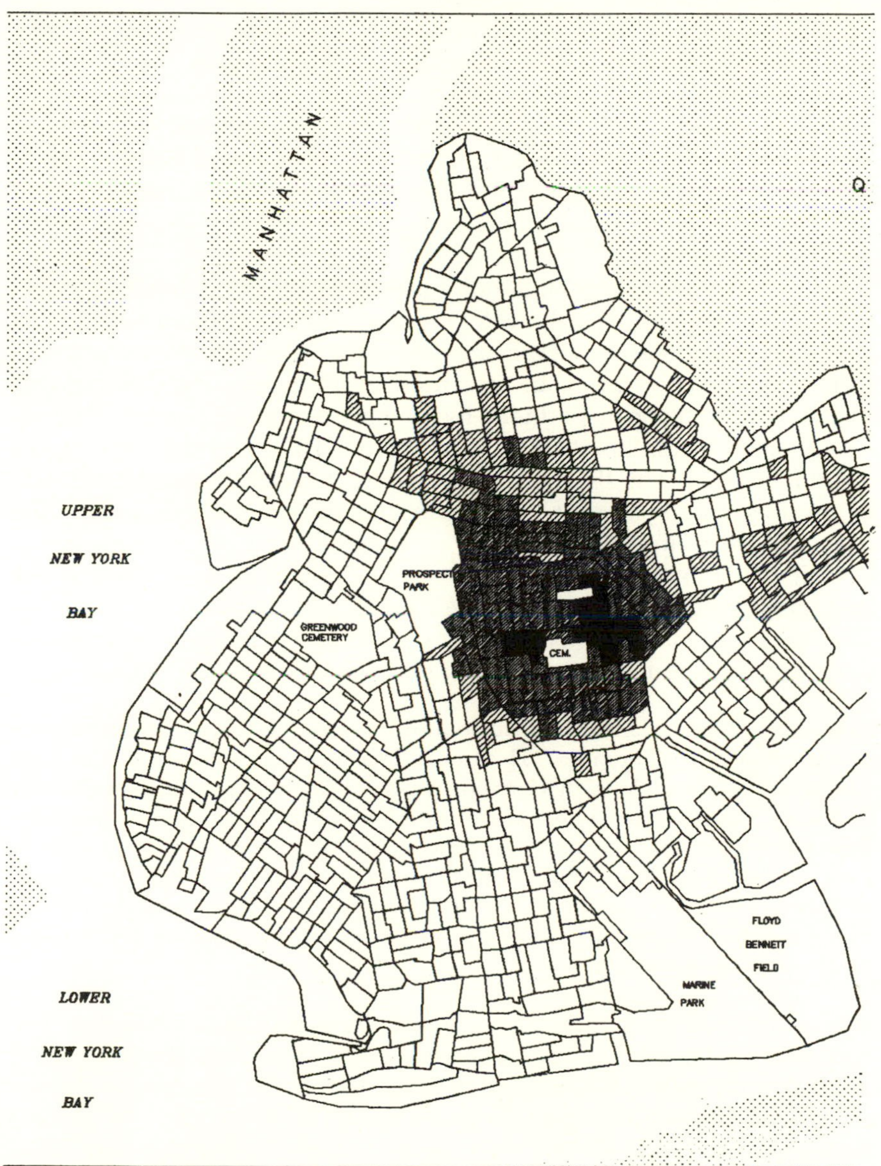

fans in the corners of the room fill the air with the drowsy hum of a summer beehive. Through a row of open windows, a Manhattan-bound Number 7 train heaves into sight, slowly curving past the factory on its elevated tracks.

About 900 industrial workers are employed at the plant; company officials estimate that at least 90 percent of them are foreign-born. Like the crew of Herman Melville's *Pequod* in *Moby Dick*, they form a sort of "deputation of all the isles of the sea, and all the ends of the earth." When employees voted to join Local 208 of the International Brotherhood of Teamsters, the election ballot was printed in 21 languages, including Spanish, French, German, Chinese, Korean, Greek, and Russian. "What you have over there," said union local president John Mahoney, "is the Tower of Babel."

Since the mid–1960s immigration has turned the entire northwest corner of Queens, from Flushing to the East River, into something of a latter-day Babel. Between 1965 and 1979 more than 304,000 immigrants from every part of the globe streamed into Queens, the 1980 census showed. Roughly half of them have moved into northwest Queens neighborhoods: Elmhurst, Woodside, Corona Park, and Jackson Heights (see Figure 6.3). The IRT Number 7, which links these neighborhoods to job sites in Long Island City and Manhattan, is sometimes called "the Orient Express" in their honor. The area has been transformed into what two New York immigration historians call "the most diversely populated immigrant neighborhoods in the world."[3]

In his book *The Dominican Diaspora*, anthropologist Glenn Hendricks describes the Latin American influx into the Corona area of Queens:

> In the early 1960s, the first known Dominican from the Cibao [a mountainous province] moved to Corona. . . . This transitional area next to Flushing Meadows had earlier been populated by Germans, Irish and later Italians; after World War II, blacks bought property in the area and this group [editor's note: actually, their children] in turn became part of the rush to the mushrooming suburbs of Long Island. They [the children] gladly rented or sold their aging two-story houses to Dominicans and other Latin Americans. The prices paid were often highly inflated—according to a local real estate agent, rents and sale prices could be doubled by such a transaction. . . .[4]

This influx has produced overcrowded housing. In Community District 4, which takes in Elmhurst, Corona, and Corona Park, the borough's most densely populated immigrant neighborhoods, the number of overcrowded houses and apartments increased by more than 50 percent between 1970 and 1980. The 1970 census recorded 4,491 dwelling units occupied by more than one person per room; by 1980 the figure had climbed to 6,693.

City fire officials say it is no coincidence that the 46th Fire Battalion,

Figure 6.3
"New" Immigrants Living in Queens

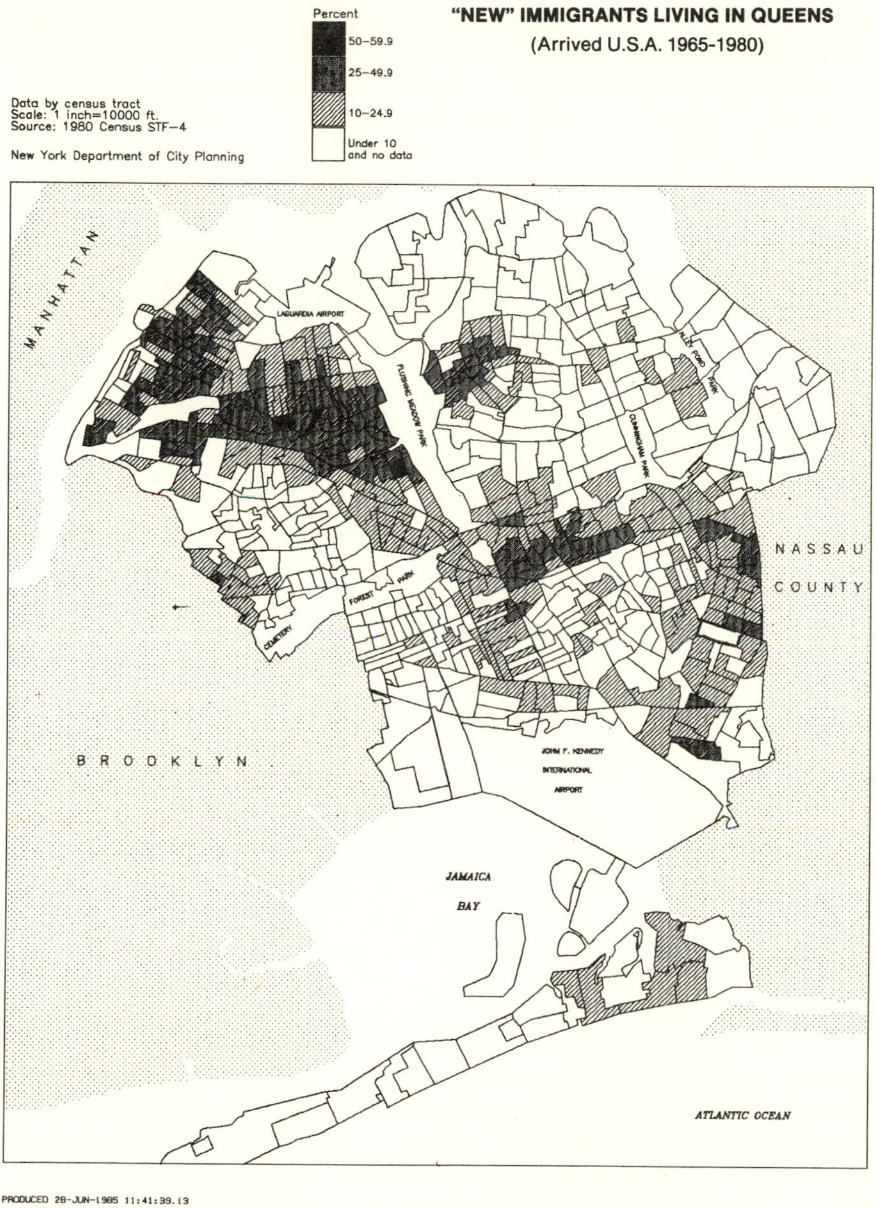

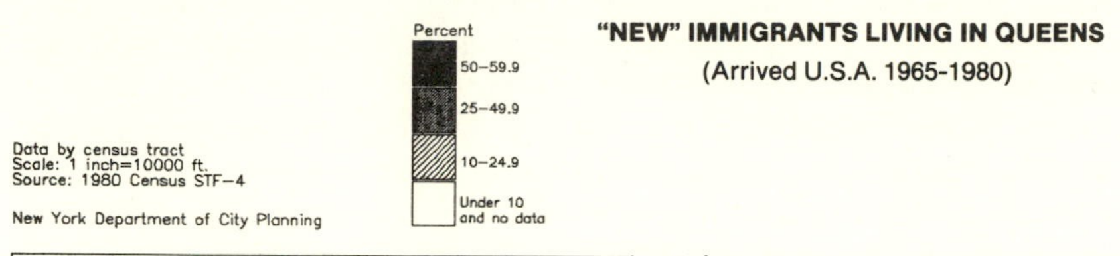

which serves these northwest Queens neighborhoods, became the busiest in the city starting in the late 1970s. Many calls, fire officials say, are to overcrowded apartment houses or to private homes that have been converted into rooming houses. Overcrowding results in excessive strain on aging or otherwise inadequate electrical systems, they say, and ovens used as heaters pose further fire hazards.

Queens neighborhoods have rarely been as sharply divided ethnically as neighborhoods in Brooklyn or Manhattan; German, Irish, and Italian families might all be found living on the same block in Queens. If anything, the new immigration has made Queens even more polyglot; at P.S. 89 in Elmhurst, for example, the pupils speak 34 different languages.

The result can be an exhilarating variety, or a bewildering one. "I came to New York so that I could learn English," a Nigerian-born woman told a *New York Times* reporter in 1982. "What I got in my life is something else. I don't know where I am. Spain? China?"[5]

Northern Manhattan: "Some Kind of Invisible Wall"

An English lesson was in progress in the classroom next to Efrain Frias' tiny office at the Northern Manhattan Coalition for Immigrant Rights on Audubon Avenue in Washington Heights. One after another, the men and women in the class, most of them in their early or mid-twenties, earnestly struggled with the lesson for the day—reciting from an imaginary letter home that inquired about the health of grandparents and reported on the exciting process of learning English in school.

In his own less-than-perfect English, Frias discussed some of the harsher realities of Dominican immigrant life in Manhattan. He is a short, energetic man of about 30 who turned down a minor league contract from the Boston Red Sox in favor of a degree in business administration at Lehman College. "From Broadway east, most of the people are Dominicans," he said. "On the other side of Broadway, where the houses are better, there are Cubans and . . . "—he searched for an appropriately sociological-sounding term—"foreign-born seniors. I don't know what it is, but at Broadway, there is some kind of invisible wall."

That wall has been there a long time. The extension of the West Side IRT subway line after World War I opened Washington Heights to development, and Irish and Jewish immigrants rushed in from other parts of Manhattan to lay claim to this new and desirable neighborhood. By the 1930s Broadway had become a dividing line between the groups, with the Irish east of Broadway, and the Jews west of it.

Economic inequities fueled religious intolerance and led to violence. Irish youths, in gangs called the Shamrocks and the Amsterdams, vandalized synagogues in Washington Heights, and attacked Jewish youngsters on the street. Jewish community leaders accused the police of ignoring their complaints about the attacks; Jewish parents organized to escort their children to and from school. But as the urban historian Ronald Bayor notes in his book *Neighbors in Conflict*, vandalism and street fighting remained common in Washington Heights right up through the end of World War II.[6]

For 20 years after the war, northern Manhattan's ethnic composition remained remarkably stable. During the 1950s there were small incursions of migrants from Puerto Rico and immigrants from Greece and Cuba. As in Flatbush, however, the demographic turning point in Washington Heights and Inwood was reached in the 1960s. The neighborhood's original residents were growing old, and their children were moving to the suburbs.

When the great Dominican migration to New York City began in the mid–1960s, Washington Heights and Inwood were natural neighborhoods for the immigrants to settle in. There was already a Hispanic presence, and the original residents were either moving out or dying. The George Washington Bridge provided an easy link to textile factory and domestic household jobs in New Jersey. By 1980 more than 38,000 of Manhattan's census count of 64,000 Dominican immigrants lived in Washington Heights and Inwood. In large part they had replaced Irish families on the east side of Broadway (see Figure 6.4).

Soon they were engaged in a battle of their own with the Jewish community west of Broadway. The precipitant was a plan to construct a new elementary school on the east side of Broadway between 182nd and 185th streets.

The children of the Dominican migration had crowded the neighborhood schools. By the early 1980s overcrowding had reached crisis proportions. For more than ten years the Board of Education had planned to build a new school, P.S. 48, at 185th and Broadway, near the geographic center of Washington Heights. The overcrowding crisis prompted it to act.

But the plan disturbed the area's Jewish leaders. Across Broadway from the proposed P.S. 48 site were a Jewish community center used heavily by senior citizens, and a yeshiva. Jewish leaders feared turf warfare if the school were built. Catholic community leaders also had misgivings about the school plan; there is a parochial school across Broadway from the proposed P.S. 48 site. The plans for P.S. 48 were stalled.

By mid–1984 a delicate compromise had been engineered. P.S. 48 would be built, but only for 700 students, not for 1,000, as originally planned, and only for grades K–4, not K–6. A larger middle school would be built ten blocks north of the yeshiva. The plan entered the design phase in 1986.

The controversy over P.S. 48 helped to arouse Dominican immigrants'

Figure 6.4
Dominican-Born Persons Living in Manhattan, 1980

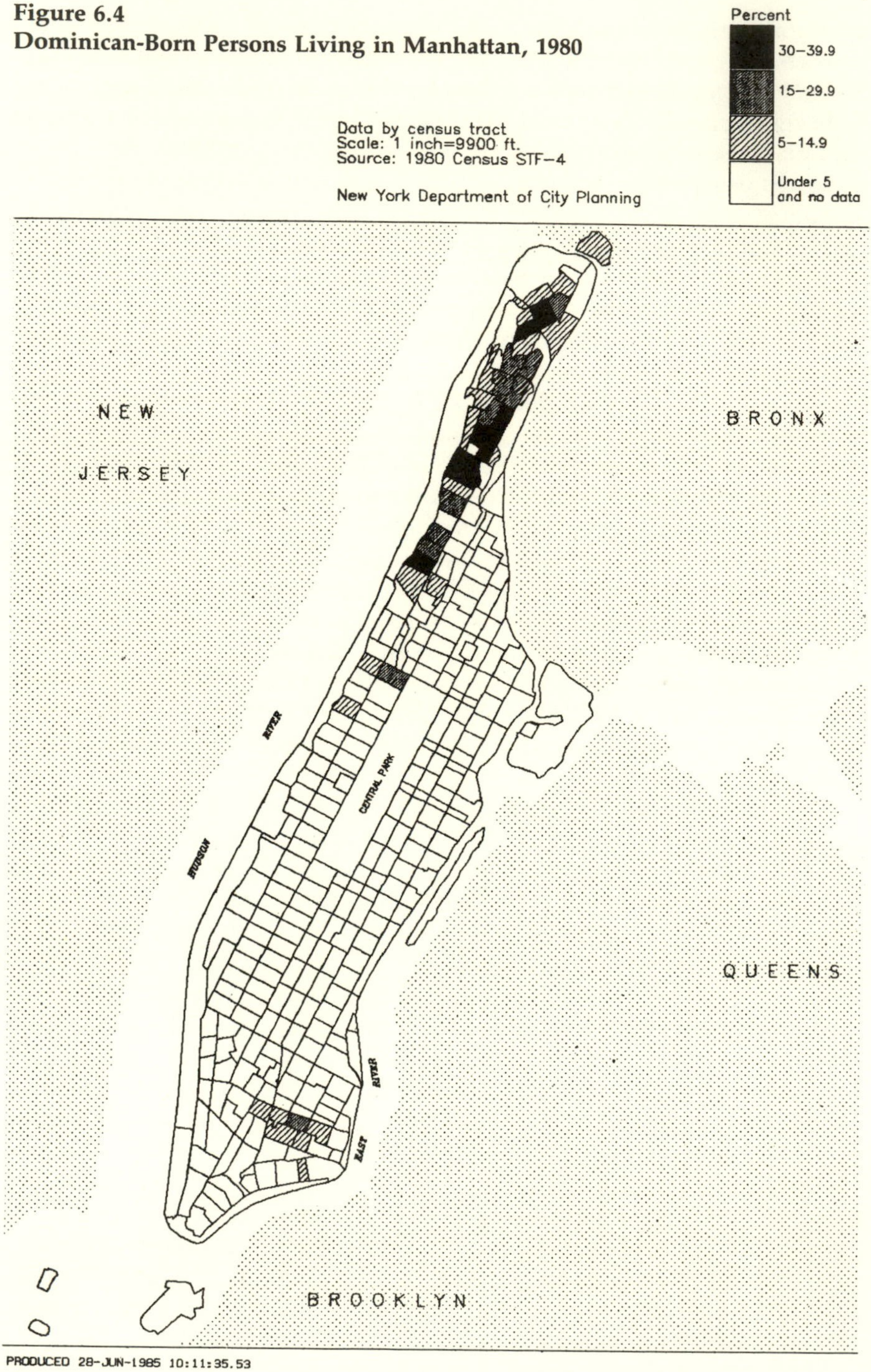

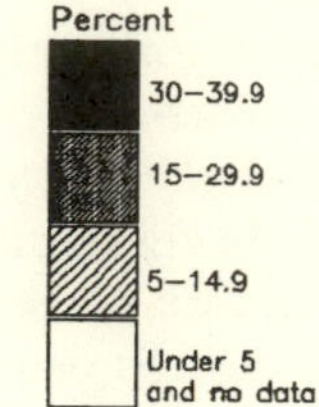

Data by census tract
Scale: 1 inch=9900 ft.
Source: 1980 Census STF–4

New York Department of City Planning

NEW JERSEY

BRONX

HUDSON RIVER

CENTRAL PARK

EAST RIVER

QUEENS

BROOKLYN

PRODUCED 28-JUN-1985 10:11:35.53

interest in local affairs, according to Efrain Frias. He reports that Dominicans are becoming increasingly interested in school issues, housing, health care—and local politics. "Until a few years ago," Frias said, "the Dominican people were not too interested in becoming citizens. Now we have four or five people a day coming to apply for citizenship. They want to participate in local matters. They want to participate in voting."

THE NEVER-ENDING STORY

For most of the 20th century, Italian immigrants have been the largest bloc of foreign-born residents in New York. The 1980 census found that more immigrant New Yorkers had been born in Italy—156,280 persons—than in any other country. Some 42,000 of these Italian-born New Yorkers were post–1965 immigrants; many of the remainder were the survivors of the great immigration waves of the early 20th century.

If current immigration trends continue, Dominican-born New Yorkers should outnumber the Italian-born when the 1990 census is taken. The Guyanese population of the city will have doubled between 1980 and 1990, as will the Asian Indian. There will be more Trinidadians living in New York than Greeks, more Filipinos than Yugoslavs. A new chapter in the city's history will be written in these numbers, and in the cohesion, chaos, and conflict of its new immigrant communities. How many more times New York City will re-create itself is anyone's guess. A new immigrant poet may have put it best. "New York," wrote Lauchland Henry of Antigua and Brooklyn, "is a story that never will all be told."

NOTES

1. Paule Marshall, *Brown Girl, Brownstones* (Old Westbury, N.Y.: Feminist Press, 1981), p. 4.

2. Robert Curvin and Bruce Porter, *Blackout Looting* (New York: Gardner Press, 1979), p. 146.

3. Thomas Kessner and Betty Boyd Caroli, *Today's Immigrants: Their Stories* (New York: Oxford University Press, 1981) p. 23.

4. Glenn Hendricks, *The Dominican Diaspora* (New York: Teachers College Press, 1974), p. 81.

5. Dena Kleiman, "A Surge of Immigrants Alters New York's Face," *New York Times*, September 27, 1982, p. B4.

6. Ronald Bayor, *Neighbors in Conflict* (Baltimore: Johns Hopkins University Press, 1978).

7 Employment Patterns Among Today's Immigrants

Ethnic enclaves in the economy are a tradition in New York City; ethnic identity has always played a strong role in determining if an immigrant works, where he or she works, and what he or she does for a living. During the 19th century, for example, Irish immigrants established dominance over work on the city's waterfront, while German immigrants were dominant as workers in the city's thriving breweries.

Today's immigrants to New York City have carved out economic niches of their own. Garment manufacturing, health care, and food retailing in grocery stores and restaurants are industries that now rely heavily on immigrant labor; employment in these industries follows clear ethnic and racial lines. Immigrant women from China and Latin America, for example, are concentrated in the garment industry, while West Indian men and women predominate in the city's hospitals and nursing homes.

Ethnic networks in the job market provide opportunities for immigrants. Connections in the grocery stores, hospitals, and garment lofts that employ immigrants afford newcomers an all-important toehold in New York. Indeed, ethnic hiring networks are an important part of the story of how the new immigrants have succeeded in finding work in New York in spite of the industrial retrenchment of the 1970s.

These hiring networks often flourish in low-wage, high-turnover businesses. They may offer subsistence, but not necessarily prosperity. Like the European immigrants of the 19th and early 20th centuries, today's Korean greengrocers, West Indian hospital orderlies, and Dominican sewing machine operators long to improve their lots, and they dream of better jobs for their children. For them, no less than for the European immigrants described by the historian Oscar Handlin in his classic work *The Uprooted*, long hours and low wages exact a price "paid in innumerable hardships of mind and body."[1]

Of course, not all of the new immigrants to New York are low-paid wage earners or overworked small shopkeepers. The 1980 census counted more than 14,000 foreign-born registered nurses who arrived in New York City after 1965. More than 5,000 new immigrants who answered the census here were practicing physicians; a similar number were accountants. What with Indian physicians, West Indian and Filipino nurses, Chinese computer experts—and the list goes on—about 20 percent of the almost 500,000 post–1965 immigrants in the city's work force were employed in professional or white-collar positions. Many more had been professionals or white-collar workers at home, but problems of language, licensing, or mere newness led to temporary or permanent underemployment in New York.

This chapter is devoted primarily to consideration of recent immigrants in blue-collar and service jobs in New York City. They are the great majority of immigrants in the city's work force, and it is from their experience that the chapter draws its major topics: the ethnic concentrations of immigrants within particular industries; the hiring networks for immigrants in those industries; and the controversial question of whether immigrants take jobs away from native-born workers, especially native-born minorities.

IMMIGRANTS IN THE WORKFORCE: WHO WORKS WHERE?

At the corner of Seventh Avenue and 39th Street, near the center of midtown Manhattan's hyperkinetic garment district, stands a monument to immigrant labor. It is a bronze statue, larger than life: a man wearing a yarmulke sits in a rickety-looking folding chair, bending over an old-fashioned treadle-operated sewing machine. The sculpture, commissioned jointly by the International Ladies Garment Workers Union (ILGWU) and the garment district's clothing manufacturers, was unveiled in October 1984.

New York's garment industry has always relied on immigrant labor, and it still does. In the early years of the 20th century, immigrant men and women from southern and eastern Europe were the backbone of the industry's workforce; the statue honors their memory. Today their places are being filled by immigrant women from China and Latin America.

The 1980 census found that more than one-third of the 118,000 workers employed in the garment industry in New York City were post–1965 immigrants. More than one-fifth were Asian and Latin American women who had immigrated since 1965. Roughly three-fourths of these women operated sewing machines for a living; the rest were pressers, hand sewers, and the like.

More of the city's post–1965 immigrants work in garment manufacturing than in any other industry in the city; about 42,000 were so employed in 1980. Other sectors of the local economy also attract immigrants. The 1980 census showed that 47.0 percent of post–1965 immigrants were concentrated in 13 industries that employed only 34.8 percent of the city's total resident work force. Because the census omitted the majority of undocumented aliens and because some are employed off the books, the concentration of immigrants in those industries may have been higher than census data suggest.

Post–1965 immigrants made up 23.2 percent of the work force in the 13 industries, although they constituted only 17 percent of the city's total work force (see Table 7.1).

Sometimes the immigrant work force clusters in single ethnic groups, sometimes not. There were no strong ethnic concentrations among the more than 40,000 post–1965 immigrants employed in banking, insurance, and real estate; all the major racial and ethnic groups were represented in numbers roughly proportional to their numbers in the work force at large. In other industries, however, the ethnic demarcation lines were striking.

- Post–1965 Asian immigrant men made up only 3.2 percent of the city's male work force in 1980, but they were 15.2 percent of the male workers in the city's eating and drinking establishments.
- Post–1965 black immigrant women, most of them from the West Indies, were 5.5 percent of the city's female work force, but they were 23.9 percent of the city's female domestic household workers, 12.6 percent of the female hospital personnel, and 21.5 percent of the women working in nursing facilities.
- Post–1965 Hispanic immigrants, male and female, were heavily concentrated in the miscellaneous manufacturing shops of the city. Hispanic immigrant males of that period were only 5.1 percent of the city's male work force, but they were 12.9 percent of all men employed in miscellaneous manufacturing. Post–1965 Hispanic immigrant women were 4.8 percent of the city's female work force, but were 18.5 percent of all women employed in miscellaneous manufacturing. Hispanic immigrants, men and women, also were concentrated heavily in hotels and motels, primarily as maintenance workers and as maids.
- Some 7,400 post–1965 male European immigrants were construction workers in New York City, more than the combined number of black, Hispanic, and Asian immigrant men employed in construction.

Job requirements contribute to these differences in immigrant concentrations. Most West Indian women who immigrate to New York, for

Table 7.1

New York City Industries with Concentrations of New Immigrants, 1980
(in rank order by number of post-1965 immigrants employed)

Industry	Total employed	Post-1965 immigrants employed	Post-1965s as percent of total employed
Total for all industries	2,897,880	492,760	17.0
Apparel manufacturing	118,540	42,760	36.1
Hospitals	185,820	41,660	22.4
Eating/drinking establishments	110,640	36,820	33.3
Banking	125,320	21,540	17.2
Construction	77,960	15,120	19.4
Real estate/building management	71,660	11,540	16.1
Private households	30,620	11,520	37.6
Nursing facilities	30,960	9,820	31.7
Miscellaneous manufacturing	32,080	9,520	29.7
Grocery stores	47,040	8,920	19.0
Insurance	76,980	8,720	11.3
Motels/hotels	25,420	7,860	30.9
Printing/publishing	74,280	7,760	10.4
Total, 13 industries	1,007,320	233,560	23.2
All other industries	1,890,560	259,200	13.7

Source: 1980 U.S. Census Public Use Microdata File.

example, are English-speaking. A knowledge of English is generally a requirement in service industries like health care. Hispanic and Asian immigrant women are concentrated in manufacturing jobs where knowledge of English generally is not necessary.

The city's evolution toward a service economy therefore has implications for immigrants. English-language skills will be increasingly necessary, and the competition for jobs that do not require English may become more intense as the market shift progresses.

IMMIGRANT JOB NETWORKS: "WHO SENT YOU?"

The rapid growth of the garment industry in Manhattan's Chinatown offers a prime example of the workings of an immigrant job network and of how both management and labor have benefited from it.

A 1983 survey commissioned jointly by Local 23–25 of the ILGWU and the New York Skirt and Sportswear Association found that the number of garment workers employed in Chinatown doubled between 1969 and 1980. The rapid growth was aided by the social cohesion of the Chinese immigrant workforce.

"Many young Chinese women," the study reported, "took advantage of family and friendships that extended from China to downtown Manhattan to form the core of a new workforce in the women's apparel industry. . . . Families and neighbors maintained their ties through the long journey from provinces in China to Chinatown, sometimes comprising nearly the entire workforce in a single shop."[2]

Familial and ethnic ties play a similar role in helping newly arrived immigrants find jobs in grocery stores, restaurants, and construction firms. Job leads are passed to cousins and countrymen. Employers, especially in loosely structured, low-wage businesses, come to rely on such hiring networks. "Hiring workers through the immigrant network," writes Roger Waldinger, a professor of sociology at City College, "strengthens an employment relationship that might otherwise prove unstable. The ethnic network provides a supply of workers whose characteristics are already known and whose behavior can be predicted with considerable accuracy."[3]

Throughout the city immigrant workers frequently are employed by immigrant entrepreneurs. The result is a paternalistic management style. "The shop is like a family—people bring me problems every day," a Dominican employer told Waldinger. "I help with applications, fill out their immigration papers, call the hospital to find out about relatives, and help with anything involving English."[4] Even in durable goods manufacturing jobs, where labor-management relations are more often governed by rules and contracts, immigrants tend to be concentrated in small, nonunion shops where more relaxed management methods prevail. There is a strong potential for abuse and exploitation in such settings, but immigrants are often willing to accept poor conditions because conditions and wages in New York are likely to be better than they are at home. Furthermore, such jobs provide opportunities to set flexible working hours, learn the rudiments of English, and make the transition to a new land.

The economist Marcia Freedman of Columbia University identified this style of business operation as a crucial factor in the success that immigrants have enjoyed in finding work in New York:

> Large-scale employment of immigrants requires an economy with many jobs in relatively unstructured settings where firms are small and labor standards poorly enforced. . . . Immigrants do not only find such places, they create them, in small businesses, in trade, construction and provision of services. And it is the network they establish for access and the informal training that takes place in these enterprises that make it possible for them to maintain their foothold in the city's economy.[5]

LABOR FORCE PARTICIPATION AND UNEMPLOYMENT

The two standard measures of labor market standing are the labor force participation rate and the unemployment rate. Labor-force participants are defined as those adults who are working or actively looking for work. The labor force participation rate answers the question: of the entire working-age population, what proportion is working or looking for work? The unemployment rate measures lack of success in finding work. It answers the question: of those who view themselves as labor force participants, what proportion are unable to find work?

Data from the 1980 census showed virtually identical labor force participation and unemployment rates among immigrants and native-born persons in their prime working years, (see Tables 7.2 and 7.3), ages 25 to 44. As indicated in Chapter 3, younger and older persons, with their unique employment problems, were excluded from this analysis.

Significant differences appeared, however, when the data were broken down by racial subgroups. In 1980 foreign-born blacks and foreign-born Hispanics had higher labor force participation rates than native-born blacks and native-born Hispanics, among men and women alike. There were no significant differences in unemployment rates between native- and foreign-born persons when analyzed by race.

The labor force participation rates of foreign-born black men and foreign-born Hispanic men were, respectively, ten and nine percentage points higher than their native-born counterparts. Among women the differences were even wider. Almost 79 percent of foreign-born black women were in the labor force, compared with 61 percent of native-

Table 7.2

Labor Force Participation of Persons 25-44 Years of Age in New York City, 1980
(percent)

	Total population	Native-born	Foreign-born by period of immigration			
			Total	Pre-1965	1965-74	1975-80
Males	88.1	87.1	90.5	91.7	92.2	86.1
White, non-Hispanic	91.8	91.9	91.5	93.0	94.1	84.2
Black, non-Hispanic	81.4	78.7	88.7	89.5	89.9	84.4
Hispanic	84.8	81.3	90.0	90.5	91.1	87.1
Asian, non-Hispanic	91.4	88.4	91.7	90.5	94.8	88.3
Females	61.5	60.9	61.9	59.6	65.8	60.1
White, non-Hispanic	65.5	68.1	53.7	54.2	53.0	54.1
Black, non-Hispanic	65.6	61.5	78.7	76.5	80.4	74.7
Hispanic	46.5	39.5	57.9	59.1	57.6	57.3
Asian, non-Hispanic	69.4	70.1	69.4	75.5	75.7	59.7

Source: 1980 U.S. Census Public Use Microdata File.

Table 7.3

Unemployment Rate For Persons 25-44 Years of Age in New York City, 1980
(percent)

	Total population	Native-born	Foreign-born
Males	6.8	7.0	6.2
White, non-Hispanic	4.6	4.6	4.7
Black, non-Hispanic	11.3	12.2	9.0
Hispanic	8.9	9.9	7.6
Asian, non-Hispanic	3.4	4.7	3.3
Females	6.9	6.6	7.6
White, non-Hispanic	5.0	4.8	6.6
Black, non-Hispanic	8.4	8.7	7.5
Hispanic	10.7	10.8	10.7
Asian, non-Hispanic	4.0	5.9	3.8

Source: 1980 U.S. Census Public Use Microdata File.

born black women. Foreign-born Hispanic women, largely from Central and South America, had a participation rate of 58 percent, compared with 40 percent for native-born Hispanic women, who were primarily of Puerto Rican ancestry.

Although the labor force participation and unemployment rates are the most common measures of labor market standing, they do not tell the whole story. For example, native-born blacks made significant advances into white-collar positions (and salaries) during the 1970s, but these advances are not reflected in labor force participation or unemployment rates. Also, the minority unemployment rate is influenced by the existence of a group of long-term unemployed whose characteristics are different from those of the rest of the minority population.

A full analysis of the complex relationships within and between immigrant employment and native employment is not within the scope of this study, but New York City needs such an analysis in order to obtain answers to questions that this chapter can merely pose.

Turning to period of immigration, census data showed that the newest immigrants—those who arrived between 1975 and 1980—had lower labor force participation rates than those who arrived in the 1965–74 period, probably because they had less time to learn English and establish job-finding contacts. The differences between the rates for the pre–1965 group and the 1965–74 group were too small to be statistically significant. Similarly, immigrant unemployment rates could not be analyzed at all by period of immigration because the numbers involved were too small.

DO IMMIGRANTS CAUSE UNEMPLOYMENT FOR NATIVES?

The 1970s were rocky economic times for New York City. Although the local economy revived as the decade ended, the city sustained a net loss of nearly 250,000 jobs between 1970 and 1980. During the 1960s unemployment in New York had been lower than in the rest of the nation; during the 1970s it was higher. Parts of the city's minority population were especially hard-hit by the economic slump.

Nevertheless, nearly 500,000 post–1965 immigrants were working in New York in 1980. Their ability to find jobs despite a flagging economy prompts the question: do immigrants take jobs away from the native-born, especially native-born minorities?

That is one of the most unsettled and unsettling questions raised in the national debate on immigration policy. It is an issue that cuts across traditional ideological lines; conservatives and liberals can be found on both sides of the fence. The issue resonates throughout American history. In times of economic expansion, immigrants have been welcomed to the United States, and praised for their thrift and hard work. In hard times they have been denounced as unfair competition for native-born workers.

The question of whether immigrants displace native workers is not currently a heated public issue in New York. The city's relative calm on the issue is probably due to its long history of receiving immigrants and incorporating them into its job market.

The prevailing school of thought on the immigrants' labor market impact in New York City was developed by a group of scholars that included Roger Waldinger at City College and Marcia Freedman and Thomas Bailey at Columbia University. They have studied immigrant workers in specific industries, including garment manufacturing and food service, and the role of recent immigrants in the economy as a whole. They do not believe that immigrants displace native workers in New York City.

Freedman summarized their conclusions about job displacement thus: "The issue of labor market competition between immigrants and native-born workers tends to be argued in oversimplified terms. Immigrants are pictured either as doing jobs that natives refuse to do, or, alternatively, as competitors who undercut standard wages and working conditions. Insofar as competition exists, it is neither general nor pervasive nor even necessarily direct."[6]

Freedman and her associates base their argument on the concept of the segmented labor market. In this view, there are several markets, not just one. The secondary market, in which many recent immigrants hold jobs, is characterized by loose administrative structure, low wages, and little job security. The preponderance of immigrants in the secondary market, Freedman holds, minimizes direct competition with native-born workers, most of whom are in the primary market.

Furthermore, ethnic hiring networks and the proliferation of immigrant-owned small businesses in the city have cut off open-market competition for jobs; there are tens of thousands of jobs in New York for which the native-born are not candidates. Whether this employment pattern over time will constitute discrimination against native workers is a matter for future monitoring.

The economist Thomas Muller, who has studied immigrants' labor market impact in California, agrees with Freedman's findings and feels that they are not unique to New York; he believes that they obtain in other urban centers as well.

Many immigrant-owned businesses rely heavily on immigrant customers; ethnic loyalty extends an economic lifeline to the businesses and their immigrant employees. Roger Waldinger writes:

> When Chinese merchants, for example, sell Chinese vegetables or fish specialties, they enjoy the advantage of a protected market from larger, possibly more

efficient competitors. Israeli immigrants in Brooklyn operate a thriving, quasi-legal cab service taxiing religious Jews who prefer a segregated lifestyle and therefore patronize Jewish concerns. In the Colombian and Dominican neighborhoods of Queens, immigrant contractors renovate buildings and homes for other immigrants who opt for the reliability and reputation of a compatriot over the lowest offer made through an ethnically open, competitive bid.[7]

Many immigrants work at low-wage jobs that offer little chance for advancement—some of the characteristics, Waldinger believes, that define "immigrant" jobs. Often immigrants intend to stay in the United States only long enough to bankroll an enterprise at home, says Waldinger—for example, a small shop or farm. Consequently they may be more willing to put in long, low-paid hours at "dead-end" jobs—at least until they decide to stay in America. Waldinger and his associates call this willingness "self-exploitation."

Census data can be interpreted to support the argument that there is little direct competition for jobs between immigrants and the native-born. Immigrant and native-born women, for example, appear to work in two discrete job markets. The 1980 census showed that the great majority of native female workers in New York were employed in offices as administrators, secretaries, and clerks. Most immigrant women were employed in manufacturing or "pink collar" service jobs such as housekeeping and health care.

Unlike the women, native- and foreign-born men were employed in many of the same occupations, suggesting a greater likelihood of competition between them. Some research suggests, however, that within a given industry, separate employment tiers exist for native and foreign-born workers. Carmenza Gallo, an economist at Columbia University, has studied immigrant employment in New York City's construction industry.[8] She found that most jobs at new construction sites were filled by native-born, unionized workers. Nonunion firms dominated the growing number of residential renovation projects, especially brownstones, and these small firms employed a predominantly immigrant work force.

The same sources can be read to support a different set of conclusions. Successful immigrant-owned businesses may crowd out native-owned businesses, along with their native-born workers. Some economists, like former Secretary of Labor F. Ray Marshall, contend that industry reliance on cheap immigrant labor perpetuates inefficient production methods, retarding productivity.

THE CASE OF THE MISSING BURGER KING

Perhaps the best argument for the proposition that immigrants take jobs away from native-born workers runs as follows: businesses that rely on immigrant labor are able to operate so cheaply that they eliminate competitors that would be likely to hire native-born workers.

The restaurant industry serves as the best example. New York City has an incomparable variety of inexpensive ethnic restaurants and fast food outlets. This ethnic smorgasbord is one of the delights of New York life. At the same time, the city has had relatively few national fast food chain outlets. Greek coffee shops and Chinese takeouts tend to outnumber Burger Kings and Pizza Huts, though the national chains are making increasing forays into urban markets. The predominance of local outlets works to the disadvantage of youthful workers, especially native minority youths who are often employed by fast food franchises.

This contention demands consideration, but there are arguments that counter it. Immigrant-owned restaurants sometimes charge higher prices than their native-owned competitors; their competitive advantage is not in price but in quality of product. New York's collective palate defies the homogeneity of taste that fast food franchises rely on and perpetuate. National grocery store chains have had difficulty in penetrating the New York City market, in part for the same reason: it is hard for a national chain to meet the widely diverse food tastes of New York's ethnically mixed population. Those tastes are more easily served by small, locally owned specialty shops.

Often immigrant businesses do not displace native-owned firms but replace businesses owned by previous immigrants. Korean immigrants have succeeded Italian immigrants as the city's foremost greengrocers. Middle Eastern and Asian immigrants operate the tobacco shops and newsstands once owned by Jewish immigrants from eastern Europe. This ethnic succession is sometimes resented by native-born customers. In Manhattan's Harlem, for example, black protests led to an agreement with Korean merchants to employ more neighborhood teenagers in the Korean-owned groceries that now line 125th Street. Nonresident ownership of Harlem stores is not a recent phenomenon, and it is only one of many reasons for the dismayingly high rate of teenage unemployment in Harlem.

WAGE DEPRESSION AND ITS EFFECTS

Immigrants, especially recent arrivals, are often willing to work at wages well below the levels accepted by native-born workers or required by the law. Many economists feel that this willingness tends to depress the wages of native-born workers in industries that employ both immigrants and natives. There is little agreement, however, on the effects of this wage depression on other industries or on the economy as a whole.

Perhaps the most thorough study to date of immigration and wage depression has been done by Thomas Muller. He found that "there is little doubt that wages in several occupations rose more slowly in Los Angeles than elsewhere as low-skilled immigrants, primarily Hispanics, entered the labor force."[9]

Julian Simon, an economist at the University of Maryland who is normally sanguine about the effects of immigration on the U.S. standard of living, believes that a large immigrant labor pool has little effect on unemployment among the native-born, but he does believe that such a pool results in a "downward pressure on wages."[10]

Is this wage depression necessarily a bad thing for native-born workers? Muller argues that it is not. One effect of immigrant-induced wage depression in Los Angeles, he found, was to "preserve the area's competitive advantage in manufacturing and to modestly increase profit margins." He contends that the depressed wages in low-skill jobs caused more such jobs to open up: "In manufacturing sectors with declining employment nationally, additional jobs for skilled and white-collar workers were created in Los Angeles to complement unskilled production jobs."[11]

Analysts of the New York City economy believe that the city's native-born may have reaped similar benefits. The garment industry is Exhibit A. The number of garment industry jobs in New York fell continuously from the end of World War II until the new immigrant influx stabilized it at its current level. Without that influx, writes economist Emanuel Tobier of New York University, the industry "would have lacked the critical mass of workers big enough to keep the industry anchored in New York City."[12] Immigrants saved jobs for thousands of native-born garment workers by keeping clothing manufacturers from going under or going to Hong Kong, Tobier contends, and also improved the condition of the city's clothing merchants "because of the greater degree of choice afforded them by the Chinese contractors in Lower Manhattan."

Other economists, however, believe that such benefits are short-term at best and are more than offset by long-term hazards. F. Ray Marshall holds that industries that rely on cheap immigrant labor wed themselves to inefficient, labor-intensive forms of production. This retards their modernization and the overall productivity of the economy. Like Tobier, Marshall uses the garment industry to illustrate his point, but argues that the "competitive advantage" of using immigrant labor is illusory: "When child-labor laws were passed, eliminating an important source of cheap labor for the garment shops, manufacturers predicted that clothing prices would rise. Instead, new methods and machinery—capital-intensive investments—were made, and clothing in the 1920s and 1950s was cheaper in real dollars than it had been in the 1900s."[13]

Michael Harrington, the author and political activists, is troubled by the social and economic implications of immigrant-caused wage depression for the native-born poor. He does not believe, as Muller and others do, that the profits gained by using immigrant labor lead to business expansion and the creation of better jobs for the native-born. Instead, he is convinced that the use of immigrant labor in menial jobs devalues the jobs for immigrants and for the native-born as well:

> If there had not been a constant inflow of immigrants into the American economy over the years, business would have been forced to upgrade the lower sectors of the labor market. Since there would not have been a cheap, docile supply of people so desperate that they would happily do menial labor at the minimum wage or less, they would have had to make these menial jobs less so, more "American." That, in turn, would have made things much better for the blacks, the Puerto Ricans and the other indigenous working poor.[14]

Whether, without immigration, such jobs would have been upgraded, or shipped out to the Third World, is an open question, but Harrington's concern for the poor—both native- and foreign-born—illuminates some hard truths. New immigrants in New York and in the rest of the nation often endure low wages, unpleasant or dangerous working conditions, and a lack of employment benefits. The usual institutional remedy for American workers facing such conditions is unionization.

The immigrant work force is divided between industries, like health care, that are unionized, and those, like the restaurant business, that are not. West Indian immigrants have played important roles in the affairs of the city hospital workers' union, District 1199 of the Retail, Wholesale, and Department Store Union.

The garment industry is split between union and nonunion shops, but the ILGWU has a strong history of immigrant advocacy. The ILGWU was established by immigrants, and since its beginnings it has encouraged immigrants to join the U.S. labor movement, without regard to their immigration status. ILGWU officials estimate that there are about 20,000 unionized garment workers in Chinatown. Thousands of these workers attended a series of rallies called by the union in 1982; their show of strength helped to resolve a contract negotiation impasse with the neighborhood's garment contractors.

Ethnic solidarity has been a powerful tool in recruiting immigrants to U.S. unions, and unionization remains one important antidote to the exploitation of immigrant labor—an exploitation that works to the detriment of natives and immigrants alike.

THE EFFECTS OF SIMPSON-RODINO

The effect that the new immigration law may have on New York City employers, employees, businesses, and industries is a matter of maximum interest and minimum certainty. To start, no one knows the actual size or location of the undocumented workforce. No one knows to what extent employers will wish to comply with the new law, nor to what extent the INS can or will force them to comply. Fraudulent work documents will certainly be available, but no one knows in what numbers nor with what freedom from detection. Some undocumented workers will surely find new job opportunities in home industry, in contract work, or in the underground economy, but no one knows how widespread these solutions will be. No one knows how many undocumented workers will get discouraged and remove themselves from the job market by leaving the United States.

Finally, should the new law succeed in discouraging large numbers of unauthorized immigrant workers, no one knows what effect this will have on New York City business and industry, nor on its unemployed. It is conceivable that new opportunities will open up for the native-born unemployed. It is also conceivable that industries will die or move out of New York, leaving native-born workers without jobs.

The greatest likelihood, however, is that there will be no vast upheaval in the labor market. Market forces, and the relationship that immigrant labor bears to them in New York, may be too strong to change drastically, either for the better or for the worse. New York industry, at least at this time, is inconceivable without its immigrant workforce.

NOTES

1. Oscar Handlin, *The Uprooted* (Boston: Atlantic-Little, Brown, 1973), p. 67.

2. Abeles, Schwartz, Haeckel & Silverblatt, Inc., *The Chinatown Garment Industry Study: An Overview* (New York: Local 23–25, International Ladies Garment Workers Union and the New York Skirt and Sportswear Association, 1983), pp. 5, 7.

3. Roger Waldinger, "Immigrants and Enterprise in New York City," *Kaleidoscope: Current Research and Scholarly Activity at CCNY* 1, no. 2 (Fall 1984):14.

4. Ibid.

5. Marcia Freedman, "The Labor Market for Immigrants in New York City," *New York Affairs* 7, no. 4 (1983):96.

6. Ibid.

7. Waldinger, "Immigrants and Enterprise," pp. 12–13.

8. Carmenza Gallo, *The Construction Industry in New York City: Immigrants and Black Entrepreneurs*. Working paper. Conservation of Human Resources (New York: Columbia University, 1983).

9. Thomas Muller, *The Fourth Wave: California's Newest Immigrants, A Summary* (Washington, D.C.: Urban Institute Press, 1984), p. 14.

10. Julian M. Simon, *Nine Myths About Immigration* (Washington, D.C.: The Heritage Foundation, 1984), p. 6.

11. Muller, *The Fourth Wave*, p. 16.

12. Emanuel Tobier, "Foreign Immigration," in Charles Brecher and Raymond Hor-

ton, eds., *Setting Municipal Priorities* (New York: New York University Press, 1983), pp. 195–196.

13. F. Ray Marshall, *Illegal Immigration: The Problem, the Solutions* (Washington, D.C.: Federation for Immigration Reform, 1982), p. 6.

14. Michael Harrington, *The New American Poverty* (New York: Holt, Rinehart and Winston, 1984), p. 166.

PART III

The Service Delivery System

8 Social Services: Welfare and Beyond

The fear that indigent immigrants might swell the nation's welfare rolls has played a large part in the recent debates on U.S. immigration policy. As Congress strove to design a legalization program for undocumented aliens who had established roots in the United States, analysts produced widely divergent estimates of potential costs in public benefits that would become available to newly legalized aliens. Concern over cost predictions and disagreement over an equitable reimbursement formula for local governments worked against earlier passage of an immigration bill.

New York City officials have insisted that the federal government provide full reimbursement to localities for social service costs incurred as a result of legalization, but their attitude was not one of great alarm or anti-immigrant sentiment. In New York City, they knew, immigrants make far less use of public assistance than do the native-born. Figures from the 1980 census suggest that foreign-headed households used public assistance at just over half the rate of native-headed households.

One reason for immigrants' lower-than-average use of public assistance is that immigration is generally motivated by the desire to find work. Many immigrants are willing to work at low-paying, low-status jobs if the only alternative is welfare. The stereotype of the hard-working, "we-help-our-own" immigrant is rooted in reality.

Like immigrants earlier in the century, today's immigrants are helped by family and countrymen who preceded them to New York. The most important agents in the immigrant adaptation process are families, neighborhood groups, ethnic associations, and small businesses, not social welfare agencies. This is true for legal and illegal immigrants alike.

The self-sufficiency of the new immigrants should not be permitted, however, to obscure their problems and needs. Although many newcomers are quickly integrated into the city's economic and social life, others have adjustment problems that cannot be solved by informal self-help networks. The 1980 census showed that 26.8 percent of the city's newest immigrants—those who arrived between 1975 and 1980—lived in households with incomes below the poverty level, compared with 16.7 percent of the total immigrant population and 21.2 percent of the native-headed households.

The immigrant poor have many of the same problems as the native-born poor in housing and feeding their families, but they are burdened with the additional handicaps of English-language deficiency, cultural difference, and a lack of know-how in obtaining resources. There are few government-funded services specifically for new immigrants, apart from English-as-a-second-language (ESL) classes and some interpreter services at local hospitals—and there are not enough of either to go around. The psychological stresses of immigration are often severe but are rarely addressed by government, and the arcane complications of immigration law frequently produce headaches for which society offers little relief.

Social service doesn't mean just welfare. It also means health care, education, vocational and personal counseling, and even legal assistance. The public focus on immigrants' use of cash assistance tends to obscure important questions about immigrants and their relationship to the rest of the social service system. How well, for example, do the city's "helping" institutions serve immigrants? Do teachers and social workers understand the widely varying child-rearing theories of the city's ethnic populations? Is enough being done to inform immigrants about affordable social services that are available to them? Are there enough interpreters at city hospitals, food stamp offices, and vocational counseling programs?

To determine whether the city was providing adequate interpreter and translator services, the Office of Immigrant Affairs (OIA) undertook a study of city language services in the fall of 1985. The OIA study was taken up and continued by the Mayor's Commission on Hispanic Concerns which issued a report in December 1986 proposing a set of language service guidelines to be adapted by each agency under the general direction of a citywide language services coordinator. In early 1987, the report was awaiting the Mayor's response.

Other questions about immigrants' relationship with the social service system can best be answered by looking at the services provided by the multitude of public, private, voluntary, and religious organizations that make up New York City's immigrant service network. To some extent, these agencies interlock, overlap, and fail to mesh—the inevitable results of diverse needs and disparate funding sources. Problems include gaps in coverage, uneconomical duplications of service, and the kind of isolationism that sometimes occurs when the competition for funding is too severe for comfort.

MAJOR SOCIAL SERVICE ORGANIZATIONS

The Human Resources Administration (HRA) administers most cash and medical assistance programs in the city; when immigrants do go on welfare, they generally do so through HRA. HRA also funds a number of service programs for refugees, such as foster care for parentless refugee children. These services are discussed further in Chapter 9. Legal immigrants are eligible for most HRA services designed for the general population. There are only a few services intended specifically for immigrants other than the refugee programs; one of those is information and referral for immigrants who might otherwise be unable to find their way into the mainstream social service system.

When immigrants need more help than their families, church, or community can give, they are likely to seek that help (if they do seek it) from one of the voluntary social service agencies that serve New York's children, elderly, and poor. Like HRA, most of these agencies do not have specific services for immigrants; their immigrant clients receive the same treatment as their native-born clients. This equal treatment has both drawbacks and benefits for immigrants.

Because such organizations are part of the mainstream social service system, their workers and administrators are highly knowledgeable about the range of services available to their clients. But because they are not oriented toward specific immigrant problems, these agencies miss opportunities to educate immigrants about the services available to them, and cultural and language barriers may hinder communication though many of the larger agencies are able to hire some staff who are conversant in other languages and cultures.

The largest of the nongovernment organizations that serve immigrants are Catholic Charities of the Archdiocese of New York, Catholic Charities of Brooklyn, and the Federation of Jewish Philanthropies. Through a multiplicity of services, the Catholic Church is the single largest agency serving immigrants in the city. Its activities in the area of immigration are discussed in Chapter 11.

IMMIGRATION COUNSELING

Immigration law and its administration are so complex that most aliens need immigration counseling and representation at some point after their arrival. Both documented and undocumented aliens need such service, whether to change from one immigration status to another, to petition for admission of a family member, to apply for political asylum, or to fight a deportation order.

After enactment of the Hart-Celler Act in 1965, a network of profit and nonprofit legal advisers grew up to meet the need for immigration counsel. The main components of the network are private immigration attorneys, nonprofit agencies that specialize in immigration counseling, immigration specialists in the local congressional offices, and informal community-based advisers who may be notaries public, travel agents, or simply knowledgeable neighbors.

About 400 attorneys practice immigration law in New York City. Some specialize in cases that involve human rights issues; others serve corporate clients bringing foreign employees to the United States for training or positions in research and management. The majority, however, are everyday working lawyers who file family reunification petitions, apply for labor certifications, and generally counsel their clients in their dealings with the INS. For immigrants the major deterrent to seeking private counsel is cost.

Immigrants without the money for a private attorney may turn to one of the 26 nonprofit agencies accredited by the INS to provide immigration representation. Few of those agencies operate full legal-service clinics. The majority restrict themselves to areas in which they feel competent—for example, naturalization or family reunification petitions—and leave the more difficult matters, like asylum petitions or deportation hearings, to the most experienced agencies. The U.S. Catholic Conference (USCC) is the largest of the accredited immigration counseling agencies and will handle any kind of case. Voluntary resettlement agencies, ethnic associations, and community organizations are other providers of counseling service.

These accredited agencies struggle under an almost impossible work load. The problem was aggravated in 1983 when the Legal Services Corporation was prohibited from using its federal funding for services to undocumented aliens. Legal Services contracts with community agencies to provide legal services to the poor. A very few of the local agencies have been able to raise private funds to maintain some level of immigration work. The Legal Aid Society of New York, another quasi-public provider of legal services, similarly has been forced to reduce the level of its immigration services.

Various provisions of the Simpson-Rodino Act will mean far more work for immigration lawyers and counselors. Aliens who may be eligible for one of the legalization programs need advice on the strength of their case and the kinds of documentation they will need to bolster it. The INS has selected a group of "qualified designated entities" to provide screening and assistance in filling out applications for the amnesty program proper. Aliens whose cases are denied will need further help.

Also in need of some kind of assistance will be aliens or citizens who believe that they have been the victims of job discrimination. The Simpson-Rodino Act set up a special counsel to review charges of employment discrimination, and many complainants are sure to want and need legal counsel.

Immigration problems are also among the matters with which congressional offices help their constituents—even if they are not yet citizens. Aides in congressional districts with large immigrant constituencies have developed considerable expertise in immigration counseling. As federal employees they are able to work directly with other federal agencies like the INS and the State Department. Congressional aides have a direct line to a congressional liaison unit at the INS, where they can get almost immediate answers to inquiries on cases that have run into delays or other problems. No one else has such access to the INS. The congressional offices also have direct contact with U.S. consulates abroad, which enables them to ascertain the status of visa applications and often to expedite the visa-granting process for relatives of constituents.

By and large, immigrants are well served by the legal services network, but there are risks and problems. The nonprofit agencies may be too overworked for maximum effectiveness; expertise varies from agency to agency and worker to worker; and though the agencies are accredited, their work is never reviewed. Some cases need, but do not get, an attorney's skills.

The immigrant who seeks help from one of the nonprofit organizations is safe, however, from overcharging and from fraud, risks to which immigrants are exposed when they deal with the few lawyers and self-styled immigration experts who prey on their ignorance and fear. Sometimes aliens are charged exorbitant fees for the most perfunctory paperwork, or for applications that have no hope of success. Sometimes they are sold counterfeit "green cards" they believe to be real. In other cases, aliens conspire with their lawyers or counselors in arranging marriages of convenience or producing fraudulent documents.

Workers in the field acknowledge that fraud and bad advice do occur, but no one knows how to root them out. The field is unregulated. Defrauded aliens, particularly if they are undocumented, are loath to report victimization—if they know it has taken place.

THE ETHNIC ASSOCIATIONS

As each new immigrant group establishes itself in the city, it develops self-help organizations designed to serve its specific social, cultural, and economic needs. Ethnic associations spring up as new immigrant groups reach large enough numbers to organize, and they multiply as differences in political, social, and economic viewpoints arise among countrymen.

Ethnic associations received their first government funding with the antipoverty programs of the 1960s and 1970s. Agencies like the Chinatown Planning Council and the Hellenic-American Neighborhood Action Committee have since grown into large, multiservice agencies providing counseling in the native language, adult education, vocational training and placement, and many other services.

The Chinatown Planning Council is an ethnic association that has been particularly successful in obtaining government support. From its establishment in 1965, it has been supported mainly by federal funds, which have been channeled through a number of city agencies: the Department of Employment, the Department of Housing Preservation and Development, the Community Development Agency, the Agency for Child Development, and the Department for the Aging. Funds have also come through the state's Refugee/Entrant Assistance Program. In recent years, about 95 percent of the council's $13 million budget has come from government grants.

Charles Wang, the council's executive director, says that his agency is the first stop for almost every Chinese immigrant to New York City. Nearly 4,000 clients a day, the majority of them recent arrivals, visit the council's 40 service sites in Manhattan, the Bronx, Brooklyn and Queens. They receive help with housing, employment, medical care, government benefits, and immigration matters. Medicaid and food stamp workers process applications for these benefits at the council's main office in Chinatown. Counselors help with personal and family problems, translate letters, and escort clients to government offices where they will need interpreters.

Many of New York's newer immigrant groups are in the process of establishing similar self-help organizations. The Haitian community gave birth to the United Haitian Association in 1977, and to the Haitian Centers Council in 1982. Both operations received technical assistance from the Community Service Society, a well-established nonprofit social service organization, and both have been the recipients of government grants. Other ethnic groups that have recently established self-help organizations include Ethiopians, Cubans, Dominicans, Koreans, and Cambodians.

The role of ethnic associations, and their relationship to the formal service delivery system, is the subject of a 1985 study.[1] These associations have a particular ability to form a bridge between the old life and the new, between the immigrant's informal social structures and the city's formal service structures.

IMMIGRANT WELFARE USE

Census takers in 1980 asked one out of every six heads of households whether he or she had received some form of welfare in the previous year. City Planning tabulations show that 7.7 percent of foreign-born heads of household said they had received some form of welfare, compared with 13.3 percent of native-born heads of household.

The data also show that foreign-born heads of household were only 18.4 percent of all New York City heads of household on public assistance, although they were 28 percent of the city total (see Table 8.1).

Census data were used for this analysis because the HRA which administers most public assistance programs for New York City residents, does not aggregate data on recipients' country of birth. HRA data show that about 12 percent of all New York City households had an open public assistance case at any one time in 1979. Although HRA and census figures are not strictly comparable because the data elements are not identical, HRA's 12 percent is close enough to the census figure of 11.7 percent for all city households to suggest that the census data are reliable.

Because this analysis relies on 1980 census data, it does not reflect public assistance use patterns among the large numbers of refugees and entrants who arrived in New York City after 1980. It is known that refugees and entrants have a higher public assistance use rate than the rest of the foreign-born population, particularly during their first years in the United States, when the federal government provides full reimbursement for local welfare costs. Refugees' use of public assistance is discussed in Chapter 9. Still, census data support the conclusion that immigrants tend to make less use of public assistance than do the native-born, despite their lower income levels.

Immigrants' rate of public assistance use varies from family to family and group to group. Alien status is one determining factor. Refugees and entrants have the highest public assistance use rate of any immigrant classification, in part because they are immediately eligible for a range of government benefits, many of which are unavailable to other immigrants. The high rate is due also to the debilitating circumstances that brought them to the United States. Other factors that influence welfare use are the job skills brought from home, psychological and physical readiness for work, the presence of a family breadwinner, nongovernmental resources available to the family, and cultural attitudes toward government assistance.

Welfare use correlates with household composition among households headed by foreign-born and by native-born, but foreign-born heads of household made less use of welfare than their native-born counterparts, regardless of the type of household in which they were living (see Table 8.2).

Table 8.1

Public Assistance Use by New York City Heads of Household, 1979

	Total	Native-born	Foreign-born
Total heads of household	2,792,540	2,011,540	781,000
Number receiving public assistance	327,020	266,960	60,060
Percentage of total recipient heads of household	100.0	81.6	18.4
Public assistance use rate (percent)	11.7	13.3	7.7

Source: 1980 U.S. Census Public Use Microdata File.

Table 8.2

Public Assistance Use by Household Type, New York City, 1979

	Total households	Native-born households	Foreign-born households
Total households receiving public assistance, as a percentage of all households in each nativity group	11.7	13.3	7.7
Family households	12.3	14.7	6.9
Married couple	3.8	4.0	3.2
Male-headed, no spouse	7.3	8.6	4.2
Female-headed, no spouse	36.3	40.3	22.5
Nonfamily households	10.6	11.0	9.3

<u>Source</u>: 1980 U.S. Census Public Use Microdata File.

Looking at the composition of only those households headed by public assistance recipients (see Table 8.3), a distinct distribution pattern emerges among the foreign-born. Among immigrant welfare recipients, larger proportions were likely to be married couples or nonfamily households than was the case among native-headed households. The incidence of nonfamily households on public assistance is explained by the presence of a large percentage of dependent elderly among the foreign-born. The incidence of married couples on welfare is harder to explain, but it does suggest that poverty among immigrants correlates somewhat less closely with female-headed household status than is the case among the native-born. One explanation may be that refugees on welfare, of whom there were some in New York before 1980, are likely to be members of married-couple families. Undoubtedly there are other reasons.

Table 8.3 compares the distribution of household types among all households and among those receiving public assistance.

Like native-headed households, foreign-headed households were more likely to be on welfare if the household head was under 25 years of age. But the public assistance use rate among foreign-headed households in this age category was only 13.4 percent, compared with 20.4 percent among native-headed households. Of the heads of households aged 15 to 24 who received welfare, more than three-quarters were females without spouses, among the foreign-born as well as the native-born. Only 43.5 percent of foreign-born female heads of household in this age group received public assistance, however, compared with 65 percent among the corresponding group of native-born heads of household.

In every age group the percentage of foreign-born receiving public assistance was lower than the rate for the native-born. In the age group 35–39, for example, 6.5 percent of foreign-born heads of household received public assistance, compared with 15.3 percent among the native-born.

HISTORY OF ALIEN ENTITLEMENTS

Earlier immigrants arrived in New York City to find an expanding economy with no public benefits; today's newcomers find a stable economy with an array of social welfare programs directed at the general population. For the immigrants of the late 19th and early 20th centuries, there were no food stamps nor Medicaid, no housing subsidies nor government-sponsored job-training programs. The help that existed for the poor and otherwise disadvantaged was provided by private charity. Immigrants were a special concern of charitable institutions; the settlement house movement, from which the social work profession grew,

Table 8.3

Distribution of Household Types Among All Households and Those Receiving Public Assistance, New York City, 1979 (percent)

	Total New York City		Native-born		Foreign-born	
	Total households	Households receiving P.A.	Total households	Households receiving P.A.	Total households	Households receiving P.A.
Total Households	100.0	100.0	100.0	100.0	100.0	100.0
Family households	63.4	66.8	61.4	67.9	68.6	61.7
Married couple	44.0	14.2	40.8	12.5	52.3	21.8
Male head, no spouse	3.0	1.9	3.0	1.9	3.2	1.7
Female head, no spouse	16.4	50.7	17.6	53.5	13.1	38.2
Nonfamily households	36.6	33.2	38.6	32.1	31.4	38.2

Source: 1980 U.S. Census Public Use Microdata File.

was created to help immigrants, and much of the early sociological research in the United States was conducted in urban immigrant ghettos.

During the period between the New Deal of the 1930s and the Great Society of the 1960s, government entitlement programs came to replace private charity as the nation's primary funder of social services. This expansion of social spending took place during a period of little immigration. Increasingly complex social welfare legislation was passed with almost no special reference to immigrants.

In 1972, however, the statute creating the Supplemental Security Income (SSI) program was written to exclude all aliens except permanent resident aliens and others "permanently residing in the United States under color of law (PRUCOL)." "PRUCOL" was not defined. From that time on, alien entitlements were restricted more and more, almost every year, at both the federal and the state levels.

These restrictions were influenced by a national immigration policy that was, and often is, contradictory, poorly articulated, and difficult to enforce. The confusions began with a lack of coordination between immigration law and social service law. Immigration law set up immigrant categories for the purpose of regulating admissions into the United States; social service law established a different classification system for the purpose of determining alien entitlements.

As alien entitlement criteria developed within the social service laws, there were contradictions between federal statutes and the federal regulations drawn up to implement them; contradictions between the policies of one agency and those of another; jurisdictional conflicts between the federal government and the states; and everywhere different interpretations of vaguely worded mandates. Finally, there were intermittent court challenges, which resulted in a shifting matrix of entitlements as new decisions changed old practices.

The cumulative effect of these confusions on social service administrators and line workers can readily be imagined. There is far too little clarity to guarantee that alien entitlements are being conferred in a consistently equitable and accurate fashion.

The problems began in 1974, as soon as the new SSI section of the Social Security Act took effect. As noted, the SSI section granted benefits only to those aliens who had permanent resident status or were living in the United States "under color of law," a phrase that created permanent confusion in alien entitlements administration because it was undefined. The statute read that PRUCOL aliens included refugees and asylees, but it did not say which other aliens were included or excluded.

Federal regulations drawn up in 1974 to implement the new program did nothing to clarify the confusion; they simply adopted the same vague language. In fact, they sowed the seeds of another controversy in that they applied the new restriction to the Aid to Families with Dependent

Children (AFDC) and Medicaid programs even though the AFDC and Medicaid statutes had not been amended. The changes in eligibility criteria came strictly through regulations.

After Congress passed the new SSI statute, with its restrictions on aliens, the New York State Legislature amended the state Social Service Law to deny public assistance to aliens "unlawfully residing" in the United States. The amendment took effect in 1974. Its purpose was to conform to the new federal rules, so it is not clear why the state used language that was different from the federal language. In doing so, it opened itself to a law suit, *Holley v. Lavine*, which became an important case in alien entitlements administration.

When the state implemented its new restrictions in 1974, Holley, a Canadian national with six U.S.-born children, was disqualified from receiving AFDC benefits for herself, though not for her children. The plaintiff had entered the country on a student visa and had stayed past its expiration date before marrying and having children. In a sense, therefore, she was an "illegal" alien. When she was disqualified from AFDC, Holley brought suit against the commissioner of the New York State DSS, claiming that the federal wording, "permanently residing under color of law," ought to take precedence over the state wording, "unlawfully residing," and that she ought to be viewed as PRUCOL because the INS knew of her presence in the country and had agreed not to deport her until her children were grown. (AFDC benefits are administered by the state and paid in part by the state though the program is federal.)

In 1977 a decision was issued in Holley's favor. The court agreed that federal wording took precedence over state wording, and that the INS had in essence conferred a quasi-legal status on the plaintiff by agreeing not to exercise its right to deport her.

The understanding of PRUCOL that emerged from the *Holley* case came to govern the state's Home Relief program as well. In 1981 the state amended its wording to conform to federal wording, and in that same year the alien restrictions in the federal AFDC regulations were finally incorporated into the AFDC statute.

The *Holley* definition of PRUCOL was broadened as a consequence of a subsequent SSI challenge, *Berger* v. *Schweiker*. Manny Berger had come to the United States from Russia on a temporary visa, and had stayed beyond its expiration to live and work here. In 1967 he voluntarily surrendered to the INS, but since it was not INS custom to deport people to the USSR, Berger was placed under an "order of supervision," which granted him permission to remain in the United States for an undetermined period of time. In 1970 Berger began to receive disability benefits from a state program that was a precursor of SSI, and he was "rolled over" to the SSI program at its inception in 1974. In 1975 his SSI benefits were discontinued, and he brought suit the following year to have them reinstated, on the ground that he was permanently residing in the United States under color of law. The U.S. Department of Health, Education and Welfare (HEW) settled the suit by entering into a consent decree agreeing with *Holley* that the INS conferred PRUCOL status if it agreed not to deport. HEW agreed further that the INS conferred permission to stay merely by not acting to deport, if it knew of an alien's presence in the country. Formal permission in writing did not have to be granted.

The case went back to court in 1982 when Berger claimed that the SSI administration was not abiding by the court judgment, and that aliens who ought to have been accepted for SSI benefits were being turned away. The court found in Berger's favor. Then the U.S. Department of Health and Human Services (HHS), the successor to HEW, went back to court in an effort to have the *Berger* decision overturned—an effort that was not successful.

Consequently, in March 1986 HHS proposed new SSI regulations that granted eligibility to aliens residing in the United States with the knowledge and permission of the INS, and whose departure the INS does not contemplate enforcing. The proposed regulations listed 14 categories of such aliens and noted that currently unspecified others might also be eligible. In early 1987, final rules had not yet been published.

The broadened interpretation of PRUCOL that was accepted by the AFDC and SSI programs was not incorporated into the Medicaid regulations, which remained more restrictive. To establish Medicaid eligibility, it was not sufficient for an alien to demonstrate that the INS had knowledge of his or her presence and had made no move to deport.

The regulations denying Medicaid benefits to undocumented aliens and the narrow definition of PRUCOL were challenged in a federal court case in New York City. The suit is discussed in Chapter 13. In brief, the plaintiffs claimed that the Medicaid regulations barring undocumented aliens conflicted with the Medicaid statute, which made no mention of alien status as a determinant of eligibility. Plaintiffs also claimed that the narrow definition of PRUCOL was arbitrary and inconsistent with the definition in effect in other entitlement programs. In July 1986, a judge ruled in the plaintiffs' favor on the grounds that the Medicaid statute clearly did not mention alienage. Congress immediately responded by amending the Medicaid statute to grant Medicaid benefits to only those aliens who were legal permanent residents or who were PRUCOL. PRUCOL was not defined in the amendment, and regulations had not been published at the time this book went to press.

While the *Holley* case was in court, the state and federal governments took other actions to restrict entitlements for undocumented aliens. In 1979 the New York State DSS issued regulations that excluded undocumented aliens from social service programs such as foster care, battered women's programs, family planning, and day care. It is worth noting that in New York City (and perhaps elsewhere) the regulations are often unenforced; documents are not always required to establish eligibility for "soft" service programs.

The restrictions on day care became the subject of a successful court challenge in *Ruiz* v. *Blum*. In 1983 a federal court ruled that the state could not refuse to serve U.S.-born children of undocumented aliens; the citizen child could not be denied service on the basis of the parents' status. The plaintiff did not challenge the ban on providing day care to undocumented children of undocumented parents, and so it remains in force.

Alien eligibility for the food stamp program was restricted through an amendment to the Food Stamp Act that took effect in 1978. (The Food Stamp Act is separate from the Social Security Act, which governs most other federal entitlement programs.) Congress circumvented the vague "color of law" language and stated specifically which categories of aliens would qualify for food stamps. Of aliens who might otherwise have been considered undocumented, the list included those who had entered the country before 1948 and those who had been granted a stay of deportation.

RESTRICTIONS ON PERMANENT RESIDENT ALIENS

Permanent resident aliens were subject to their first limitation of benefits in 1980 when Congress tightened the financial eligibility criteria for receiving SSI. A combination of forces, including the effects of a decade of economic uncertainty and a growing conservatism, put Congress in a restrictive frame of mind.

In 1978 the U.S. General Accounting Office (GAO) had issued a report that carried the warning "Number of Newly Arrived Aliens Who Receive Supplemental Security Income Needs to Be Reduced." The GAO found that a third of the elderly aliens who arrived (legally) in the country during fiscal years 1973–75 were receiving SSI benefits at the end of 1976. One explanation subsequently advanced in the media was that immigrant landlords were sponsoring their elderly relatives for immigration, signing them up for SSI benefits, then using part of the benefits as rent.

Congress moved quickly to stop this alleged practice. Senator Charles Percy of Illinois sponsored a bill stipulating that if a permanent resident alien applied for SSI benefits within three years of entering the United States, the income of the alien's sponsor would be considered in determining the alien's financial eligibility for benefits. Such a stipulation is known in welfare legislation as a "deeming" provision; that is, some particular asset—in this case the sponsor's income and resources—is "deemed" to be available to the applicant.

The term "sponsor" does not appear in immigration law. It is used in social service law as a designation for a person who signs an affidavit of support for a prospective immigrant. Immigration authorities sometimes require such an affidavit as a guarantee that a prospective immigrant will not become a public charge. An affidavit of support is not required of all applicants—that is, not all immigrants have sponsors. The deeming provisions come into play only when an immigrant has a sponsor.

Since 1980 deeming provisions have been applied more widely among entitlement programs, and they have begun to be challenged in court. In 1981 a deeming provision was incorporated into the AFDC section of the Social Security Act, and the New York State Legislature adopted one in the Home Relief Law. The state law is currently being challenged in court on the grounds that it violates the state constitutional responsibility to provide for all the needy. Plaintiffs also contend that it violates due process to determine an applicant's benefits on the basis of a sponsor's resources if the applicant is not receiving them. In 1985 State Supreme Court Justice Elliott Wilk denied a motion to dismiss the case (*Minino* v. *Perales*). His decision not to dismiss virtually took the form of an opinion that the provision does violate the New York State Constitution. Years of litigation are probably ahead before the matter is resolved.

In 1982 the federal government incorporated a deeming provision into the Food Stamp Act. In 1984, for the AFDC program, Congress redefined "sponsor" to include sponsoring organizations as well as sponsoring individuals.

Paradoxically, the deeming provisions make it more difficult for some permanent resident aliens to obtain public benefits than it is for aliens who are here under color of law. It was certainly not the intent of Congress to provide more liberal benefits for PRUCOL aliens than for permanent residents; the inequity arose in the absence of coordination and comprehensive legislative planning. (See Table 8.4 for a summary of alien entitlement restrictions.)

Deeming provisions have not been incorporated into the Medicaid law. The policy in the New York State Medicaid program is to consider the sponsor's resources only if they are an actual source of income for the applicant. If the sponsor does not actually contribute, his or her resources are ignored. The distinction is an important one because sponsors are not legally bound to contribute to their sponsorees' income, even though they have signed affidavits of support. Still, for the entitlement programs where deeming provisions are in force, the sponsor's income and resources are considered even if they are not actually contributed.

The Simpson-Rodino Act of 1986 created several new alien classifications, the most important of which for New Yorkers is temporary

Table 8.4

Evolution of Alien Entitlement Restrictions

Undocumented Aliens		Documented Aliens	
1972	Congress creates SSI program and confers benefits only on citizens, permanent resident aliens, and aliens "permanently residing in the United States under color of law" (PRUCOL).	1980	Congress restricts SSI benefits for permanent resident aliens during their first three years in the country by requiring that their sponsor's income be taken into consideration in determining eligibility (a "deeming" provision).
1974	When regulations are written to implement new law, undocumented aliens are denied AFDC and Medicaid benefits as well as SSI.	1981	A deeming provision is added to the AFDC statute.
	New York State Social Service Law is amended to deny state-funded cash and medical assistance to aliens "unlawfully residing" in the country.		Deeming provisions are incorporated into state-funded cash assistance programs, but not into Medicaid, through changes in state law and regulations.
1976	State regulation bars undocumented aliens from "soft" service programs like daycare.	1982	Federal Food Stamp Act is amended to incorporate a deeming provision.
1978	Undocumented aliens are barred from Federal Food Stamp Program through amendment to Food Stamp Act.	1984	Through an amendment to the AFDC statute, the income of sponsoring organizations, and not just sponsoring individuals, is now deemed as a resource available to AFDC applicants.
1982	The 1974 regulations barring undocumented aliens from AFDC are now incorporated into AFDC statute. Medicaid section is unchanged, and alien eligibility continues to be interpreted under regulations.	1986	Most aliens who achieve legal status under amnesty provisions of Simpson-Rodino Act are denied some federal benefits, such as AFDC, Food Stamps and Medicaid, for five years from date of legalization. The elderly, blind and disabled are exempted from these restrictions, and federal Medicaid is available to pregnant women, children under 18, and emergency cases.
1986	Medicaid statute is amended to grant benefits to permanent resident aliens, PRUCOL aliens (not defined) and, in emergency cases only, undocumented aliens.		

Source: New York City Department of City Planning.

resident alien. An alien who qualifies for legalization under the amnesty program spends 18 months as a temporary resident alien before he or she is eligible to apply for legal permanent resident status. Temporary resident aliens are ineligible for certain federal benefits such as AFDC and food stamps and Medicaid, and they continue to be ineligible for their first five years in legal status. In the case of Medicaid, exceptions are made for pregnant women, children under 18, and emergency cases. The elderly, blind and disabled are exempted from all these amnesty program restrictions; they are eligible immediately after legalization for SSI, Medicaid and food stamps.

NOTES

1. Shirley Jenkins, Mignon Sauber, and Eva Friedlander, *Ethnic Associations and Services to New Immigrants in New York City*, (New York: Community Council of Greater New York, 1985). See also Hailu Kebede, *Immigrant Services in New York City: An Agency Directory*. New York: Department of City Planning, Office of Immigrant Affairs, 1986.

9 Refugee Resettlement

New York City continues to fill its historic role as a haven for the victims of war and persecution. Since the mid–1970s, it has welcomed more than 90,000 refugees and entrants, most of whom were forced to leave their homelands as a result of international events that were front-page news: the Vietnam War and unrest in other nations of Southeast Asia; civil war in Ethiopia; the Soviet invasion of Afghanistan; the Mariel boatlift from Cuba. New York City's refugee population is the second largest in the country, exceeded only by that of Los Angeles.

Until 1980 New York City and other localities struggled to resettle their newly arriving refugees under the burden of an erratic, under-funded federal refugee policy. The Refugee Act of 1980 brought greater order to the refugee resettlement system. Refugees now arrive in the United States through an organized resettlement program that extends from the countries where they first took refuge, to the national resettlement agencies that arrange for their admission to the United States, to the local agencies that assist them in finding and furnishing their new homes, sending their children to school, and acquiring the skills and jobs that will enable them to become self-supporting as quickly as possible.

NATIONAL REFUGEE POLICY

Since the end of World War II, more than 2 million refugees have been resettled in the United States with the approval of the federal government and the assistance of the nation's voluntary resettlement agencies, commonly known as "volags." Despite minimal and erratic federal funding, the volags resettled 400,000 displaced persons in the period immediately after World War II, and 100,000 Hungarian refugees after the failure of the 1956 revolution.

The massive flow of refugees from Cuba after 1959, when Castro assumed power, prompted Congress to define its financial responsibility for refugee resettlement. (About 200,000 Cubans fled to the United States between 1959 and 1961.) Under the terms of the Cuban Adjustment Act of 1966, the volags received a per capita grant for each Cuban refugee they resettled in the United States. State and local governments were reimbursed for the costs of public assistance and other services to Cuban refugees.

Nevertheless, U.S. refugee policy remained a policy of crisis. The Hart-Celler Act of 1965 set an annual refugee ceiling of 10,500, but the Attorney General used his parole authority to admit far larger numbers as crises arose overseas.

The massive refugee resettlement problems in the years after the Vietnam War moved Congress in 1980 to articulate a refugee admissions policy and to establish mechanisms for carrying it out. The Refugee Act of 1980 did the following:

- Gave Congress and the president responsibility for setting the refugee ceiling at the beginning of each year.
- Established the Office of Refugee Resettlement (ORR) in HHS to coordinate and administer refugee programs.
- Authorized a benefits package for new refugees and reimbursement to localities for public assistance, health, education, and other social service expenditures incurred during refugees' first three years in the United States.
- Established a contractual relationship among the federal government, volags, and service providers for resettlement activities at the local level, and gave the states leadership roles in those relationships.
- Redefined "refugee" to conform with the United Nations definition: any person who has left his or her country and is unable or unwilling to return because of persecution or a well-founded fear of persecution based on race, religion, nationality, membership in a particular social group, or political opinion.

The new definition extended eligibility, at least in theory, to refugees from all political systems, not just from Communism. In practice, however, most persons viewed as refugees by the U.S. government are fleeing from Communist or Communist-invaded nations. As always, admissions decisions are based on a combination of humanitarian considerations and foreign policy interests.

The Refugee Act underwent a test in its first year: waves of Cubans and Haitians appeared without authorization on the shores of Florida, seeking refugee status. Because they had not applied from a country of first asylum, they did not fit the specifications of the Refugee Act, so President Carter created for them a special designation, "Cuban/Haitian entrant." Congress subsequently granted them resettlement benefits that were virtually identical to those of refugees and incorporated them within the same service delivery system. Their unique history is touched on in this chapter and discussed at greater length in Chapter 10.

On October 18, 1986, Congress reauthorized the domestic refugee resettlement program for an additional two years and appropriated $362 million for fiscal year 1987.

NEW YORK CITY'S REFUGEES

In the last fifteen years, New York City has resettled about 37,000 Soviet Jews, 18,000 Indochinese, 20,000 Cuban and Haitian entrants, and 15,000 refugees of other origins. These figures do not include secondary migrants, refugees and entrants who were formally resettled in other parts of the country but subsequently moved to New York. Some observers believe that as many as 16,000 secondary migrants ought to be added to New York's refugee total; but refugees also leave New York, and there may be an even exchange of refugees entering and leaving the city by secondary migration.

About three-quarters of the refugees who arrived in the United States between 1975 and 1985 were Indochinese. New York City received only a small percentage of them—2.7 percent between October 1, 1980 and December 15, 1986, the period when accurate resettlement data became available for New York City. Los Angeles received more than twice as many Indochinese refugees as New York.

Statistics on New York City's refugee inflow for this period have been compiled by the Refugee Data Center in New York, the data repository of the American Council for Voluntary International Action (known as Interaction), which administers refugee resettlement in the United States (see Table 9.1). Their data show that about 29,000 refugees were resettled in New York City in this period 5.6 percent of the U.S. total. (These figures do not include Cuban and Haitian entrants, whose period of eligibility for entrant designation was coming to an end as this data period began.)

New York City was the nation's largest receiver of European refugees in this period, with 18.2 percent of the U.S. total. The city also received 10.5 percent of the country's refugees from the Near East, 4.1 percent of African refugees, and 1.5 percent of those from Latin America.

The individual nations most heavily represented among New York City's refugees for this period were Vietnam, with 20.5 percent of the city's total; the Soviet Union, with 19.2 percent; Cambodia (Kampuchea), with 15 percent; Poland, with 13.3 percent; Romania, with 12.1 percent;

Table 9.1

Refugee Resettlement in New York City,
October 1, 1980 - December 15, 1986

Country of Origin	Number	Percent of NYC Total
Total	29,121	100.0
Europe	14,163	48.6
Albania	133	0.5
Austria	4	*
Bulgaria	115	0.4
Czechoslovakia	497	1.7
France	1	*
Greece	1	*
Germany (West)	10	*
Hungary	372	1.3
Italy	2	*
Poland	3,881	13.3
Portugal	1	**
Romania	3,513	12.1
Turkey	18	0.1
Soviet Union	5,590	19.2
Yugoslavia	22	0.1
Unidentified	3	*
Africa	575	2.0
Ethiopia	536	1.8
Mozambique	5	*
South Africa	4	*
Somalia	1	*
Uganda	1	*
Zaire	25	0.1
Unidentified	3	*
Indochina	10,853	37.3
Cambodia (Kampuchea)	4,375	15.0
China	176	0.6
Laos	305	1.0
Vietnam	5,969	20.5
Unidentified	28	0.1
Near East	3,472	11.8
Afghanistan	2,724	9.4
Iran	633	2.2
Iraq	53	0.2
Israel	2	*
Syria	60	0.2
Latin America	58	0.2
Cuba	43	0.1
El Salvador	15	0.1

* Less than 0.1 percent.

Source: Refugee Data Center. Prepared by: Department of City Planning.

and Afghanistan, with 9.4 percent. Together, these nations accounted for 89.5 percent of the city's total for the period.

Two-thirds of New York's Soviet Jewish émigrés were resettled between 1979 and 1982, when the Soviet Union temporarily opened its doors to large-scale Jewish emigration. The agency primarily responsible for resettling Soviet Jews in New York is the New York Association for New Americans (NYANA), an operating arm of the Hebrew Immigrant Aid Society (HIAS). Soviet Jews have been resettled largely in southern Brooklyn (Brighton Beach, Coney Island, and Borough Park), Forest Hills in Queens, and Washington Heights in Manhattan.

More than half the city's Southeast Asian refugees are from Vietnam. Some left after the Communist takeover in 1975, but the majority left in 1978 and 1979, in a mass exodus by sea, driven by the Communist government's expropriation of all private businesses and a new monetary system that together destroyed the middle class. Most of the middle class were ethnic Chinese, as they are in much of Southeast Asia. As a visible and resented bourgeoisie, they made a ready target for government persecution. About 40 percent of New York City's Southeast Asian refugees are ethnic Chinese.

The Vietnamese were followed to New York by some 4,000 Cambodians, who were among the 500,000 people who left Cambodia in 1979, when Vietnam invaded. These Cambodians, already victims of war and the brutalities of the Pol Pot regime, were held in camps in Thailand for two years before the United States agreed to accept 20,000 of them. About 500 families, most of them from rural backgrounds, were resettled in the Bronx and Brooklyn in the spring of 1982.

Eight voluntary agencies participate in the resettlement of New York City's Southeast Asian refugees. NYANA, the International Rescue Committee (IRC), and Catholic Charities of the Archdiocese of New York together resettled two-thirds of the total. Southeast Asians have been resettled throughout the city, particularly in the Fordham area of the Bronx, Astoria in Queens, and Flatbush in Brooklyn.

The 1980 influx of Cuban entrants occurred when Castro briefly and capriciously opened the port of Mariel, permitting 125,000 Cubans to make their way to the United States. Previously Castro had forbidden emigration, even for relatives of Cuban-Americans. Most Cubans have been resettled in New York City by Catholic Charities of New York and Brooklyn, IRC, Church World Service, and the Lutheran Immigration and Refugee Service. Most Cuban entrants were resettled in Washington Heights, the South Bronx, and Brooklyn.

Haitians have been leaving their country continuously since the early 1970s because of economic hardship and political repression. Haiti is the poorest nation in the Western Hemisphere; in 1980 its annual per capita income was $270. The Haitian emigration rate increased at the same time

Castro opened the port of Mariel, in part because of increased political repression and in part because Haitians believed that President Carter would be as welcoming to them as he seemed initially to be to the Cubans. Haitian entrants have been resettled in New York largely by the U.S. Catholic Conference, the Lutheran Immigration and Refugee Service, and Church World Service. They live primarily in the Flatbush, East Flatbush, and Crown Heights neighborhoods of Brooklyn.

Since 1982, the influx of refugees from the Soviet Union, Indochina, and the Caribbean has leveled off or decreased. Now New York is home to increasing numbers of refugees from other parts of the world, particularly Poland, Romania, Afghanistan and Ethiopia. Their numbers at the moment are only in the thousands, not the tens of thousands, but the numbers are growing. Again, political stresses are largely responsible. The Polish government crackdown on the Solidarity labor party in 1981 led to the flight of many Polish dissidents; the Soviet invasion of Afghanistan in 1979 propelled many Afghans to the United States; Ethiopians began to flee their country during the bitter civil war that followed Emperor Haile Selassie's overthrow in 1974 by a leftist military government; and Romanians have been coming to the United States in steady numbers since the end of World War II and the Communist takeover in their country.

NEW YORK IS "REFUGEE-FRIENDLY" (MOSTLY)

It might surprise some New Yorkers to know that social service agencies consider New York a good place to resettle refugees despite the difficulties and dangers of life there. The city's sheer size and ethnic diversity make it hospitable to newcomers. In New York refugees are just another thread in the complex social fabric, and it is likely that they will find fellow countrymen nearby.

Despite their deterioration in the wake of the city's fiscal crisis of the 1970s, New York's public services are a boon to refugees. The subway and bus systems provide them with a convenient means of travel. The public schools provide English-language instruction for children and adults. Interpreter services can be found at some health installations, and there are many hospitals and clinics to which refugees have access. Although the city's industrial base shrank in the 1970s, refugees, like other immigrants, are generally able to find jobs.

Finally, because of New York's long history of receiving immigrants, the city has developed an extensive network of public, private, and voluntary agencies that provide services to refugees and entrants, often in the language of their homeland.

Even though considerable help is available to refugees and entrants, many still find the city a baffling or frightening place. Work may be a succession of dead-end jobs (assuming that work is found); home isn't necessarily very affordable, attractive, or safe; police locks can't always protect you from crime. Many of these problems are endemic to life in a big city, but they are particularly troublesome to people who do not speak English, who have no familiarity with the customs of the country, who may not be from urban backgrounds, who may lack social or ethnic connections, and whose psychological and physical health is weakened by the stress of forced migration. New York is a mixed blessing.

REFUGEES' USE OF SERVICES

Refugees and entrants make more use of social services, both public and private, than any other immigrants. Their disproportionate use is due to two factors: the government's generosity in granting them eligibility for a variety of financial and social services that are available to no other immigrant group, and their unusually high need for service, particularly in the first months or years after arrival. Most refugees have fled war or persecution, risked severe dangers in flight, spent months or years in refugee camps awaiting permanent resettlement, and lost family members and most or all of their possessions. Viewed from the perspective of what is available to other immigrants, the services available to refugees are generous. Viewed from the perspective of their needs, the resources available to rebuild their shattered lives and to orient them to a totally alien culture are woefully inadequate.

New York City need bear very little of the cost of resettling its refugees and entrants for their first three years in the United States. During this time the federal government supports its refugee policy with 100 percent reimbursement to localities for cash and medical assistance. In addition, the Department of State makes per capita grants to New York's 11 volags for 90 days of resettlement services. The volags receive $560 for each refugee they resettle. There is an alternative matching grant program under which the Office of Refugee Resettlement (ORR) offers per capita grants of $1,000 if the grants are matched by the volags in cash or in kind. However, few volags, other than those that resettle Soviet Jews, can raise the matching funds.

Most of the grant money goes for immediate needs such as food, clothing, rent, and transportation. The volags also provide orientation to living and working in the United States, referral to health facilities, assistance with school enrollments and public benefit applications, and job placement services. The larger volags, using privately raised funds, often offer ESL training, counseling, and vocational preparation. In 1982 Interaction estimated the average per capita resettlement cost to be $709.

In addition to the resettlement funds available from the Department of State, ORR makes grants to the states to fund a variety of ancillary

Figure 9.1
Elements of the Refugee Service Network, 1986

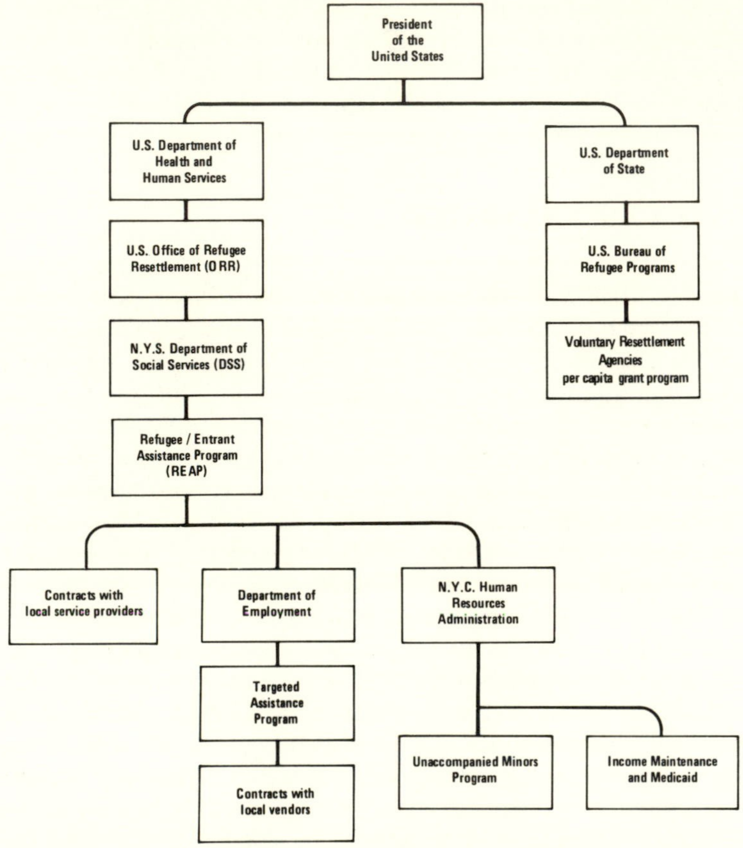

social services for refugees, including ESL, counseling, and various forms of vocational assistance. The New York State DSS contracts with some volags and with other private, nonprofit agencies to provide these services. The state's annual allocation is based on its refugee resettlement figures for the previous three years. New York State received $3.6 million in fiscal 1983, $5.4 million in fiscal 1984, and $6.2 million in fiscal 1985. Now, the allocation to states is based on the actual numbers of refugees living in the state at the start of each fiscal year.

In New York part of the ORR money is distributed through the DSS and its Refugee/Entrant Assistance Program (REAP). Another part, intended particularly for employment activities, has been channeled through the city's Department of Employment as its Targeted Assistance Program. The Refugee Reauthorization Act of 1986 eliminated Targeted

Assistance funding for 1987, but the program continued to run on accruals.

Ethnic associations founded by immigrants act as grass roots advocates and ultimate gap fillers for their ethnic clientele. The federal government has encouraged the ethnic associations to become formal refugee service providers by providing funds for their activities. In this formal role the ethnic groups are called "mutual assistance associations." In 1985 the state DSS distributed a total of $181,000 in ORR funds to six New York City mutual assistance associations serving the Afghan, Cambodian, Ethiopian, Soviet Jewish, Polish, and Vietnamese refugee communities.

The city's HRA administers the cash and medical assistance programs for refugees and entrants. It also runs a foster care program for refugee children with no adult relatives in the United States.

PUBLIC ASSISTANCE

Achieving economic self-sufficiency for their refugee and entrant clientele is the primary goal of all refugee service agencies, but there are deeply felt—and poorly researched—differences of opinion on how best to achieve this goal. Program planning is hampered by a dearth of information on patterns of refugee welfare use, and on the success of various strategies now in use for keeping refugees on or moving them off welfare. Furthermore, the bifurcation in the funding stream that supports refugee services results in some ambiguity in service goals and procedures; ORR grantees and Department of State grantees need not necessarily coordinate or agree on goals and procedures for achieving the successful resettlement of their clients.

Officials of the New York State DSS estimate that 32.4 percent of refugees resettled in the state between October 1982 and October 1985 were on public assistance in October 1985. Their estimate for New York City was 37.0 percent. DSS counted refugees who had been in the United States for three years or less because that is the period during which the federal government is obligated to provide New York State and New York City with 100 percent reimbursement for refugee public assistance costs.

The city's refugee public assistance rate was much higher than its rate for the general population, which was 11.7 percent, according to 1980 census data. (That is the individual rate; the 13.3 percent figure that appears elsewhere in this book is the household rate.) The New York refugee rate was, however, much lower than the national refugee rate, estimated by the federal ORR at 55.5 percent for the period October 1982 through October 1985. California's rate for that period was 90.4 percent, according to ORR records.

To some extent the New York State and New York City estimates were the products of interpolation and educated guessing because the city's HRA had not developed reliable procedures for identifying refugee public assistance cases. DSS based its estimates on refugees in the rest of the state, where recordkeeping was better. It used some city information on Indochinese refugees, whose public assistance applications were processed separately from the rest of the city case load, and for whom there were more reliable data than for other refugee groups.

The HRA data problems were of concern to the state because of the consequent loss of federal reimbursement. If the city could not count its refugees on welfare, neither the state nor the city could claim federal reimbursement. It seems possible that the loss to state and city was in the range of $2 to $5 million in each of several years. Since 1984, however, HRA has made progress in improving its data collection system, and the annual loss to state and city combined has been reduced to an estimated maximum of $1 million.

Not only is it important for the city and state to count recent refugees on welfare, it is also important for them to count refugees who remain on welfare beyond the three-year federal reimbursement period. After three years the state and city must pick up their standard share of welfare costs. Without knowing the numbers or characteristics of long-term welfare cases, they cannot evaluate the long-term costs of refugee resettlement, nor can they design effective procedures to reduce these costs.

Refugee service agencies, both public and private, are making efforts to reduce public assistance use among their clientele, even though the use rates are not accurately known. Enabling refugees to apply for Medicaid benefits without making contact with the welfare system is one method being used. Most refugees arrive in the United States with health problems that require immediate attention, according to the staff of the ORR-funded Refugee Health Project. In order to afford medical care, many refugees must turn to publicly subsidized programs like Medicaid. The fact that Medicaid enrollment is often tied to receipt of cash assistance has encouraged a higher cash assistance rate than absolutely necessary.

In an effort to sever the automatic connection between Medicaid and cash assistance, the New York City Medicaid office since 1980 has deputized caseworkers from three volags—NYANA, IRC, and Catholic Charities—to complete Medicaid applications at the volag offices rather than at income maintenance centers. In addition, the Yorkville income maintenance center runs a Medicaid-only unit for Indochinese refugees.

In a similar effort to provide health care without cash assistance, the volags have established relationships with a number of municipal and voluntary hospitals at which refugees can receive low-cost medical care even without Medicaid. The cooperating hospitals include Beth Israel in Manhattan; Montefiore and Einstein in the Bronx; Kings County,

Caledonian, Maimonides, and Coney Island in Brooklyn; and Elmhurst General in Queens. Some of these hospitals have interpreters on staff.

The federal government has contemplated another way to avoid or minimize refugees' entry into the welfare system. The Lungren Amendment at one time before Congress would forbid public assistance for the 90-day volag grant period, and the volags would receive some additional funding to make up for the missing public assistance benefits. Congress has not acted on this proposal.

Although they agree on the undesirability of welfare dependency, refugee service workers are in passionate disagreement on some aspects of the issue. How do you best prepare a refugee or entrant for self-sufficiency? Do you immerse him in English-language training five days a week—even though he'll have to enroll on public assistance during the period before he is employed—on the theory that the job he finally gets will be far better, and far more easily obtained, if he can speak English? Or do you help her find a job, any job, as quickly as possible, on the theory that she will learn English on the job, avoid contact with the welfare system, and avoid developing any expectation of public support? How important are job training and skills upgrading, services that are available to very few refugees and entrants?

Differences of opinion on these matters can be creative and useful when translated into programs that can be tested and evaluated. The problem in New York is that there is no systematic effort under way to measure the efficacy of these varying approaches.

OTHER PROBLEMS IN SERVICE DELIVERY

The volags are limited in the duration and scope of service they can provide to their refugee clients. The $560 per capita resettlement grant is not enough to pay for food, clothing, shelter, and transportation, plus English-language instruction, counseling, and job referral. It is certainly not enough to pay for such services beyond the 90-day grant period. There is neither money nor federal requirement to assist or monitor the resettlement process past the initial 90 days.

Yet it is often after that first three months, when the shock of newness has worn off and when social services have been reduced or eliminated, that serious problems arise. At that point, refugees may begin to feel the delayed effects of the violent and traumatic events that brought them to New York. Then the grinding realities and loneliness of life in New York begin to take their toll. Physical or emotional illness may develop in response to stress, and families may be strained to the breaking point.

The larger volags, with larger independent budgets, are able to keep in touch with their former refugee clients by mail, phone, or an occasional appointment for a year or more total. The smaller volags generally end their contacts at the end of 90 days. The longest client contacts are kept by the ethnic associations; consequently, these organizations are often a good source of information about the employment status of their clients, their health, their use of public assistance, and so on. But the ethnic associations serve only a small proportion of the city's refugee population.

Each volag keeps records on its services to clients, but these data are not compiled citywide to give a profile of refugee life in New York. In general there has been little study of refugees' progress in integrating into society, their physical and mental health, their employment history and income, or their use of public assistance and other tax-supported programs. Church World Service has produced a report on its refugee program that addresses many of these issues.[1]

The Refugee Data Center in New York maintains individual and general information on all refugees resettled throughout the United States. Its current practice is to aggregate data by state, not by city, though it has the capacity to do both. The New York City data in this chapter were produced on special request.

Among the many agencies that could profit from more information about refugee resettlement in New York City are community boards and local social service agencies. They are not official members of the refugee resettlement network, but refugees are among their most vulnerable constituents. A widely publicized example of the problems that can arise when communication is inadequate occurred in April 1983 when several Cambodian refugee families, totaling 44 people, were moved out of North Flatbush after being beaten and robbed on several occasions. In their distress over these incidents, local Community Board 14 and the Flatbush Development Corporation established a task force to study the refugee resettlement process. Their report concluded that no system existed in New York to monitor refugee resettlement, and they recommended the creation of one.[2] The task force also recommended the creation of an office with central responsibility for immigrant issues, and the establishment of community-based walk-in resettlement centers in those neighborhoods receiving large numbers of new immigrants and refugees. The creation of the city's Office of Immigrant Affairs in essence implemented one of their recommendations. In addition, the Flatbush Development Corporation obtained funding from REAP to provide refugee services.

Inadequate per capita funding is not the only financial burden under which the volags operate. Their task is made harder by yearly changes in the number of refugees they are asked to serve, consequent shifts in staffing levels, and the changing linguistic and cultural backgrounds of their clientele. Their budgets and staff rosters are often in flux. Federal refugee admissions tell the story: in fiscal 1980 the United States admitted

81,000 refugees; in fiscal 1981 the figure was 155,000; in fiscal 1982 it was 61,500; in fiscal 1984 it was 70,000; and in fiscal 1985 it was 67,800.

THE THANHS: A PORTRAIT IN REFUGEE RESETTLEMENT

Whatever the problems of the refugee resettlement network, it still helps thousands of people to build new lives in the United States. How its agencies work is illustrated by the story of the Thanh family. The Thanhs are a composite portrait of New York's Indochinese refugee families. Their story depicts the service system functioning at its best; this is the work of which the network is capable.

The Thanh family's odyssey from Ho Chi Minh City (formerly Saigon) ended, 15 months after it began, in an apartment on University Avenue in the Bronx. It started when the Thanhs, their six children, and Mrs. Thanh's widowed sister fled their homeland in a small fishing boat. The journey was harsh. Mr. Thanh, who had been a merchant in Saigon, liquidated his assets and spent his savings on provisions for the long boat voyage to Malaysia. The family's few remaining possessions were taken in a pirate raid. Mrs. Thanh's sister died at sea.

In many respects the Thanhs were luckier than thousands of their countrymen who fled Vietnam after the collapse of the Saigon government in 1975. The Thanhs were interned in a Malaysian refugee camp for only slightly more than a year; many Indochinese refugees spent years in such camps. And after the Thanhs arrived in New York, under the sponsorship of the IRC, the refugee assistance network worked smoothly to help them adjust to their new home.

The Thanhs and their six children, ages 2 to 19, were greeted at John F. Kennedy Airport by Mr. Ngo, an older brother of Mrs. Thanh who had fled Vietnam four years earlier. He took the Thanhs to his apartment in the Bronx for a joyful family reunion. The newcomers spent their first night in the United States sleeping on the Ngos' living room floor.

In the morning Mr. Ngo took the Thanhs to IRC's office on Park Avenue South in Manhattan, where they were introduced to their caseworker, Mrs. Nguyen, herself a refugee from Vietnam. Mrs. Nguyen assessed the family's immediate needs and helped the Thanhs fill out applications for Social Security cards, Medicaid, and food stamps. She made appointments for health checkups at Montefiore Medical Center and gave the Thanhs a check for $80 to cover their first week's food, clothing, and transportation expenses.

During the next three months, Mrs. Nguyen monitored the Thanhs' progress through interviews at her office, home visits, and telephone calls. She counseled members of the family individually, and introduced them to agencies that could provide services beyond the scope of IRC.

Within two days of their arrival in New York, the Thanhs were settled in a two-bedroom apartment next door to the Ngos. IRC paid their first month's rent, their security deposit, and their utility costs, a total of $975. IRC also furnished the apartment with five beds, a dinette set, linens, blankets, cookware, dishes, and other household goods.

By their second week in the city, the four school-aged Thanh children were attending three local public schools. The youngest of the four, a five-year-old kindergartener, was soon picking up English from her classmates. The three older children were assigned to classes in ESL, in addition to their regular classes.

Mr. Thanh went to the Refugee Employment Project for help in finding his first job in New York. The project, a cooperative venture undertaken by nine voluntary agencies in 1980, was set up to find employment for newly arrived Asian boat people and was subsequently funded by REAP. It has found jobs for more than 5,000 refugees of various origins.

Mr. Thanh had been a moderately prosperous merchant in Vietnam, but he arrived in New York penniless, unable to speak English, and without salable job skills. He was determined to find a job as quickly as possible, no matter what job or at what salary. His philosophy accorded with that of the Refugee Employment Project, which encourages the quickest possible entry into the job market, even if the first job is at the entry level. By his third week in New York, Mr. Thanh had begun work as a warehouseman in Long Island City at $3.50 an hour.

Mr. Thanh wanted his oldest son, who had been a promising student in Vietnam, to continue his education. It was obvious, though, that Mr. Thanh's wages—$115 a week after taxes—could not support his large family. Bowing to this reality, Mr. Thanh permitted his son to accept an evening job as a busboy in a Manhattan hotel restaurant. He was pleased when his son began to study English with refugees from eight other countries in an intensive six-week cycle of daytime classes at the Riverside Adult Learning Center in Manhattan, another REAP grant agency.

Within three months of their arrival in New York, most members of the Thanh family were busy at work or school, and were learning the language and customs of their new country. The exception was Mrs. Thanh. She remained at home to care for her two-year-old daughter and to manage the household. Although her children were learning English rapidly, she found it difficult even to ask for directions or to communicate with local merchants. Frightened by stories of violence against refugees, she was reluctant to leave the house unless accompanied by family members or neighbors. She felt helpless to deal with such everyday problems as peeling paint or too little heat. A woman who had been an energetic and resourceful provider in Saigon, working next to her husband in the family business, was becoming a depressed and frightened recluse in New York.

At Mrs. Nguyen's suggestion, Mrs. Thanh received some counseling from social workers at the Vietnamese American Cultural Organization, a mutual assistance association funded by DSS and staffed by former refugees. With their encouragement Mrs. Thanh worked out a child-care sharing arrangement with her sister-in-law that enabled both of them to attend ESL classes at the McBurney YMCA's ELESAIR Program in Manhattan. Both benefited from the "survival skills" taught by ELESAIR (another REAP grantee). Their instructors used everyday situations, like the purchase of furniture on credit, to teach English vocabulary and grammar. Mrs. Thanh's self-confidence grew with her command of English, and she began to look forward to her daily trips to the YMCA in Manhattan.

At the end of their first year in New York, the Thanhs appeared to be winning their struggle for financial self-sufficiency. Mr. Thanh was now working as a factory cleaner for Allied Maintenance Corporation at a wage of $9 an hour, plus benefits that included family health insurance. His goal for the future was to open a Southeast Asian produce market in partnership with his brother-in-law.

The oldest son, now 20, had recently entered Adelphi University's Training Program in Human Services Counseling, which prepares refugees for jobs as bilingual counselors in schools, hospitals, nursing homes, and other social service agencies. As his field assignment he accompanied caseworkers from the HRA Unaccompanied Refugee Minors Program on home visits to families providing foster care to Vietnamese refugee children without parents.

Mrs. Thanh joined her Vietnamese and Cambodian neighbors in a tenants association that was working for improved conditions in their apartment houses. They were assisted by community workers from the Urban Skills/Community Action Program, a joint project administered by several New York volags with REAP funding. The community workers taught Mrs. Thanh and her neighbors how to get tenant complaints resolved, and how to establish useful links with community boards, churches, and local police precincts. Life was not trouble-free, but the Thanhs had come a long way from Vietnam.

NOTES

1. *Making It on Their Own: From Refugee Sponsorship to Self-Sufficiency* (New York: Church World Service, 1983).

2. *Task Force Report: Refugee Resettlement and Neighborhood Impact* (New York: Brooklyn Community Board 14 and the Flatbush Development Corporation, 1983).

10 Cuban/Haitian Entrants: A History

War, famine, international politics, humanitarian impulses, and national guilt—these are the stuff of which U.S. refugee policy is made. Perhaps because it has been established so often in the eye of a storm, U.S. policy on "displaced persons," "refugees," or "asylees" has tended to lurch from crisis to crisis, leaving behind a trail of inconsistent decisions.

A case in point is President Carter's 1980 decision to create a Cuban/Haitian "entrant" category for the Cuban and Haitian boat people who flooded into the Florida Keys that year. Carter's action came when the ink was barely dry on the Refugee Act of 1980—the act that was supposed to bring order to U.S. refugee policy.

Carter's decision promoted confusion in several ways: it linked Cubans and Haitians, groups for whom U.S. admissions policy had been very different; it invented a new admissions category, "entrant," which bypassed the new Refugee Act and its definitions; and it left in limbo the future status of the new entrants. Congress contributed to the confusion by allocating benefits only for those Cubans and Haitians who arrived during part of the crisis. These executive and legislative actions set off a chain of legal and social problems that have affected Cuban/Haitian entrants wherever they have settled, as well as the agencies that serve them.

To link Cubans and Haitians in one admissions policy was to make an apparent turnabout in U.S. foreign policy. U.S. relations with Haiti and with Cuba have been markedly different, and the difference has been reflected in the way the United States has dealt with Cuban and Haitian requests for asylum or refugee status. For Cubans in flight from Castro's Communist regime, there were programs of welcome; for Haitians who were in flight from the Duvalier regime, with which the United States had friendly diplomatic relations, there was unrelenting rejection. U.S. policy makers contended that Haitians generally left their country in search of economic opportunity, not to flee political repression. Economic distress, under U.S. law, does not constitute grounds for refugee or asylee status.

What Cuban and Haitian entrants had in common, in the eyes of the U.S. government, was their unauthorized arrival on the shores of Florida in the spring of 1980. Haitian immigrants had been arriving this way for years, but their numbers increased dramatically in 1980 and 1981 when they saw that the Cuban boat people were being admitted in large numbers. Most estimates suggest that about 40,000 Haitians entered southern Florida illegally by boat between 1972 and 1982. Cubans, on the other hand, had not generally entered illegally, nor in such large numbers as they did in 1980.

Early in 1980 Castro was faced with a political crisis. Hundreds of thousands of Cubans gathered at the Peruvian Embassy to seek political asylum in Peru. Peru granted asylum, but Castro would not permit the prospective asylees to leave until worldwide pressure forced him to reverse his position. To his embarrassment, there were soon more than 10,000 people at the embassy. To counter the bad publicity, he staged massive demonstrations of political support for his regime, and he announced that anyone who could find a boat to board could leave from the port of Mariel, a few miles west of Havana.

Most of the asylum seekers at the Peruvian Embassy found safe harbor in Peru and other Latin American nations. Thousands more descended on the tiny port of Mariel to head for the United States. When Castro announced the opening of the port, Cubans in the United States sprang into action, sending boats to Mariel to rescue friends and relatives who remained behind. In April thousands of Cubans began to arrive in Florida each day. By mid-June their numbers had reached 125,000.

The Carter administration received the news of the rescue operation at first with joy ("We welcome the Cubans with open arms and open hearts") and then with consternation as the number of "Marielitos" grew. The dismay grew further when Castro began to send Cuba's convicts and mentally ill to Florida as part of the boatlift.

The administration responded erratically. It issued threats to blockade or fine boat owners, but it continued to admit Cuban arrivals. Ultimately Castro ended the boatlift by closing the port of Mariel.

While thousands of Cubans were being admitted daily, Haitian and other black leaders demanded equal treatment for Haitian boat people. Their situations were so similar that Carter could not avoid acceding to the Haitian demands.

The new Refugee Act of 1980 had no clear category to fit the Cuban and Haitian boat people. They were not refugees because refugees were people who applied from abroad to enter the United States. They could not be processed as asylees because asylum applications had to be made individually, and it would have been an impossible administrative task to process so many applications. Furthermore, it soon became apparent that it would have been difficult to qualify many of the boat people under the "well-founded fear of persecution" standard required for refugee or asylee status.

Carter solved his problem by inventing a new admissions category that applied both to Cuban and to Haitian boat people and that bypassed the Refugee Act entirely. He called the new category "Cuban/Haitian entrant; status pending." Cubans and Haitians who entered the country during the boatlift crisis (by June 19, 1980; later extended to October 10, 1980) could qualify as entrants, along with any Haitians who had entered the country earlier and were known to the INS. A total of 125,000 Cubans and 14,000 Haitians qualified for entrant status. They were granted temporary admission, with their future status to be decided by Congress.

In choosing to circumvent the Refugee Act, rather than bend it to grant refugee status to the boat people, Carter was influenced by several provisions of the law. If he invoked the act, it would limit his personal authority to deal with the crisis because the act required that Congress be consulted on refugee admissions. Furthermore, the designation "refugee" would automatically trigger a three-year financial benefits package and eligibility for permanent resident status after one year. Carter did not want to make that kind of commitment to such a large group of people who had not been screened before entry.

Instead, Carter asked Congress to provide temporary funds for the entrants and to establish their future right to permanent status. On October 10, 1980, Congress passed the Fascell-Stone Amendment to the Refugee Education Assistance Act of 1980. This amendment awarded the entrants virtually the same 36-month benefits package available to refugees under the provisions of the Refugee Act. In so doing, Congress undid Carter's efforts to avoid granting refugee benefits to the new entrants.

On the question of entrants' future status, Congress did not reach a decision. Entrants remained "status pending," with no assurance of permission to remain in the country permanently, and without the right to petition for relatives to join them.

For four years the entrants remained in their ambiguous status. When the dates on their temporary admission papers expired, the authorities tacitly extended their special status. The Simpson-Mazzoli Immigration Reform Bill of 1984 included a measure that would have legalized all entrants and other Haitians who had entered the country between October 1980 and January 1982. Thus far, Cuban and Haitian entrants had been treated alike. But after the Simpson-Mazzoli Bill died, the INS announced that Cuban entrants would be handled under the terms of the Cuban Adjustment Act of 1966, which would make them eligible for permanent resident status and ultimately for citizenship. No such action was taken on behalf of the Haitians.

The INS decision on behalf of the Cuban entrants came about as the result of a lawsuit brought by Cuban entrants in southern Florida. The plaintiffs claimed eligibility for benefits under the 1966 Cuban Adjustment Act. The suit had been held in abeyance during the Simpson-Mazzoli debate because Simpson-Mazzoli would have solved the problem legislatively. When the bill failed, the INS acceded to the Cubans' demands without waiting for a court decision. Haitian entrants, however, remained in limbo.

The ill-fitting yoke that linked the Cuban and Haitian entrants did not outlast the boatlift emergency. After the fall of 1980, Haitian asylum applications were once again rejected. In May 1981 the Reagan administration began to incarcerate ("detain") all Haitian arrivals. In June 1982 the courts struck down this practice as discriminatory, but the detainees were released with their status still unresolved. In September 1981 the Coast Guard began to intercept boats suspected of carrying Haitian immigrants and send them back to Haiti, with the agreement of the Haitian government.

ENTRANTS IN NEW YORK

Not all entrants remained in Florida; many resettled elsewhere in the United States. After Miami, New York City became the second largest receiver of Haitians and the third largest receiver of Cubans, after Miami and northern New Jersey. There are no hard data on the numbers of entrants in New York City, but the figure is generally estimated at about 20,000, divided fairly evenly between Cubans and Haitians. Haitian leaders contest these figures; they believe the number of Haitian entrants in New York is far larger than 10,000. The Cuban figure is not contested. When Cuban entrants were permitted to register under the terms of the 1966 act, about 6,000 registered in New York. The 6,000 did not include those Cuban entrants who had already gained permanent resident status because they were close relatives of U.S. citizens.

Cuban and Haitian entrants are eligible for various resettlement services from REAP. More than a third of REAP agencies included entrants in their case loads as of 1982. In welcoming their Cuban and Haitian clients, they inherited the confusions created by unresolved federal policy. The entrants were eligible for the same resettlement and social service benefits as refugees, but there were difficulties in determining who was an eligible entrant. Their documentation differed from that of refugees, and many entrants had documents that were stamped with expiration dates that had passed. Federal authorities allowed it to be known, quietly, that expired documents were acceptable, but local agency staff often remained unaware of this unpublicized policy.

Agencies that served Haitian entrants endured particular frustrations. Entrants were eligible for various language and job training programs, but Haitians without entrant status were not. In their demographic characteristics and their service needs, the entrants and nonentrants were virtually indistinguishable; most of the nonentrants had arrived in the United States just before or just after the official entrant period. Agency staff found it painful to turn these nonentrants away. There were large numbers of them, too; the number of undocumented Haitians in New York has been estimated at 150,000.

Cuban entrants presented a different problem. There is no doubt that the Cuban entrant population included some mentally ill and/or criminally inclined young men who made trouble in Cuba and who continued to make trouble in the United States. Some of these entrants have tended to depend on public assistance and other social service supports. This problem-ridden portion of the entrant population has no ties to New York's established, largely middle-class, and highly law-abiding Cuban-born community of about 50,000 people. These middle-class Cubans view the troublesome entrants with resentment for the negative image they create.

Lack of clarity about their status has been a source of anxiety for all entrants, but especially for the Haitians. By 1985, many Cubans became secure in their eligibility for permanent resident status, if they met the general requirements for immigration through the use of the 1966 Cuban Adjustment Act. Haitians, however, saw their hopes go down in defeat in 1985 and 1986 as versions of the Simpson and Rodino bills stumbled toward what looked like inevitable failure. Both bills contained provisions that would have provided for adjustment of Cubans' and Haitians' status.

When President Reagan signed the Immigration Reform and Control Act on November 6, 1986, he brought a resolution to the problem of the Haitian entrants, who finally achieved the right to adjust to legal permanent resident status—and to do so as of Jan. 1, 1982, so that they are eligible to apply for citizenship as soon as they obtain their green cards. Cubans with entrant designation achieved the same rights, as did other Cubans and Haitians who arrived in the United States before Jan. 1, 1982, and established any kind of dealings or communication with the INS. *Not* eligible are Cubans and Haitians who arrived on valid temporary visas, such as students and tourists—unless they applied for political asylum before Jan. 1, 1982.

Applications for adjustment to permanent resident under this program will be taken through November 6, 1988. After that date, there will still be undocumented Cubans and Haitians in New York who were not able to legalize under any of the existing legalization programs, but by and large, the story of the Cuban-Haitian entrants will be over.

11 The Catholic Church and Its Services to Immigrants

The religious institutions of New York City are indispensable members of the immigration service network. The USCC, the Federation of Jewish Philanthropies, the Protestant-supported Church World Service, and the Lutheran Immigration and Refugee Service are among the largest sectarian agencies, and smaller religious organizations, including individual churches and synagogues, are also helping immigrants to adjust to their new home.

The work of all the denominations is essential, but the Roman Catholic Church stands out as the largest private provider of services to immigrants in the city, and in the country as well. The Church has a network of agencies that offer refugee resettlement, legal guidance, mental health counseling, English classes, job referrals, and emergency aid ranging from food and shelter to money for immigration court bail. Although the Church agencies were created to meet the needs of newly arrived parishioners, they serve all faiths.

It is not merely the size and breadth of the Church's services that distinguish it, but also its dual role as service provider and spiritual leader for the many immigrants who are Catholic. While the Church is serving its immigrants, it is being transformed by them. In this dynamic relationship the Church is a microcosm of the city.

The Church has a long history of serving and absorbing immigrants. In the 19th century it faced the task of accommodating streams of Irish, German, Italian, and Polish Catholics without splitting along ethnic lines. These immigrant groups had come to the United States from homogeneous churches, bringing with them their own languages, their own priests, their own liturgical traditions, and their own national saints.

The heterogeneity of the Church in New York was an unsettling mixture of the strange and the familiar.

Gradually the Church evolved two strategies for incorporating its diverse membership while maintaining its hierarchical unity. First, it established a far-reaching network of social services that carried immigrants from their European points of departure to Ellis Island, and thence to new homes and new lives within its sheltering arms.

Second, Church leaders accommodated the immigrants' desire to build their own national churches within the parish system already established here. In these national churches, immigrants could be ministered to by their own priests and nuns, in their own language, without compromising their allegiance to a united Church.

These strategies succeeded. The New York Church remained intact and stable through the mass migrations of the late 19th and early 20th centuries, and on into the postwar period of minimal migration. The lull in migration between 1921 and 1965 gave the Church a chance to consolidate its position ethnically, liturgically, financially, and politically. By 1965 the old immigrants and their descendants had for the most part become prosperous, assimilated, middle-class New Yorkers.

With the post–1965 wave of migrants from Latin America, Asia, and Europe, the Church has become once again a church of immigrants—but not exclusively so. Today's migrants are entering an established church, a church facing challenging internal pressures for change. The philosophical turmoil generated by Vatican II, women's pressure for a greater leadership role, the decline in religious vocations, and the financial difficulties in maintaining church schools are some of the issues with which today's Church must grapple. Yet the sheer number of immigrants demands the Church's attention. Hispanics, the largest group of new arrivals, are rapidly approaching 50 percent of the Catholic population of New York.[1]

The Church knows that new tools are needed to integrate these immigrants. Hispanics present a special challenge. The Church cannot rely on a native Hispanic priesthood to advocate and plan for them; under the colonial system through which Catholicism came to Latin America, the native priesthood remained small. In the interest of its Hispanic parishioners, therefore, the Church has had to train its priests and other personnel in the language and culture of the newcomers. The Church has been both agent and subject of change.

Furthermore, the homeland-to-new-land social service network of the early 20th century has metamorphosed from a cluster of small agencies designed for specific immigrant groups into a network of professional services aimed at the poor in general. The system has had to be retooled to face the renascent immigrant need.

More important, Hispanics have challenged the Church to accommodate them as full participants, not merely as clients.[2] This accommodation inevitably will bring some redistribution of resources and power within the Church. In its effort to make room for newcomers without displacing established constituencies, the Church stands as a poignant and universal example of an institution confronting change.

THE CATHOLIC CHURCH IN NEW YORK

Mention the Catholic Church to tourists or non-Catholics, and what generally comes to their minds is St. Patrick's Cathedral and the prestige of the Archdiocese of New York. But there are two dioceses in the city: the Archdiocese of New York, which takes in Manhattan, the Bronx, and Staten Island as well as seven upstate counties; and the Diocese of Brooklyn, made up of Brooklyn and Queens. The two dioceses differ in constituency and character. The archdiocese is wealthier, and Irish prelates have predominated in its strong central hierarchy. The Diocese of Brooklyn gives the impression of greater informality, and Italians have achieved notable representation in its hierarchy.

In colonial times, Catholics had to struggle for a place in Protestant-dominated New York. Until the American Revolution, Catholic clergy were barred from the colony. The new state constitution of 1777 removed that bar but prohibited foreign-born Catholics from becoming citizens and prohibited all Catholics from holding public office. These barriers were gradually removed in the early 1800s.

The Church grew rapidly in the 19th century. In 1815 there were only an estimated 16,000 Catholics in New York, one-eighth of the city's population. The Irish influx between 1830 and 1860 swelled New York's Catholic population to 400,000, a third of the population of the city. The Irish set to work building a church that could prevail despite hostility and discrimination, and whose growing political activism could advance the entry of Catholics into American society.

The pivotal figure in this remarkable Irish achievement was Rev. John Hughes, who arrived in New York in 1838 and was appointed archbishop in 1842. Hughes was the first in a line of Irish archbishops that is unbroken to this day. By the time of his death in 1864, he had transformed the loose network of parishes into a well-integrated organization in which priests assumed administrative and financial responsibilities as well as pastoral ones. Archbishop Hughes developed the parochial school system; founded the Emigrant Savings Bank to make loans to Catholics who were discriminated against by other banks; and encouraged an array of energetic social service organizations that were vital to the immigrants' well-being and to their continued loyalty to the Church.

The Church was the principal source of help for needy Catholics. Indeed, private charities of all faiths provided most 19th-century social services; the city limited itself to basic institutions, such as hospitals for the sick and almshouses for the poor. The Catholic Church opened orphanages and boardinghouses, found housing and jobs, and helped to locate relatives who had arrived earlier.

By the end of the century, the network was complete. Catholic agencies in Europe notified their counterparts in the United States of the names and arrival dates of new immigrants. Charity workers met the newcomers at the docks, offered assistance, and directed them to their ethnic neighborhoods. There, parish priests awaited their coming.

Diverse immigrant groups were incorporated into the structure of the Church by the establishment of national parishes. When a new group achieved significant numbers in a parish, a priest of that nationality was installed, or a second church was built. Before 1880 there were a few German, Spanish, and French national parishes, but the majority were Irish.

The large numbers of Italian immigrants who arrived after 1880 sought national parishes, and some German Catholic leaders went further, requesting that a diocese system be organized along ethnic lines. Fearful that ethnic fragmentation would threaten the unity and authority of the Church structure, Church leaders at first tried to assimilate the Italians into existing parishes, but subsequently agreed to their demands.[3]

This development may have delayed the Italians' entry into the archdiocesan hierarchy because they were concentrating their energies in their national parishes. Between 1884 and 1915 the Italians built 19 churches in Manhattan and the Bronx, a remarkable feat of financing and labor at a time when many were struggling to survive. Italians were slow to achieve influential positions in the archdiocesan leadership, however; the first Italian auxiliary bishop was ordained in the early 1950s.

RETOOLING SOCIAL SERVICES

The local parish is still the first stop for many Catholic immigrants, both because it offers help and because it is familiar: a priest celebrating Mass or a nun teaching classes provides a reminder of home. After 1965, when the number of Catholic immigrants in New York began to rise again, parish workers were the first to realize it. When they turned to the traditional Catholic social service agencies to get help for their new parishioners, they realized that adjustments had to be made.

At the turn of the century, the multitude of immigrant agencies had been brought under central control, and Catholic Charities was established as an umbrella agency in each diocese. Over the years the focus shifted from immigrants in particular to the needy in general. Catholic Charities, assisted by independent lay charities such as the St. Vincent de Paul Society, offered modern social services, including mental health

Figure 11.1
Network of Catholic Agencies Serving Immigrants, 1986

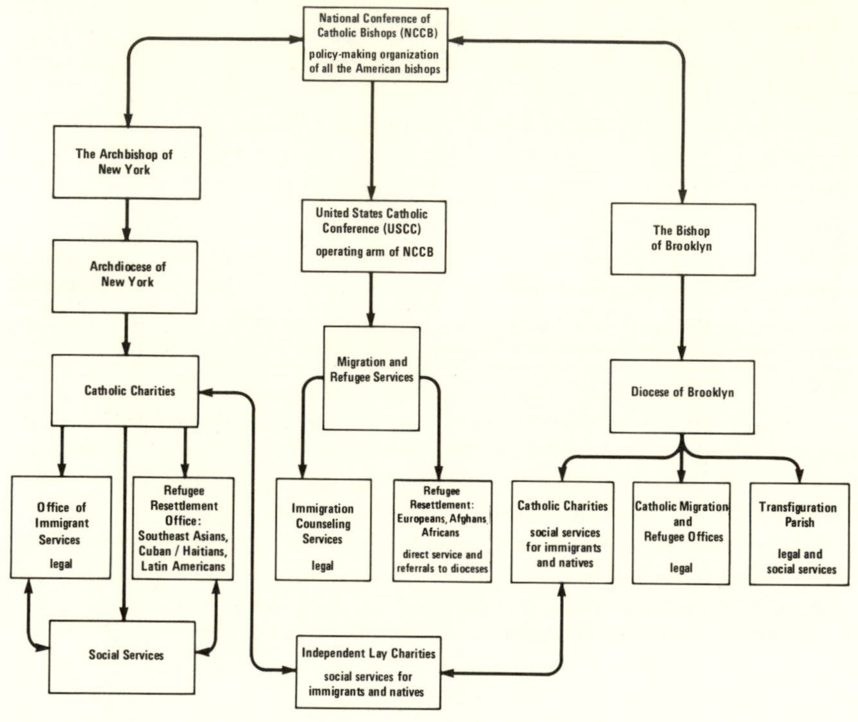

counseling, foster care, job training, assistance with government benefit applications, and emergency food and shelter.

The influx of refugees after World War II first revived the need for services specific to immigrants. The need grew with the larger immigrant influx that began in the mid–1960s. Although immigrants could use the general social services, they needed culturally attuned mental health counseling, interpreters, language classes, and private sources of assistance when they were ineligible for government programs. In particular, immigrants need advice on immigration law. The law was now so complex, and its year-to-year application so affected by U.S. foreign policy, that few immigrants, documented or undocumented, could negotiate it on their own.

The Church readapted its agencies to its new clients, and it now provides an extensive network of immigrant services (see Figure 11.1). Program staff members are more aware of the language and cultural requirements of immigrant clients, and new programs have been created to fill gaps in service. The greatest response has been in the area of legal

Photos by Harvey Wang

Establishing themselves in the United States has not been easy for Kaen Singkeo and his wife, who arrived in New York in 1981 from a mountain farming village in Laos. The two never attended school in Laos and never learned to read or write in their native tongue. Their young daughters' histories will be far different, however; the girls, age 7 and 11, are enrolled in Brooklyn public schools and already are speaking and writing in English. Joining the Singkeos in this portrait is a five-year-old neighbor, Pasith Vatthanavong, whose family comes from the same Laotian village.

It could be Hong Kong but it's Union Street in Flushing, where Chinese-, Japanese- and Korean-owned businesses cater to their large Asian clientele.

Gladys Sanchez and Jaichindernauth Jodharam work for the same garment manufacturer in lower Manhattan. Ms. Sanchez arrived from Cuba in 1980 with her teenage daughter, who has now completed college. Mr. Jodharam emigrated from Guyana in 1978; his parents had been emigres from India. He and his wife Chandai have four sons, all of them enrolled in Bronx public schools.

Medical professions run in the family of Sidney and Eldoris Elliot. Mr. Elliot was a public health inspector before the family's emigration from Jamaica in 1966. (He is now a loan and security clerk at a large bank.) Mrs. Elliot is a registered nurse. One son is a physician, married to a registered nurse. The Elliots' children also include an accountant and a college student. They live in Laurelton, Queens.

Chinese and hispanic women make up the majority of sewing machine operators in today's garment trade.

Homero Guerrero is about to open a car repair business with his son Homero Jr. The elder Mr. Guerrero emigrated from Ecuador with his wife Sara in 1966. He recently sold his taxi fleet to raise funds for the new business. The Guerreros live in Kew Gardens, Queens.

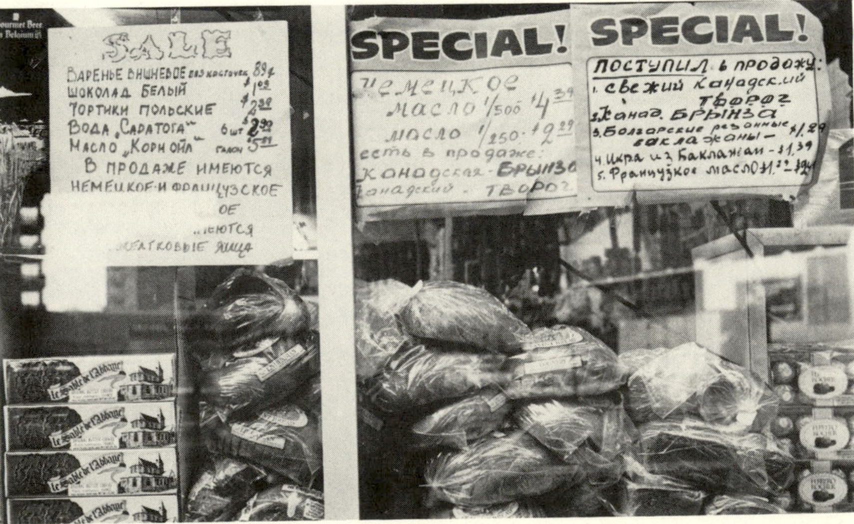

Sale signs in Russian on Brighton Beach Avenue attest to the large numbers of Soviet emigres who have settled in southern Brooklyn.

The family of Dimosthenis and Christina Pavlakos assemble in their Astoria home after church services each Sunday. Mr. and Mrs. Pavlakos arrived in the United States from Greece in 1966. Their grandchildren all attend a Greek church school; maintaining the Greek language, religion and culture is extremely important to this family.

Many of the vegetable stands in the Flatbush area of Brooklyn are owned by Koreans, but they carry items demanded by their predominantly West Indian customers: cabbages, yellow turnips, sweet potatoes and yuca.

The century's earlier immigrants included craftsmen like Siegfried Liebmann, a refugee from Hitler's Germany who arrived in the United States in 1938. Mr. Liebmann made mannequins for jewelry display.

and paralegal services. Through an effort encompassing national, diocesan, and parish organizations, the Catholic Church now provides most of New York's low-cost legal counseling for immigrants. The largest legal service agency is run by the USCC, a national Catholic welfare agency directed by the National Conference of Catholic Bishops. In addition, each diocese has opened a migration office, and one Brooklyn parish has mounted its own immigrant assistance program.

These offices have been shaped by the specific needs of today's immigrant parishioners and by the personalities of the church workers who responded to those needs. The USCC office takes its character in part from the dynamic Ukrainian refugee who has supervised the daily operations for many years; the Brooklyn diocesan office reflects the activism of the lawyer/bishop who founded it; the archdiocesan office operates with the professionalism one would expect there; and a small Brooklyn parish office reflects the personal commitments of staff members in its special work with women and Salvadoran asylum seekers.

In 1986 USCC immigration office staff members filed INS applications in 4,000 cases ranging from political asylum cases to applications for naturalization. Those 4,000 cases probably represented somewhere between 25,000 and 40,000 individuals, according to the office director, Rev. Peter Zendzian.

Lydia Savoyka, the senior counselor, was rescued by a Catholic relief organization in 1948, when she was a 14-year-old orphan in the Ukraine. Her office is a clutter of boxes and files piled on the floor, the windowsill, shelves, and chairs. She is in perpetual motion as she switches from case to case and language to language. (She speaks 12.) After nearly 35 years in the business, she is dean of immigration workers in this city, and her walls are covered with awards and hand-drawn pictures from grateful clients. An enlarged newspaper photo shows her with Pope John Paul II; he requested a meeting with her to discuss Polish refugees.

The office supplements its ten-member staff with volunteers, many of them immigrants waiting for their cases to be resolved. A Sri Lankan teenager who overstayed a visitor's visa is waiting to find out if he will be deported. Meanwhile, he does the office photocopying. An Afghan asylum applicant goes out to get coffee for visitors while Savoyka calls the INS on his behalf. Will he be allowed back into the country if he leaves the United States temporarily to visit his ailing mother?

About a third of the office's $750,000 budget comes from client donations ranging from $10 to $500, and the rest from the National Council of Catholic Bishops. Its service is a bargain in a city where a private attorney may charge $500 just to open a client's case. Like the other Catholic legal service offices, USCC takes no government grants for this work, lest that restrict its freedom to serve undocumented aliens.

Even after 35 years, Savoyka still makes a point of ending each client's interview with the words "Don't worry. Just go. Let me worry." She has good reason to worry. Many of her clients hope for rulings that she knows the INS will not make. The office has received about 13,000 political asylum requests from Salvadorans alone. Salvadoran applications have a high rejection rate. The Salvadoran files wait beside folders for Afghans, Egyptians, and Poles. At last count Savoyka's own case load was more than 3,000.

There wasn't any good news that day for the Afghan applicant, yet when she broke the news, there was hopefulness in her voice, a note that implied, "That's the answer today, but tomorrow something may change it."

The New York Archdiocese and the Brooklyn Diocese both run immigration offices that are similar to the USCC's in the range of legal services they provide and in the special passion for immigrants' rights that inspires their staff despite the increasing frustrations of the field.

Anthony Bevilacqua, now bishop of Pittsburgh, founded Brooklyn's Catholic Migration and Refugee Office (CMRO) when he was serving in New York. Bishop Bevilacqua, an attorney, led the national immigration debate among Catholic prelates when he was chairman of the National Council of Catholic Bishops' immigration committee. When he left Brooklyn for Pittsburgh, he left behind an extensive network of immigration field offices in the Brooklyn Diocese that have now been consolidated into four under the leadership of Bishop Rene Valero. In addition to providing legal advice, CMRO arranges English classes for immigrants and solicits free medical care from Catholic hospitals.

Rev. Francisco Dominguez heads the archdiocesan immigration office, located on First Avenue and 55th Street in Manhattan. The office has a staff of seven, including three clerical workers to help with the interminable paperwork that is required in most immigration cases. Father Dominguez and one of his two staff counselors make monthly trips to their offices in White Plains and Newburgh, and a counselor makes weekly visits to clients at the INS detention center on Varick Street in Manhattan. In 1986 the office logged nearly 13,000 requests for information and referral, and it worked on 4,500 cases. Its services are supplemented by several parishes.

Father Dominguez also provides an important service to the archdiocese. The Church relies on increasing numbers of foreign clergy and religious—Irish nuns in the schools and Mexican brothers in the parishes, for example—to supplement its declining native-born staff, and Father Dominguez processes the labor certifications and visa applications that are necessary to bring these workers to the United States.

Brooklyn's Transfiguration parish in Williamsburg became active in immigrant services in the late 1970s, when increasing numbers of undocumented immigrants, primarily from Central America, began to enter the parish. These immigrants could not be served adequately by the parish social service agency—the Southside Community Mission—because most of its services involved referral to government-sponsored programs for which undocumented aliens were not eligible. The parish priest, Rev. Brian Karvelis, asked a nun, Sister Peggy Walsh, to start a program that could serve undocumented aliens—a program that would be funded entirely by private donations. The Southside Community Mission Annex came into being, within the church building itself, to give its clients a sense of security and sanctuary. The annex offers the same range of legal services as the other Catholic migration offices, along with some social services that are specific to the needs of its clientele, such as hospital escorts and loans for immigration court bail. Annex staff members also visit the INS detention center, where they offer legal assistance to undocumented aliens who have been arrested by the INS and have no way of affording private legal services.

On one visit to the detention center, Sister Peggy's first client was a young Dominican woman who had been arrested at Kennedy Airport for entering the country with a false passport. Sister Peggy knew that the best her client could hope for was a voluntary departure; she could admit she had entered with false papers, and give up her right to a deportation hearing, in exchange for the government's dropping its fraud charge against her. It was hard for the woman to admit that her passport was fraudulent. Sister Peggy spent a long time with her, speaking in quiet, careful Spanish, assuring her that she needn't be ashamed of having tried to enter the United States by whatever means she could find. Sister Peggy views it as no sin to try to improve one's life. She was angrier at the swindler who took $1,000 of the Dominican woman's money for a patently false passport than she was at the woman herself. Sister Peggy took a deep breath before moving on to her next client, an Ethiopian who had a certificate of marriage to an American woman—a ticket to legal entry if the marriage is more than an attempt to circumvent immigration law—but who didn't have so much as his wife's telephone number.

Because of its long history of service to immigrants and its extensive immigrant counseling network, the Church naturally has an important role to play in fulfilling the intentions of the Simpson-Rodino amnesty program. The USCC, the diocese and the archdiocese, like a number of other private and religious organizations, have contracted with the INS to be "qualified designated entities"—that is, organizations that can counsel, screen and assist in the paperwork for amnesty applicants. Applications that appear to meet all criteria are forwarded to the INS for final approval.

Local parishes are being used as information and application centers, staffed by counselors who have been trained by USCC. A legalization director in each diocese oversees the outreach and application program.

Although the INS has two application centers within New York City, it is assumed that aliens will feel safer if they consult first with a qualified designated entity such as USCC. The government set up this agency designation system on the understanding that this would be so.

HISPANICS AS PART OF THE CHURCH

The Church is not just a service provider for immigrant Catholics; it is, and must be, their spiritual leader, as it was for the immigrants of the 19th and early 20th centuries. But the constituency of the Church has changed. It is now a settled, middle-class group that must stretch to accommodate the new immigrants, who are arriving as immigrants usually do—often poor, unable to speak English, and attached to their own linguistic, cultural, and religious traditions.

The migration with which this "establishment" Church is faced is predominantly Hispanic. Although Puerto Ricans are native Americans and have been treated as such in this book, Puerto Ricans have to be painted into any accurate picture of the "Hispanicization" of the Church. The Hispanic migration to New York City began with the Puerto Rican influx after World War II. Puerto Ricans were the main Hispanic newcomers throughout the 1950s and well into the 1960s, when they were joined by large numbers of Cubans. From the 1970s on, Hispanic immigration has been primarily from the Dominican Republic, Central America, Colombia, and Ecuador.

Most of these Hispanics are Catholic, at least in name. The Church's Hispanic constituency grows proportionately larger and larger as non-Hispanic Catholics leave the city for the suburbs, and as newcomers—younger and more fertile than the nonimmigrant Church membership—arrive and reproduce.

Far less militant than the German and Italian Catholics of 19th-century New York, these Hispanics nonetheless present the New York Church with a powerful challenge. To maintain its spirit of Catholicism and its numbers, the Church must make room for them. Yet there is much about their style of Catholicism that is hard for the American Church to understand, and they themselves are hampered by having few champions within the church structure.

Catholicism in colonial Latin America discouraged the development of a native priesthood. Its priests were European and North American, and too few in number to accompany their parishioners to the United States. The numbers tell the story. In 1955 there was 1 priest for every

560 Catholics in the Archdiocese of New York; there was 1 for every 7,250 in Puerto Rico.

Because of the shortage of priests in their native lands, Hispanic Catholics developed observances that were personal, informal, and centered on family and fiestas. Hispanics value the spirituality, intimacy, and warmth of religion more than they value institutional involvement. A 1982 study conducted by the archdiocese showed that Hispanics tend to accept Catholic beliefs but are uninformed about Catholic liturgy, and are less likely to attend Mass, go to confession, or receive Communion than are non-Hispanic Catholics.[4]

Furthermore, Hispanic Catholicism is not a single pattern of religious expression. African, Caribbean, and Protestant practices have influenced the Latin nations in various ways. These influences differ in their compatibility with European-American Catholicism. Some practices, like Bible study worship services at home, are relatively easily integrated. Others are more difficult to accept, like the practice of *santeria*, whose saints are thinly disguised versions of African gods.

Among today's Hispanics, particularly Puerto Ricans, the Church is facing competition from evangelical Protestant religions whose storefront churches, with their family orientation and opportunities for lay leadership, are attracting increasing numbers of followers.[5] Many Hispanics participate in both religions, regularly attending evangelical services but relying on the Church for baptisms, confirmations, and marriages. To meet the Hispanics' need for culturally meaningful forms of religious expression, the Church offers marriage encounters, *cursillos*, and other kinds of retreats that use group techniques to build excitement, involvement, and a sense of community. The charismatic movement offers born-again evangelism within a Catholic framework. Spanish-language programs in lay leadership training are held at centers in the Bronx and Manhattan. And throughout the archdiocese, religious services and educational programs for both children and adults are offered in Spanish.

Hispanics did not tend to enter the priesthood in their native countries, and they do not tend to do so in the United States. Their immigrant experience reinforces the pattern: newcomers are interested in jobs that pay them enough to survive and to bring their families into the United States. Most Hispanic immigrants lack the college degree necessary for the priesthood. Celibacy runs counter to prevailing Hispanic values. Nationwide, Hispanics complain that there are few Hispanic role models in the church hierarchy. A survey made in mid–1985 showed that of the ten auxiliary bishops in the New York Archdiocese, none were Latin American, although one was a Basque from Spain; of four in the Brooklyn Diocese, one was a Latin American from Venezuela.[6]

Religious vocations are decreasing among all American Catholics;

Church projections suggest that the number of priests will halve by the year 2000. The American Church may of necessity come to resemble the Latin American Church in its small ecclesiastical hierarchy and its large, decentralized network of lay workers and leaders.

DECLINE OF NATIONAL PARISHES

Hispanics arrived in New York at a time when the Church had strong reasons not to create new national parishes. The national parishes, which had served the first generation of immigrants so well, could not hold on to the children and grandchildren of immigrants. Suburbanization was drawing many of the city's Catholics away from the city and its churches; some church buildings were only half full.

In 1939, as Puerto Ricans were arriving, Francis Cardinal Spellman decided that integrated parishes would best meet the Church's needs. Whenever possible, priests who spoke Spanish would be transferred to parishes in which there were large numbers of Hispanics, and the cardinal asked all priests to become familiar with their new parishioners' language and culture. Some priests responded to his call for self-education; others did not.

In the early 1950s the Church began to articulate its awareness that the needs of its Hispanic parishioners were not being met fully. In 1952 an archdiocesan study team reported that many priests were reluctant to accommodate Hispanic language or religious practice, and the team recommended mandatory Hispanic studies for priests.[7] The archdiocese immediately began language training programs for new seminary graduates—but new graduates were only a small proportion of the priestly population.

In the midst of these discussions, there arrived in New York a young Yugoslav priest who was to become an outstanding ecclesiastical champion of Hispanics. In 1951 Ivan Illich left a promising Vatican diplomatic career to come to New York. Now known widely for his iconoclastic writings on social change, such as *Deschooling Society* and *Tools for Conviviality*, Illich was assigned to Incarnation parish on 175th Street and St. Nicholas Avenue in upper Manhattan. He became fascinated by the religious culture of his Puerto Rican parishioners. On vacations he hitchhiked through Puerto Rico, sleeping on church steps and saying Sunday Masses wherever he went. He loved the familiar, daily observances of Hispanic Catholicism, which he viewed as closer to the heart of Christianity than the urbanized, once-a-week Catholicism of the mainland.

Illich was convinced of the need to train priests in a Puerto Rican style of ministry. In 1957 he obtained Cardinal Spellman's support for the establishment of the Institute for Intercultural Communication in Ponce. There, newly ordained New York priests spent eight weeks in Hispanic language and cultural training, followed by six weeks of service in a rural Puerto Rican parish. Strictly speaking, the training was cultural, not political, but it was inevitably shaped by Illich's radical adoption of Hispanic Catholicism. The institute profoundly influenced a generation of priests, religious, and lay people; its graduates are found everywhere among the thinkers and doers of today's Church.

The social activism of the 1960s, inside and outside the Church, supported and amplified Illich's work. Outside the Church the civil rights movement began to eat away at the institutional props for poverty and inequality. Inside the Church the Second Vatican Council (1962–65) placed new emphasis on lay participation, and diversity of language and practice. Throughout the 1960s the Church experimented with folk Masses, fiestas, consciousness-raising sessions, and Church-affiliated civic activities. The Spanish Catholic Action Office, established by Cardinal Spellman in 1953, became the creative agent for the experiments of the 1960s.

The creative ferment of the Great Society was not to last. When Cardinal Spellman died in 1967, it fell to his successor, Terence Cardinal Cooke, to institutionalize the Hispanic advances, a difficult and controversial duty. Saying that Hispanic integration had been achieved,[8] Cardinal Cooke moved Hispanic programs out of their own offices and into general chancery offices. The Spanish Catholic Action Office, by then renamed the Office of Spanish-Speaking Apostolate, was disbanded and reorganized. It operates today as the Office for Hispanic Affairs.

Critics protested that Cardinal Cooke's moves interrupted the momentum of Hispanic integration, but the critics did not prevail. Illich's institute closed its doors in 1972 as interest flagged and money dried up. Illich himself had left in 1960, a casualty of ecclesiastical and secular politics, when his support for a Puerto Rican political party ran counter to the position of the island's bishop. He is now a writer and visiting professor at universities in Europe and the United States.

Although Cardinal Cooke was criticized for breaking up the Hispanic offices, he did in fact emphasize the importance of Hispanic ministry on every level of church life. In that way he continued the work that Cardinal Spellman had begun. In the years shortly before his death in 1983, Cardinal Cooke initiated two major projects on behalf of his Hispanic constituents: a study of Hispanic values and beliefs, and a commission to develop a plan for a Hispanic ministry.

The study, a two-volume report on the attitudes, beliefs, and needs of Hispanics in the archdiocese, was published in 1982 and is cited in this chapter. The report of the commission, *A Pastoral Plan for Hispanics,* was presented to the new archbishop, John J. O'Connor, in September 1984. It recommended reactivating the language and cultural programs for priests, nuns, and lay workers.

Implicit in these activities is the acknowledgment that Hispanics have not yet achieved their place in the Church. The letter of the U.S. bishops, *Hispanic Presence: Challenge and Commitment,* has been a call to Catholics on behalf of their Hispanic coreligionists. It is the kind of call that might well be made to many of New York's public and private institutions.

NOTES

1. See Robert L. Stern, "Evolution of Hispanic Ministry in the New York Archdiocese," in *Hispanics in New York: Religious, Cultural and Social Experiences*, Vol. 2 (New York: Office of Pastoral Research, Archdiocese of New York, 1982); and Joseph P. Fitzpatrick, *Puerto Rican Americans: The Meaning of Migration to the Mainland*: (Englewood Cliffs, NJ: Prentice-Hall, 1971), ch. 8.

2. See *Hispanic Presence: Challenge and Commitment*, a pastoral letter of the American bishops responding to the recommendations of nationwide Catholic Hispanic assemblies (Washington, D.C.: United States Catholic Conference, 1984).

3. See Silvano Tomasi, *Piety and Power: The Role of the Italian Parishes in the New York Metropolitan Area, 1880–1930* (New York: Center for Migration Studies, 1975).

4. See Hispanics in New York vol. 1 (New York: Office of Pastoral Research, Archdiocese of New York, 1982), pp. 207–209.

5. See Renato Poblete and Thomas F. O'Dea, "Anomie and the Quest for Community: The Formation of Sects Among Puerto Ricans in New York," *American Catholic Sociological Review*, Spring 1960, pp. 18–36.

6. In the February 1986 issue of *Clergy Reports* (Vol. 16, No. 2, p. 7), a newsletter for priests, the archdiocese reported progress in achieving Hispanic representation in the archdiocesan hierarchy. High-level Hispanics included the chancellor of the archdiocese, two vicars (one a bishop), the director of the Office for Hispanic Affairs, 80 priests, 14 pastors, and 43 deacons. The newsletter also reported efforts to increase the numbers of Hispanic and bilingual employees and the use of bilingual materials in many Catholic offices including Catholic Charities, the Catholic Home Bureau, the Hospital Apostolate, and the Catholic Center.

7. See summary of a study by George Kelly in Stern, "Evolution of Hispanic Ministry," pp. 298–99.

8. See Stern, *op. cit.*, pp. 324ff.

12 The Role of Public Education

Trina Melloy teaches third grade at P.S. 89 in Elmhurst, Queens. Three-quarters of her students were born abroad. Most of her pupils have recently come to New York with their families from Asia, Latin America, and the Caribbean. Her class roster lists names like Swarup Bandyopayay, Kin Chan, and Andre Esquerra; and when she leads her class in stretching exercises, Mrs. Melloy counts the beats in English, Spanish, Chinese, and Tagalog.

The high proportion of immigrant children in Mrs. Melloy's class is not unusual at P.S. 89, where an estimated 90 percent of the student body is foreign-born. That percentage is much higher than average for the New York City public schools, but every school in the system has its Andre Esquerras and Kin Chans. The "new" immigration to New York City is seen nowhere more clearly than in the public schools, which function, as they have for more than a century, as the primary institution of acculturation for the children of the worldwide diaspora.

Strictly speaking, children can be termed immigrant only if they were born abroad. But many of New York's immigrant families have children who were born here. Andre Esquerra, Kin Chan, and Swarup Bandyopayay were born abroad, but they probably have younger siblings who were born in New York. Loosely speaking, these younger siblings are "immigrant" children too, even though they are native-born.

Analysis of 1980 census data shows that more than a quarter of the city's public school children—27.2 percent—came from immigrant households; and of those children, more than half were born in the United States. More than a third of the city's nonpublic school children—

35.4 percent—were from immigrant families; and of those children, nearly four-fifths were U.S.-born (see Table 12.1).

City Planning demographers reached these findings by analyzing the composition of the city's households, those that were headed by someone of native birth and those that were headed by an immigrant. Then, households were analyzed to see where their children were born.

These figures are for children aged 3–19 in grades K–12. "Children of Native-Headed Households" and "Children not Living in Households" include about 7,700 foreign-born children, most of them born abroad of a U.S.-born parent. Of that 7,700 total, 6,440 were in public schools and 1,260 in nonpublic schools.

These are census data, not actual school enrollment figures. The schools do not aggregate data on birthplace of parent or child, so this type of analysis cannot be done from school figures. Total school enrollment figures for 1980 were close enough to census figures to suggest that the data were valid.

Puerto Ricans by definition are not foreign-born; they are native-born Americans. Consequently there is little discussion of them in this study. Their presence adds to the multilingual and multicultural environment of the city and its schools, however, and it compounds the task of teaching American language and customs to the children of non-Anglo ethnicities. If Puerto Rican households are analyzed as immigrant households were analyzed, what emerges is that in 1980, 17.4 percent of the city's public school children came from families that were headed by someone born in Puerto Rico, and about 20 percent of those children themselves were born in Puerto Rico. The rest were born on the mainland (see Table 12.2).

Adding first- and second-generation Puerto Rican children to first- and second-generation immigrant children, City Planning analysts found that 447,500 (44.6 percent) of the city's public school children were newcomers or the children of newcomers.

Public school children from families headed by immigrants represented 134 nations in 1980, and they spoke 56 languages. Generally following citywide immigration trends, their primary countries of origin were the Dominican Republic, Jamaica, China, Guyana, and Trinidad and Tobago, in that order. An image of a miniature United Nations composed of New York City public school children emerges from these statistics. The presence of children from such diverse backgrounds infuses the school system with added excitement. Cultural exchanges take place far from the diplomatic sphere—in Trina Melloy's third grade classroom, for example.

Immigrant children contribute to the classroom environment by broadening the horizons of their classmates. At the same time they have educational needs that make particular demands on their teachers. Lan-

Table 12.1

Children of Native- and Foreign-Headed Households in New York City Schools

	Total enrollment	Children of native-headed households	Children of foreign-headed households			Children not living in households
			Total	U.S.-Born	Foreign-Born	
Public Schools						
Number	1,003,220	726,940	273,120	143,680	129,440	3,160
Percent	100.0	72.5	27.2	14.3	12.9	0.3
Nonpublic Schools						
Number	309,880	199,740	109,580	84,340	25,240	560
Percent	100.1	64.5	35.4	27.2	8.1	0.2

Note: Because of rounding off, totals may not equal 100.0 percent.

<u>Source</u>: 1980 U.S. Census Public Use Microdata File

Table 12.2

Children of Puerto Rican-Born Householders

in the New York City Public Schools

	Total	Mainland-Born	Island-Born
Number	174,380	138,320	36,060
Percent of total enrollment	17.4	13.8	3.6

Source: 1980 U.S. Census Microdata File.

guage poses one obvious difficulty for any non-English-speaking newcomer to the United States. Consequently, bilingual education and ESL classes are components in the education of many immigrant children. An examination of the New York City Board of Education's bilingual and ESL programs reveals a strong base of needed service, accompanied by gaps in data collection, program evaluation, and program planning. Many school staff members have given thought to the areas in which improvements are needed, and various school offices have taken steps to fill the data gaps, but the Board of Education has yet to coordinate these efforts.

Adjustment to life in the United States involves more than language. Immigrant children must make psychological and cultural transitions as well. New federal funding in the 1984–85 school year encouraged New York City educators to look at these larger issues.

HISTORY

The history of the New York City public school system is inseparable from the city's immigration history. The school system was the product of conflict and competition between Irish Catholic immigrants of the early 19th century and their English Protestant predecessors.

Diane Ravitch, an educational historian, writes that "Each major reorganization of the school system was the result of intense political struggle, and . . . each of these battles coincided with a huge wave of new immigration."[1] Ravitch sees the schools as "the battleground where the aspirations of the newcomers and the fears of the native population met and clashed."[2]

New York City had no government-operated schools until 1842, when the New York State Legislature created the New York City Board of Education. Earlier in the 1800s, public funds had been used to support a quasi-public system of schools run by the Public School Society, a charitable organization established by the city's prominent citizens to educate the children of the poor. The Public School Society schools were free and ostensibly nonsectarian, but New York's first Irish Catholic archbishop, John Hughes, believed them to be Protestant in religious orientation, anti-Irish, and anti-Catholic.

As Ravitch tells the story, Hughes wanted public funding for his fledgling parochial school system. He found an ally in New York's aristocratic but libertarian governor, William Seward. Seward did not think Catholics should have to send their children to schools they found offensive, nor should they have to keep their children at home in order to avoid unacceptable teachings. He believed in universal education and whatever was required to achieve it.

Catholic school proponents and public school proponents warred verbally in the churches, meeting halls, and newspapers of the city. From there the fight went to the legislature in Albany. "When the struggle was concluded," Ravitch writes, "the city had a public school system, publicly funded and publicly controlled by elected local school boards, an outcome which none of the participants had sought. The Catholics won their battle to disestablish the private society which monopolized public education funds, but lost their war for a share of the money."[3]

By 1880 the Irish were no longer the "new" immigrants. Northern Europeans had been succeeded by migrants from southern and eastern Europe who, by 1900, were pouring into New York at a rate never equaled before or since. Many "old" New Yorkers worried about the assimilability of the Jews and Italians, and they turned, says Ravitch, to the public school system as the appropriate institution to cope with the newcomers' problems.

> In the nineteenth century, the public school was only one of many acculturation devices; it was expected to provide a seat for the child, lecture him on good habits, and drill into him enough schooling to get him into the world of work on a competitive, if minimal, basis. But in the early twentieth century, the public school was transformed into a vast, underfinanced, bureaucratic social-work agency, expected to take on single-handedly the responsibilities which had formerly been discharged by family, community and employer. Of course, the immigrants continued to be acculturated through work, politics, religion, the press, and their own communities, but the idea took hold that the public school was uniquely responsible for the Americanization and assimilation of the largest foreign immigration in the nation's history.[4]

That crisis also passed. By the 1940s the children of the great immigration had had children of their own, and the city's schools were populated by second- and third-generation children of European ancestry. "The schools had not conquered the problems of first-generation immigrant pupils," Ravitch writes, "but rather had survived them."[5] Now the schools met another shock: new waves, not of immigrants, but of Puerto Ricans and American blacks migrating from the South. These migrants made new, and newly political, demands; blacks wanted integration and community control; Puerto Ricans wanted bilingual education.

BILINGUAL EDUCATION

The school system's bilingual and ESL programs have achieved their size and permanence as a result of two lawsuits of the 1970s, one brought in New York by a Puerto Rican advocacy group, the other brought in San Francisco by a group of English-deficient Chinese children. Based primarily on civil libertarian concepts, these suits were part of the nation's stepped-up civil rights activism of the 1960s and 1970s.

Hundreds of thousands of Puerto Ricans migrated to New York City during the 1950s and 1960s, and enrolled their children in the city's schools. In the late 1960s the Board of Education hired several bilingual teachers and instituted bilingual programs in some schools.

The Puerto Rican advocacy group, Aspira, was not satisfied with the scope of these efforts. Aspira and other Hispanic groups and individuals sued the Board of Education in 1972, asserting that all Spanish-speaking children were entitled to bilingual education on the grounds of equal educational opportunity. An out-of-court settlement known as the Aspira Consent Decree (1974) mandated a much expanded bilingual program for Spanish-speaking or Spanish-surnamed students who were deficient in English. The curriculum provided for major subject instruction in Spanish, intensive instruction in English, and a simultaneous development of Spanish-language skills.

The final draft of the Aspira Consent Decree drew on a similar San Francisco case, *Lau* v. *Nichols*, as legal precedent. In 1970 non-English-speaking children of Chinese ancestry brought a class action suit against the San Francisco Unified School District. Plaintiffs claimed that they suffered unequal educational opportunity because of their limited English proficiency, and that the school district had failed to provide adequate language programs.

In a unanimous 1974 decision the U.S. Supreme Court sided with the plaintiffs, overturning lower court rulings. Justice Douglas wrote for the Court, "Students who do not understand English are effectively foreclosed from any meaningful education. . . . [Such students] are certain to find their classroom experiences wholly incomprehensible and in no way meaningful."

Over the years since the *Aspira* and *Lau* cases, the New York City public schools have established bilingual programs in an increasing number of languages as immigrants have changed in ethnicity. All new language programs follow Aspira Consent Decree guidelines. In the 1985–86 school year the schools provided bilingual classes for 41,000 students whose low scores on a standardized test of English-language proficiency qualified them for language instruction. About 15,000 students who scored just above the cutoff also were enrolled.

Of those students who scored below the cutoff and enrolled in bilingual classes, 70 percent spoke Spanish, 11 percent spoke Chinese, and 5 percent spoke Haitian Creole. The remaining 14 percent, in declining order of magnitude, were speakers of Korean, Vietnamese, Italian, Arabic, Greek, Khmer (Cambodian), Hindi, French (Haitian), Urdu, and Russian. Although the number of Hispanics was by far the largest, the proportion of non-Hispanics is on the increase; and within the Spanish-speaking group, bilingual program staff members have observed an increase of foreign-born Hispanics over Puerto Ricans.

Parents of children who are selected for bilingual education can opt for ESL-only instead. Unlike enrollees in the full bilingual program, ESL-only students take their major subjects in mainstream, English-speaking classes. They separate from the mainstream only for ESL. School staff members observe that Hispanic parents tend to prefer full bilingual programs for their children; Asian parents are more likely to make use of the ESL-only option. Various ethnic groups can, and do, mix in ESL classes, since the classes are conducted in English. In 1985–86, 30,600 students were enrolled in ESL-only.

State regulations developed pursuant to the Aspira Consent Decree require that bilingual education be provided in schools where there are 20 or more children of the same grade and language group who are deficient in English. Finding bilingual teachers can be a problem, particularly for new, small language groups. Where full bilingual classes are not provided, either because a language group is too small or because a bilingual teacher cannot be found, state regulations require that ESL instruction be made available.

Although the Board of Education works hard to adhere to court- and state-mandated language program guidelines, it is not always successful. In 1985–86, for example, nearly 89,000 students were eligible for language programs, but only 81 percent of them were placed in full bilingual or ESL programs. The remaining 19 percent received only a partial program, or their status was unknown.

The Board of Education's procedures for data collection and analysis, program evaluation, and program planning have not yet reached the thoroughness that many school staff members desire. In January 1984, however, the Office of Educational Assessment undertook the task of creating a longitudinal data base to use as a language program evaluation tool, and published a report entitled *An Educational Profile of Language-Minority Students in the New York City Public Schools*. The authors of the report intended it to be the first in a series; in early 1987, a second was cleared for distribution.

Continual debate takes place among parents and educators over the goals and effectiveness of bilingual education. The Board of Education treats bilingual education as a transitional phase in a child's academic development. Maintaining the native language and culture are not official objectives of the program, although many parents and educators consider it important. Views differ widely; some oppose any use of a native language in school; others want a gradual transition from the native language to English; and still others place a high value on retention and refinement of the native culture.

Some critics who oppose native-language retention see it as a screen for other, more political goals; others see it as an impediment to English-language learning. From a strictly educational standpoint, learning English is by no means incompatible with native-language retention; on the contrary, good language skills are readily transferable in either direction. But critics fear that the goal of English-language proficiency is being lost, and that some bilingual program enrollees are spending too many years outside the mainstream. The debate sometimes leaves the realm of educational theory for that of ethnic politics. Hispanics primarily, but other ethnic groups as well, want to ensure the longevity and appreciation of their culture, and their fight with the forces of homogeneity is carried out partly on the fields of bilingual education.

In recent years, school systems across the country have begun to focus attention on the particular needs of Hispanic schoolchildren, whether or not they are technically deficient in English. Issues include a high dropout rate, inadequate vocational preparation, educational difficulties, problems in social and cultural adjustment, and the desirability of retaining native language and culture. Some commentators believe that English-language deficiency may be part of a wider range of learning problems that demand responses over and above language instruction. It is not clear whether these problems differ for Hispanics born abroad, Hispanics born in Puerto Rico, and Hispanics born on the U.S. mainland.

In New York City, Hispanic schoolchildren are not the only group warranting further inquiry. Jamaica sends the second largest group of immigrant children to the New York City public schools. Children from Jamaica and other ostensibly English-speaking countries of the Caribbean are not eligible for language programs because their official language is English. In fact, however, many of these children speak a Creolized form of English that is virtually a foreign language when the Creolization is deep. Their language problems recently have come under study by a task force of public school and university educators.

In 1985 Chancellor Nathan Quinones reconstituted the Chancellor's Citywide Commission on Bilingual Education and charged its members with developing an educational policy for all language-minority children in the public schools, not just those who were deficient in English. In 1986 the commission recommended that all public school students develop proficiency in two languages (one of them English), whether their or not primary language was English or not. The Board of Education adopted the recommendation as school policy, and a task force was set up to make recommendations for implementation. In early 1987, the chancellor had before him the task force recommendation for a pilot project.

An evaluation of current bilingual and ESL programs was not part of the Citywide Commission's mandate.

AID FOR IMMIGRANT CHILDREN

When immigrant children arrive in this country, they must make a transition that is social, cultural, psychological, educational, and linguistic. In 1984 the U.S. Department of Education acknowledged that these needs merit special efforts on the part of the public schools when it created the Federal Emergency Immigrant Education Assistance Program (FEIEAP). Before FEIEAP the only immigrant children for whom the federal government provided special education funds were refugees, and the dollar amounts were small.

Of the $30 million nationally available in FEIEAP's second year, New York City received a total of $3.4 million for its public and nonpublic schools. The city received a per capita allotment for each immigrant child who had been in a U.S. school for three years or less. The Board of Education identified about 45,700 such children. Because the board identifies children by their country of last address rather than their country of birth, these figures omit immigrant children who may have lived in another U.S. city before coming to New York.

Each eligible district and the Division of High Schools created its own plan for the use of its share of the FEIEAP funds. Most proposals emphasized the development of English-language skills, but some involved cross-cultural communication through recreation and cultural programs. The Division of High Schools allocated funds to help students explore educational and career goals.

In addition to FEIEAP funds, the federal government provides some financial support for the education of refugee children, using a formula based on each child's length of time in the United States. New York City received about $194,000 in 1985–86, when about 970 refugee children were credited to the public schools and 140 to nonpublic schools. The methods that have been devised for counting refugee children do not catch all of them, school officials believe, so it is unlikely that New York City is receiving its correct per capita share.

Refugee children, like all other immigrant children, are incorporated into the standard school programs, including bilingual education and ESL-only if needed. The federal aid is used for materials for the language programs.

ISSUES IN DATA COLLECTION AND ANALYSIS

The Board of Education has the capacity to know much more than it does about its foreign-born students, its language-minority students, and the students enrolled in its language programs. Only recently have school staff members realized the potential usefulness of the data, and efforts are under way in several parts of the school system to evaluate the schools' data needs and data collection procedures.

For maximum utility, student data must be transferred onto the Board of Education's central computer file, known as the "bio" file, so they can be cross-tabulated with other data items. Then the data must be tabulated in a form that can be used by data analysts and program planners. Various important elements are collected by the schools, but they are not necessarily being entered onto the bio file or printed out for program planning purposes. Within the family of nationality and language issues under discussion here, some of the more important data elements are the following:

- *Country of birth.* This is collected for most pupils at the home school, but it is entered onto the bio file only for language program participants, and it is not tabulated. If it were tabulated for the entire school population, it could be used to ensure maximum funding from FEIEAP; to evaluate the use of the language programs by, and their effectiveness for, various nationality groups; to study the educational needs of foreign-born students who are not technically defined as English-deficient; and to assist the city in following immigration trends in the ten years between censuses.
- *Country of last address.* This is summarized for the FEIEAP application as a substitute for country of birth.
- *Language spoken at home.* This is collected for every student, but it is not entered onto the bio file, though discussions are under way at the Board of Education on the possibility of adding it.
- *Parents' country of birth.* No agency of which City Planning is aware collects this information. It could be used to evaluate the educational needs of children whose parents are immigrants or island-born Puerto Ricans.
- *Length of stay in a language program.* The data have been on the bio file since 1982, but they are not regularly tabulated or used for program evaluation and planning.
- *Educational achievement of language-minority children.* This includes those never in language programs, formerly in language programs, or currently in language programs. The data have been on the bio file since 1982 and were used in the *Educational Profile of Language-Minority Students* discussed earlier in this chapter.

UNDOCUMENTED ALIENS

Before the U.S. Supreme Court settled the matter in 1982, the nation's public schools struggled with the question of whether to educate the children of undocumented aliens, and whether to educate them free. The New York City public schools confronted these issues during the mid–1970s, and by 1978 the Board of Education had reached a decision to educate all resident children, at no fee, regardless of immigration status. School administrators were instructed not to ask the immigration status of an enrolling child.

In 1953 the INS began granting student visas to children of undocumented aliens who wanted to attend school. It authorized the Board of Education to admit them and to charge tuition—$664 a year for elementary students and $1,943 a year for secondary students. Tuition was levied on the theory that undocumented aliens were not paying taxes, so they ought to pay tuition.

There were problems with the policy. In some district alien status was scrutinized; in other districts it was not. The Board of Education did not enforce the tuition requirement, and very little money was collected. It became apparent that few residents were making use of the visa process, which was used primarily by foreign children to gain legal entry to the United States.

These revelations, combined with changing public attitudes toward the education of undocumented children, caused the school system to reevaluate its position during the mid–1970s. Members of the public joined school officials in their concern that children of undocumented aliens might be staying away from school because their parents could not afford the tuition or because they feared being reported to immigration authorities. In 1978, when the Board of Education adopted its open admissions policy, it stated that "the monitoring of the immigrant status of a child or parent is not a proper function of the New York City Board of Education."

When the Supreme Court spoke in 1982, it was ruling on the case of *Plyler v. Doe*, a class action suit filed in 1977 on behalf of undocumented children in the Tyler Independent School District of Smith County, Texas. In 1975 the Texas Legislature had enacted a law that excluded undocumented children from the state's public schools and prohibited the use of state funds for their education. The Supreme Court held that the law violated the equal protection clause of the Fourteenth Amendment, and it ruled that the public schools could not deny undocumented children the free public education provided to other children in the state.

Despite the Supreme Court ruling and New York City's own policy, some undocumented children are thought to be staying away from school because their parents fear detection by the immigration authorities. It is unlikely, however, that the numbers are large. Some undocumented families prefer to enroll their children in parochial schools out of greater trust in nongovernmental institutions. Again, the numbers are not known.

ENGLISH-LANGUAGE INSTRUCTION FOR ADULTS

Immigrant children almost always outpace their parents in learning English. In 1980, census data indicate, 142,000 of the city's adults could not speak English at all, and another 329,000 could not speak it well. Of the 471,000 total, about 70 percent were foreign-born, and most of the rest were born in Puerto Rico.

Immigrants to New York have always been able to find jobs that required no English nor formal schooling. But the city's industrial sector has declined, and jobs in the growing information and service sectors demand English proficiency, a high school diploma, and often a college degree. The premium on English proficiency is growing.

Adults who want to learn English can choose from several types of classes: free ESL classes offered by the public schools' Division of Adult Basic Education or by various community organizations that receive government money for the purpose; low-cost ESL classes at Adult Continuing Education Centers in the public schools; low-cost classes at community colleges; and fee or nonfee classes offered by dozens of private for-profit and nonprofit language schools whose fee arrangements vary considerably. In a 1984 survey of Manhattan language schools, fees ranged from $282 to $425 for 100 hours of instruction.

The Division of Adult Basic Education of the public schools provides most of the free ESL classes in the city. Between 1983–84 and 1984–85, the schools more than doubled the number of adult ESL students they served, from 5,700 to 13,500, as a result of new state and city appropriations for the purpose. The city had not used tax levy funds for adult ESL since the fiscal crisis of the mid–1970s. The number served rose again in the 1985–86 school year, to an estimated 16,000.

There are never enough slots. "The demand far exceeds our ability to meet it," says Aris Papargyriou, coordinator of instructional and administrative services for the Division of Adult Basic Education. Waiting lists at ESL centers grow so long that they have to be closed so as not to encourage false hopes of early acceptance.

Passage of the Simpson-Rodino Act is going to mean longer lines. Applicants for permanent residence under the amnesty program will be required to demonstrate a knowledge of English and civics, or show that they are enrolled in English and civics classes. It seems probable that the city will try to provide more slots to meet the increased need.

Classes are taught by licensed ESL instructors, meet from 6 to 15 hours a week, and average 20 students per class.

Adults attend classes for different reasons. Some want to learn enough English to function in their new country. Others are studying to pass a job test. Young mothers want to be able to help their children with homework, or to get a job outside the home.

About 380 adults attend classes held in the former P.S. 179 building on West 102nd Street and Amsterdam Avenue in Manhattan, next to a public housing project. Most come from the neighborhood, which has a large Hispanic population.

One day not long ago, 13 men and women gathered for their morning lesson in an old classroom with a knee-high sink in the corner and faded linoleum tile on the floor. Posters, maps of the New York City subway system, and pages of verb conjugations were tacked to the walls. The students' assignment for the morning: write one or two paragraphs about "something that's been on your mind lately," and then explain it out loud.

Not surprisingly, the conversation touched on jobs, money, family, and marriage. A young Haitian named Antoine described his night job as a security guard in an apartment building. After he goes off duty at eight in the morning, he walks to his nine o'clock English class. "I come to school to learn something more in life," he said.

Throughout the discussion the teacher encouraged self-expression, explained colloquial expressions like "going steady," referred students to programs and services, and promised one young man to get details on the plumber's licensing exam.

Like the Board of Education, some unions offer free ESL classes, though only to their members. The New York locals of the ILGWU, most of whose members are Hispanic and Chinese women, have a long tradition of educational service, according to Kathy Andrade, educational director of Local 23–25.

Mrs. Andrade is herself a product of the union's educational program. She came to New York from El Salvador in 1949, got a job as a machine operator for a garment manufacturer, joined the ILGWU, learned English in a union class, and, with the help of the union, became a citizen. Later she attended classes in labor history, public speaking, and union contracts.

Mrs. Andrade now directs the education program for her local. "We are always after them to continue their education," she says of her constituents. ESL classes are the first step. In 1985, 295 Hispanic women and 480 Chinese women attended the local's ESL and citizenship classes; the latter prepare newcomers for the U.S. naturalization exam. After completing union ESL classes, many students attend high school equivalency classes run by the Board of Education.

HIGHER EDUCATION

Immigrants can, and do, continue their education beyond high school. Census figures show that in 1980, 6 percent of the foreign-born were attending institutions of higher learning, the same percentage as the native-born. Immigrants made up exactly their proportionate share of the college and university population: 101,000 out of 427,000 (23.7 percent).

Almost three-quarters of foreign-born university students attended public institutions, mainly the 18 colleges of the City University of New York (CUNY). Like the Board of Education, CUNY offers programs and courses for students who need help in English. Most courses at CUNY's bilingual college, Eugenio Maria de Hostos in the Bronx, are offered in Spanish and English.

No data are available on the academic success of the city's foreign-born students, but immigrants have a long-standing reputation for academic accomplishment that probably is well-deserved. The following facts aren't conclusive, but they are indicative: The valedictorian of the 1984 City College graduating class was Chi Luu, an ethnic Chinese refugee from Vietnam; the salutatorian of the 1985 graduating class was Alejandro Rey, an immigrant from Argentina; in 1986 both top slots were filled by immigrants—Marie-Elena John, born in Antigua, was valedictorian, and the salutatorian was Egyptian-born Waiel Abdelwahab.

NOTES

1. Diane Ravitch, *The Great School Wars* (New York: Basic Books, 1974), p. xiii.
2. Ibid.
3. Ibid., p. xiv.
4. Ibid., p. 176.
5. Ibid., p. xv.

13 Issues in Health Care

For 19th-century immigrants good health was a triumph of constitution over environment. New York City's immigrant neighborhoods were literally pestholes of dank, unventilated apartments, overflowing outhouses, and garbage-filled streets. When epidemics of cholera, dysentery, and typhus swept the city, the heaviest tolls were in the overcrowded immigrant tenements.

The foul living conditions of the 19th century have largely been eradicated, although residential overcrowding in some neighborhoods still fosters the spread of some infectious disease. The stress of immigration, and long hours at grinding jobs, increase the vulnerability of today's immigrants to illness, just as they did for the immigrants of yesterday, but the most serious health problems faced by immigrants are no longer the results of their present environment. Rather, they are health problems brought from homelands where modern medical care may be virtually nonexistent.

Data from the New York City Department of Health (DOH) and from health care workers around the city show that some of today's immigrants arrive in New York with such communicable diseases as tuberculosis and intestinal parasites, and untreated chronic ailments such as scoliosis and hypertension. Dental problems are common. So is the absence of vaccination.

Immigrants' health generally improves in the United States because of better treatment and better hygienic conditions. Tuberculosis and parasitic infections are readily treated. Furthermore, new immigrants have age in their favor; they tend to be young and resilient.

At present it is unclear whether immigrants' health problems have increased the incidence of any infectious diseases among the native-born population. Native-born Americans appear to be protected by immunities and by the good hygienic conditions in which they were raised. The native population most at risk probably consists of immigrants' U.S.-born children. Still, the question of contagion to the native-born, particularly of tuberculosis, requires further study.

Most new immigrants come to the United States from developing nations where public hygiene is inadequate and medical personnel are scarce. Ironically, access to health care remains a problem for immigrants even after they reach the medically sophisticated United States. Here their access is limited by their lack of knowledge of the health care system, the cost of care, and their initial lack of health insurance. The financial impediments to care are most pronounced in their first years after arrival, when their need for care is greatest.

At the start most immigrants are too poor to afford medical care, and they are likely to work in businesses like retail shops, restaurants, and taxi services, where health benefits generally are not provided. Their access to Medicaid is limited by their earnings, which need not be very great to exceed the Medicaid income criteria, and by confusing and controversial Medicaid criteria governing the eligibility of various classes of aliens. Often they fail to seek low-cost care at municipal hospitals and clinics because they do not realize that they are eligible for such care, or because they dread the complicated paperwork that is sometimes required in order to receive it. Fear of being reported to immigration authorities—a fear that once had substance but does no longer—discourages many undocumented aliens from seeking care. It also discourages some documented aliens who do not understand their rights well enough to know that they are safe.

Cultural barriers also impede immigrant access to health care, barriers as simple as language and as complex as radically differing concepts of sickness, health, and treatment. City hospitals in immigrant neighborhoods often have foreign-language speakers on staff, and some staff are attuned to different cultural outlooks on health care, but there are not enough of either group to go around.

New York's immigrants are too diverse to present a single health profile, and these general remarks should not be construed as applying to all new immigrants. Not all immigrants come from medically underdeveloped nations, not all come with health problems, and not all are too poor to pay. Even among the most recent immigrants, 1980 census data suggest, about 20 percent are employed in white-collar jobs that are likely to provide health insurance. Furthermore, a substantial number of new immigrants, particularly women, are attracted to the heavily unionized garment and health industries, in part because of the availability of health benefits. Ethnic associations are beginning to step into the insurance breach. For example, the Korean Produce Sellers Association offers a health insurance plan for its self-employed members.

DATA SOURCES

As in many other areas of immigrant research, public knowledge of immigrant health needs is limited by lack of data. Immigrants are largely unstudied as a patient group. One cannot look to the census for data on health. The municipal hospital system does not routinely aggregate data on patients' country of birth, though it does for its specific service planning studies. The city's DOH did not aggregate such data until 1985.

Now the DOH records country of birth in several of its data systems. The new computerized patient information system in the eye, dental, child health, and tuberculosis clinics includes country of birth. The school health program is recording country of birth of those children whose health problems are being followed medically. The vital statistics computer system is coding country of birth from birth and death certificates.

In addition, the DOH is collecting and analyzing information on refugees, the one immigrant group for which the federal government provides funding and requires data collection. It also conducts occasional studies on specific immigrant health issues.

Few statistical data on immigrant health issues were available at the time of this writing, but health care workers throughout the system had accumulated considerable information. This analysis relied upon their knowledge and upon the special studies conducted by the DOH.

HEALTH PROBLEMS AMONG IMMIGRANTS

Some of today's immigrants come to the United States from parts of the world where diseases are prevalent that have nearly been eliminated in this country. The most serious and rigorously documented of these diseases is tuberculosis, which is widespread in Latin America and Asia. It occurs three times as frequently among New York's immigrants as among the native-born, according to a 1976 DOH study. Immigrants had 51 cases per 100,000 residents; the native-born had 18.

There is reason to believe that the incidence of tuberculosis among the foreign-born may be higher than the DOH data indicate. Although prospective permanent resident aliens are screened for tuberculosis before they are permitted to enter the United States, students, tourists, and aliens who enter secretly are not. If undocumented aliens do carry tuberculosis, they may be reluctant to seek treatment; DOH data are for cases that have been medically diagnosed and reported to the department.

It is not known whether the incidence of tuberculosis of foreign origin affects the TB rate among native-born Americans. The disease is associated with poverty and overcrowding, conditions not limited to immigrants. High rates are found among the homeless and in several crowded New York City neighborhoods. Some of them, such as Chinatown, have many immigrants; others, such as Central Harlem, have few.

Even more than tuberculosis, leprosy is an immigrant disease. Though its absolute incidence is very low, the number of cases reported per year in New York City has risen with the new immigration, from about 5 a year before 1976 to 25 a year now. A 1982 DOH study showed that 99 percent of reported leprosy patients were foreign-born.

Despite its reputation for contagion, leprosy does not appear to pose a health threat to the native-born population. It is not very infectious, and it is easily controlled. There has been no documented case of transmission to a native-born American; DOH staff members speculate that native-born Americans have a natural immunity to the disease.

Some immigrants arrive with chronic health problems that have gone undetected or untreated at home. School nurses report a higher-than-average incidence of untreated strabismus (crossed eyes) and scoliosis (curvature of the spine) among foreign-born children, a rate of dental cavities twice that of American-born children, and poorer immunization histories. Workers with Soviet Jewish refugees note numerous cases of strokes and circulatory problems resulting from untreated diabetes and dangerously high levels of hypertension. Public health studies show a high rate of late-stage cervical and breast cancer among Caribbean-born black women.

Immigrants tend to bring other, less serious health problems, especially parasitic infections. Cambodian, Laotian, and Vietnamese refugees are particularly likely to carry them; medical screenings have shown an incidence of nearly 50 percent. But these conditions are easily controlled, and the likelihood of recurrence is lessened by this country's hygienic conditions. The DOH operates two tropical disease clinics for treatment of such ailments; the majority of patients are foreign-born, and many have recently returned from trips abroad.

One can hardly call pregnancy a health problem, but maternity care does loom large among immigrant health needs. In 1980 the birth rate among the city's immigrants was 20.3 per 1,000, compared with the native rate of 13.5 per thousand. The Health and Hospitals Corporation (HHC), which operates the city's 16 public hospitals, does not routinely keep data on its maternity patients' country of origin; but a 1983 study of the undocumented alien patient population showed that 51 percent of undocumented inpatients were maternity cases, many of whom had received inadequate prenatal care.

There are many reasons for the high immigrant birth rate. First, immigrants tend to migrate in their young adult years; 56 percent of recent immigrants were between the ages of 20 and 44, according to the 1980 census, while only 36 percent of the native-born population fell within that age range. Refugee families may wish to have many children to replace family members lost in war. In many developing countries, large families are the norm.

THE MENTAL STRESS OF MIGRATION

Virtually no data are available on the mental health needs of New York's immigrants, but mental health workers repeatedly cite mental health problems as a primary immigrant health issue. Symptoms such as disorientation, depression, anxiety, and mood swings are common among new arrivals.

Migration carries many stresses. New York's heterogeneity can be bewildering. A new language must be learned; and even then, the immigrant is surrounded by a babble of unknown tongues and a confusing variety of customs and values.

Familiar support systems may have been lost. Families may be separated until the first arrivals earn enough money to send for the rest of the family. Even in united families there is stress. Husbands and wives find their roles changing when wives work outside the home for the first time, perhaps earning more than their husbands. Children learn the English language and American ways more quickly than their parents, thereby exacerbating generational conflict.

Stressful change extends to the work place. Many immigrants find themselves working less skilled jobs than they held at home because they do not speak English well enough to function at their highest level or to pass professional licensing tests. Others struggle with differences in the economy. Soviet refugees who open their own businesses, for example, report difficulty in adjusting to the aggressiveness and risks of the capitalist marketplace.

Some Southeast Asian refugees have been affected by a pattern of depression and guilt that is similar to the "survivor syndrome" manifested by European Jews who survived the Holocaust. About six to ten months after their arrival here, when their immediate survival needs have been met, the new refugees may become severely depressed as they begin to grieve for dead family members and to feel guilty that they have survived when others have not.

Few mental health programs have the language capability[1] and cultural knowledge to serve the new immigrants. Refugee resettlement agencies provide counseling for their clients, but usually not after the first year in the United States. Immigrants play a part in their failure to be served;

often they are reluctant to acknowledge mental distress or to seek help from U.S. institutions.

THE COSTS OF CARE

How to pay the high cost of health care is an issue that affects the city's immigrants and its health care providers equally. The HHC, the DOH, the Medicaid system, and immigrants themselves all are up against cost problems that are national in scope, but the problems are more severe for immigrants than for the native-born.

HHC is committed to providing low-cost health care to all needy New Yorkers, but there are costs attached to that commitment, especially when immigrants do not have health insurance or the ability to pay out of their own funds. The problem has been particularly acute among undocumented aliens, who are likelier than other immigrants to lack adequate funds or insurance, and whose access to Medicaid has been blocked by eligibility criteria that have been the subject of court challenge, new legislation, and continuing controversy.

The Department of Health operates many neighborhood clinics that focus on specific public health problems, such as venereal disease, tuberculosis, and well-child care. These clinics are not intended as substitutes for primary health care, but they are free to all New Yorkers, regardless of immigration status.

When needy HHC and DOH patients are Medicaid-eligible, the city is reimbursed 75 percent of the cost of care. When such patients are not Medicaid-eligible, the city pays 100 percent.

HHC has no regular mechanism for aggregating data on the immigration status of its patients. To estimate its cost of service to uninsured, undocumented aliens, in 1983 it hired a private research firm, Mathematica Policy Research of Princeton, New Jersey. The Mathematica researchers concluded that 3 percent of uninsured patients in municipal hospitals were "positively" or "probably" undocumented aliens. Had these patients been eligible for Medicaid reimbursement, HHC would have received about $21 million for their care.

If outpatients had been studied, the estimate of lost reimbursement would have been much higher. The brevity and intermittency of outpatient visits made it too difficult for Mathematica to establish alien status, but undocumented aliens are thought to make considerable use of outpatient services. Most of these services are relatively inexpensive compared with inpatient treatment; one exception is kidney dialysis, a highly expensive long-term treatment. HHC estimates that in the period 1980–84 it absorbed $1.4 million in dialysis costs at Kings County Hospital alone for undocumented aliens ineligible for Medicaid.

HHC commissioned the Mathematica study in support of the lawsuit challenging the Medicaid exclusion of undocumented aliens. The suit, joined by the city in 1982, is discussed later in this chapter.

Although HHC is committed to treating undocumented aliens who are residents of the city, hospital administrators are concerned that some aliens are coming to New York City solely for treatment of serious conditions that are likely to require long and expensive care. In immigration law there is no visa category for aliens who wish to enter the United States specifically for medical treatment. A temporary visitor's visa may be granted to such aliens if they can guarantee that the costs of their care will be paid. Some aliens apparently enter the United States without making it known to immigration authorities that their sole purpose is to obtain medical care. It is understandable that aliens may dodge the law to seek U.S. health care if their lives depend on it. It is also understandable that city officials do not want the municipal health care system to have to bear the heavy costs of these aliens' care.

ACCESS TO CARE

Undocumented status has been only one impediment to Medicaid benefits for aliens. Like the native-born working poor, many immigrants make a little too much money to qualify. In addition, many immigrants—even some health care workers—believe that Medicaid is available only to welfare recipients. The working poor often fail to apply for Medicaid, not realizing that they may be eligible. They also may not realize that it is possible to qualify financially for in-hospital Medicaid even if not for outpatient Medicaid.

Confusion and controversy over the legal and financial criteria for care discourage some immigrants from seeking care at municipal hospitals. Many immigrants and immigrant advocates appear to believe that indigent immigrants are accepted only for emergency care, particularly if they are undocumented. This is not the case. HHC policy is to provide necessary care, at a cost the patient can afford.

When an indigent alien seeks care at a municipal hospital, HHC policy requires that the hospital undertake a financial procedure that is identical with that for native-born patients. First, the hospital determines whether the patient is eligible for Medicaid or any form of third-party payment. If not, applicants are classed as self-pay patients. As such, they can negotiate with the hospital for fee reduction or participation in a sliding-scale fee system. It is the patient's responsibility to trigger the fee negotiation process; patients who do not do so are billed at full fee.

In most cases the system works quite well, but sometimes immigrants are not told about the system, or perhaps they do not understand it well enough to request it. Some estimates suggest that about 2 percent of uninsured patients fail to trigger the fee reduction system, and their unpaid bills frequently go to collection agencies.

Some aliens, particularly those whose immigration status is uncertain, are reluctant to undergo an HHC financial screening for fear of being reported to immigration authorities. Before 1984 that was a well-founded fear, but it is no more. Between 1977 and 1984 the names of some aliens who applied for Medicaid were submitted to the INS for verification of their immigration status if they lacked documents to demonstrate that status. Applicants were not always informed that this INS check would be made.

The INS followed up on only a small percentage of the reports, but it did use hospital-supplied information on aliens in whom it had an active interest. For example, in January 1984 Medicaid screeners at Kings County Hospital sent the name of Immacula Abraham, an undocumented Haitian immigrant who had been a patient, to the INS. Abraham had failed to appear for an INS hearing, so the INS used the hospital-supplied information on her whereabouts to visit her home and question her children. Abraham, who had an advanced case of uterine cancer, was readmitted to the hospital on the day of the INS visit and died two days later.

The Haitian community, convinced that Abraham's death was hastened by the trauma of the INS visit, demanded that the HHC stop sending names to the INS. Through a confluence of circumstances, HHC did change its procedures. In September 1983 the city Medicaid program had instituted a policy by which an applicant's written consent had to be obtained before a check was made with the INS. HHC adopted the same policy. In addition, HHC had become concerned about INS requests for information on the cost of care to aliens. Consequently, in February 1984 HHC strengthened its efforts to ensure that the new procedure was being followed. INS checks were made only with the patient's written consent. Furthermore, if hospital workers had reason to believe that a patient was an undocumented alien, HHC terminated the Medicaid application process and absorbed whatever costs of care the patient could not pay, in spite of his or her consent for an INS check.

The policy not to communicate with the INS about an applicant's status received reinforcement from Mayor Edward Koch in October 1985 when the Mayor issued a memorandum to all mayoral agency heads ordering them not to report unauthorized aliens unless the aliens were involved in some kind of criminal activity. The Mayor did not want to discourage essentially law-abiding aliens, even those who were living in the United States without authorization, from making use of public services that they needed.

Under the old reporting policy, HHC made INS checks only to further the Medicaid application process; its intention was not to report undocumented aliens, though that was sometimes the effect. Some aliens still fear the possibility of being reported to the INS, and they avoid hospitals and the Medicaid application process as a result.

There is a state law on the books that requires social service agencies to make reports to the INS when aliens apply for state-funded benefits without being able to produce evidence of legal immigration status. The law, however, is not enforced.

THE MEDICAID SUIT

Long before it commissioned the Mathematica study, HHC was aware that the city was losing substantial amounts in potential Medicaid reimbursement for classes of aliens who were excluded from Medicaid eligibility. This knowledge prompted the city in 1982 to join a civil action against the Medicaid hierarchy.

The original suit, *Lewis et al. v. Krauskopf et al.*, was filed in 1979 by a group of undocumented aliens in an effort to broaden the Medicaid eligibility criteria. The suit was against the city, state, and federal components of the Medicaid hierarchy: the city's Human Resources Administration, the state's Department of Social Services, and the federal Department of Health and Human Services.

The city and HHC joined the suit against the state and federal Medicaid administrations. Although named in the original suit, city Medicaid officials contended that they were simply following state and federal regulations, and had no interest in disqualifying aliens.

The plaintiffs' primary contention was that the federal Medicaid statute made no mention of alienage; to promulgate regulations basing eligibility on alien status was therefore to violate the intent of the statute. Alienage restrictions, they maintained, even if authorized by statute, are unconstitutional, particularly with respect to children and pregnant women.

Plaintiffs also contended that the Medicaid list of eligible alien classes was too restrictive, in that it excluded many aliens on whom immigration law conferred the right to reside in the country. They argued that any alien who was living in the United States with the knowledge and acquiescence of the INS should be viewed as living here "under color of law," the wording used to describe the eligible class. They also argued that aliens' Medicaid eligibility should not be more restricted than their eligibility under the SSI program, which, like the Medicaid program, is governed by the Social Security Act. Under the plaintiffs' interpretation, any resident alien who entered the country on a valid visa, or had an application before the INS, was living here with INS knowledge and acquiescence, and "under color of law." The plaintiffs' standard would exclude aliens who had entered the country secretly and had made no move to regularize their status, aliens who were under active deportation orders, and aliens who were here on temporary visas, such as tourists and students.

The city further argued that the federal government was responsible for the presence of all aliens in the United States because immigration control is strictly the province of the federal government; therefore, the federal government ought to absorb its fair share of their medical costs.

The suit was originally filed in 1979 by Lydia Lewis, a Haitian national who was ruled ineligible for Medicaid because of her lack of permanent resident alien status. Mrs. Lewis arrived in the United States at age 11 on a student visa and lived here continuously thereafter. She eventually married an American citizen. Mrs. Lewis was eligible for permanent residency on two counts: her husband's citizenship, and her mother's status as a permanent resident alien. Her "green card" application was still pending when she applied for Medicaid assistance for the births of her first two children, and her Medicaid application was denied. Mrs. Lewis' story illustrates the city's contention that most aliens turned down for Medicaid because of alien status were on their way to permanent residency—and eventual Medicaid eligibility.

Mrs. Lewis' situation was serious and important, but it was not as medically dire as the situations of some other aliens who were affected by the Medicaid restrictions. Take, for example, the case of Andre Francis, an undocumented Trinidadian alien who was also a plaintiff in the *Lewis* suit. Francis was admitted to Kings County Hospital in 1980 with spinal injuries causing quadriplegia. He remained at Kings County long after his condition was stabilized because no long-term rehabilitation center, including those run by the city, would accept him without insurance or Medicaid. Too handicapped to be discharged, but with no prospect of getting the treatment he needed, Francis lay in a ward for weeks at a cost to the city of $317 a day. He joined the *Lewis* suit in 1981, after which he was granted temporary Medicaid benefits pending resolution of the case. He was subsequently transferred to a municipal rehabilitation center, where he improved immensely. In 1984 he completed the New York City Marathon in his wheelchair.

On July 14, 1986, Judge Charles P. Sifton found for the plaintiffs; the Medicaid statute contained "no express restrictions on alien eligibility," he ruled, so that aliens could not be excluded from eligibility on the basis of regulations. As a result of Justice Sifton's decision, financially qualified persons became eligible for Medicaid regardless of alienage.

Congress quickly responded to Sifton's decision, and its implications for widespread Medicaid use, by changing the Medicaid statute. On October 17, 1986, Congress passed an amendment to the Budget Reconciliation Act which denied Medicaid benefits to undocumented aliens except in emergency cases. Medicaid benefits were reserved for those aliens who were permanent legal residents or who were "permanently residing in the United States under color of law" (PRUCOL). PRUCOL was undefined in the law, which went into effect on January 1, 1987, without benefit of regulations which would offer clarification.

The *Lewis* suit did not die when Congress changed the Medicaid statute. The suit had been based on many arguments other than the statutory one, and those aspects of the case are still under Justice Sifton's consideration.

Congress enacted another Medicaid restriction through the Simpson-Rodino Act. Temporary resident aliens for the most part are not eligible for federal Medicaid benefits, though states with Medicaid programs may offer benefits if they wish to do so. At this writing, it appeared that New York State and City would grant Medicaid benefits to temporary resident aliens, although it was not clear whether the federal government would reimburse them for it despite the law's provisions for reimbursement of state costs attendant upon the amnesty program.

NEW SIGHTS AND SOUNDS AT LOCAL HOSPITALS

One of the first tasks faced by all health care institutions in making themselves hospitable to immigrants is overcoming the language barrier. Kings County Hospital recruits doctors, nurses, and social workers who speak French and Haitian Creole so they can communicate with the hospital's large Haitian patient population. Elmhurst General Hospital, located in one of the city's most ethnically diverse neighborhoods, relies heavily on volunteer interpreters. At last count these interpreters spoke more than 35 languages, and hundreds of Indian and Arabic dialects.

The city's refugee resettlement agencies negotiate for interpreter services at voluntary hospitals used by their clients. Many Cambodians who live in Brooklyn travel to Mount Sinai Hospital in Upper Manhattan because they know Mount Sinai has a Cambodian interpreter.

Hospitals throughout the city have begun to print patient information pamphlets, menus, and TV rental agreements in languages other than English. The Chinatown Planning Council has produced a Chinese-English medical phrase book in which, for example, a nurse can point to the phrase "Take one teaspoon at bedtime" and the patient can read the Chinese version.

The increasing numbers of new immigrants working in the city's health professions provide a built-in interpreter service. A third of the New Yorkers employed in local hospitals are new immigrants. Most of them are English-speaking Jamaicans, but there are also many Chinese, Filipinos, Indians, and Koreans with foreign-language facility.

The presence of immigrant health providers is not an unalloyed benefit in the eyes of all immigrant patients, however. Immigrants may be pleased to find a doctor who speaks their language, but some may be suspicious that their countryman is not as good as a "real" American doctor.

On the other hand, immigrants' attitudes toward Western health care contain a good deal of suspicion. Immigrants may prize American medical technology, but they are reluctant to abandon their traditional methods and medicines, especially when they are having to abandon so much else that is culturally familiar. Many immigrants settle on a two-tiered approach to health care. Their first recourse in illness is the Chinese herb shops, Hispanic *botanicas*, or equivalents that flourish in other immigrant communities. For more serious ailments they turn to hospitals.

Consequently, American health care providers have had to become familiar with the signs of traditional treatments. The first doctors to treat Southeast Asian refugees often mistook red welts on children's bodies for signs of child abuse. They soon discovered that the marks were left by *cao gio*, a practice of rubbing salve into the skin with the edge of a coin to draw out "bad blood." Some mothers are still reluctant to bring their children for care if they have done coin rubbing, for fear of being accused of child abuse.

Sometimes the signs of traditional treatments provide important diagnostic clues for health care workers. Cambodians often treat headaches by heating a glass, pressing it to the forehead, and pulling it away after a vacuum has been formed by the cooling, shrinking air. The mouth of the glass leaves a red ring on the forehead. One social worker with a Cambodian clientele noticed that headache was often a mask for depression; when she saw a client whose forehead bore a ring, ostensibly a sign of headache, she made a point of eliciting information about the client's state of mind.

Sometimes serious health problems can result from traditional remedies. In 1982 the DOH investigated the case of a four-year-old who had serious neurological symptoms. It was found that the mother had been treating the child's diarrhea with an herbal remedy containing mercury. Further study showed that other herbal mixtures contained mercury, arsenic, or small quantities of other heavy metals. Subsequently the DOH undertook an educational campaign in Asian neighborhoods on the dangers of these herbal remedies.

Assimilating the new immigrants into the city's health care system is not easy, but it is happening.

NOTE

1. In December 1986, the New York City Department of Mental Health, Mental Retardation and Alcoholism Services published an "Inventory of Languages Spoken at Manhattan Mental Health Services." Among the 25 languages listed were Arabic, Cantonese, Haitian Creole, Mandarin, Pharsee, Shanghai, Toisun, Urdu and Vietnamese.

14 Immigrants and the Criminal Justice System

New York City has long received its immigrants with a certain ambivalence—a mixture of welcome and distrust. Despite evidence to the contrary, some people still suspect that immigrants are more criminally inclined than the average New Yorker.

During the 1850s, for example, many of the city's leading citizens believed that Irish and German immigrants were devoid of respect for the law. In an address to the city's Common Council in 1855, Mayor Fernando Wood warned that the "evil influences" of immigrants upon society, and the "contaminating effects upon all who come within range of their depraved minds," had become a matter "exceedingly serious and demanding immediate and complete eradication."

By the turn of the century, new groups of immigrants had arrived in the city, and they came in for their share of accusations. In a 1908 article in the influential *North American Review*, New York City Police Commissioner Theodore Bingham blamed half the city's crimes on "Hebrews," mostly of Russian birth. He went on to complain of the ostensible criminality of the city's Italians and Chinese. Such views were not universally held, even at the time; and after a storm of criticism, Bingham was forced to write a retraction. Nonetheless, the fact remains that his views readily found their way into print, and they reflected a substantial segment of public opinion.

Modern social historians believe that the incidence of immigrant crime has often been exaggerated. Historian Robert Ernst reports, for example, that 55 percent of persons arrested in New York City in 1859 were Irish-born, but most of them were arrested on minor charges such as petty thievery, drunkenness, and disorderly conduct. Ernst suggests that the police of the day "kept a sharp eye out for slight misdemeanors committed by persons of no political influence."[1] In other words, to some degree crime is in the eye of the beholder.

Immigrant crime nevertheless remains a headline grabber. When a judge proclaimed in 1982 that 85 percent of the drug cases in Brooklyn criminal courts involved undocumented aliens, newspapers reported his remarks without attempting to verify them. A 1984 article on Cuban Mariel entrants noted their achievements in many walks of life, but the article was headlined "Castro's 'Crime Bomb' Inside U.S."[2] Colombian-American leaders in New York City have complained for years that press coverage of the world of international cocaine trafficking has defamed their community. The Colombians feel much as the Italians felt before them: the criminal activities of the few are too often attributed to the many.

It does appear to be true that "organized" crime is often organized along ethnic lines, as it has been throughout the city's history. It also appears to be true that the cocaine trade is dominated by Colombians, and that Chinese and Southeast Asian immigrant gangs have come to control a portion of the country's heroin trade. And it is true that in February 1985, a federal grand jury in Manhattan indicted 25 reputed members of the Ghost Shadows Chinatown youth gang on racketeering charges involving accusations of extortion, robbery, kidnapping, and murder.

There is no evidence, however, to suggest unusual criminal tendencies among immigrants as a group. Most crime is not organized crime, and there is little reason to believe that immigrants commit a disproportionate amount of any kind of crime.

How prevalent is immigrant crime? By whom, and against whom, is it committed? At present our knowledge of these matters is scanty. Since 1982 the New York City Police Department has kept records on the country of birth of all persons arrested in the city. But the records can provide only a rough sketch of immigrant crime, largely because country of birth is elicited from suspects themselves and is not checked for veracity. Criminal justice researchers agree that arrest statistics have many other flaws as indicators of the true state of crime in America; for example, they do not account for unreported crime; they can be skewed by priorities in police work; and they reflect apprehensions, not convictions.

Nevertheless, the city's arrest data seem to suggest that immigrants as a class are at least as law-abiding as the native-born. The city data tend to be supported by the results of a prison census conducted by the New York State Department of Correctional Services in October 1984. Like the city data, the state data were obtained strictly by self-report and, also like the city data, were not verified.

Although the state data showed that foreign-born inmates were underrepresented in the state prison population, state analysts were concerned about a marked upward trend in foreign-born commitments, which nearly doubled between 1978 and 1982. It is important to note, however, that 1980 was a peak year in recent immigration, and that the upward trend did not appear to continue after 1982.

Lawrence Sherman, a former research analyst with the New York City Police Department who later became research director for the Washington-based Police Foundation, speculates that immigration may involve a type of self-selection for noncriminality. "If the arrest rate is much lower for immigrants," he says, "it may well be that the kinds of people who come here are less likely to throw away everything they have achieved, by committing crimes." A field worker for the Victim Services Agency in New York takes a less sanguine view. The city's large undocumented population fears that contact with the police or courts will lead to deportation; consequently, he thinks, "they are scared into being law-abiding."

Fear and distrust of police are common sentiments among immigrants, documented and undocumented. Many street criminals and con artists prey on immigrants for that reason; they believe that immigrants who are victimized will not go to the police. Immigrants' reluctance to report crime means that some crimes committed by and against them never reach police attention. That is one reason to mistrust arrest data as an indicator of immigrant crime.

In an effort to improve relations with immigrant groups and to involve them in crime prevention programs, Deputy Police Commissioner Wilhelmina Holliday in 1985 set up a seven-member New Immigrants Unit in the department's Community Affairs Division. In addition, the department overhauled its police recruit training to broaden instruction on the city's rapidly changing ethnic composition.

MEASURING IMMIGRANT CRIME

In 1931 the Wickersham Commission, a blue-ribbon panel appointed by President Herbert Hoover, issued a 12-volume report on the nation's Prohibition-era crime problems. Volume 10 was entitled *Crime and the Foreign-Born*. After analyzing arrest statistics from 30 of the nation's largest cities, the commission's researchers concluded that any presumption of "excessive criminal propensities among so-called 'foreigners' . . . is at variance with the facts." The researchers found that immigrants were far less likely than the native-born to be arrested for "crimes for gain," but they approached the native-born in "crimes of personal violence."

Recent New York City arrest data, if valid, would tend to confirm the

Wickersham finding that immigrants are more law-abiding than the native-born. In an analysis of all arrests made during the first nine months of 1986, the Police Department's Crime Analysis Unit found that the (self-reported) foreign-born accounted for 16.3 per cent of all felony arrests—15,991 out of a total of 98,306—although the foreign-born make up far more than 16.3 per cent of the city's population. Even if immigrant arrests are underreported, it is unlikely that immigrants represent more than their "fair share."

The fact that country of birth is self-reported and unverified is the greatest reason to suspect that the immigrant felony arrest rate may be higher than 16.3 percent. Crime analysts in the Police Department believe that some foreign-born Hispanics report their place of birth as Puerto Rico—the United States—in order to escape the attention of immigration authorities. Without further research, it is impossible to estimate how much immigrant crime is misattributed in this fashion.

An October 1984 state prison census showed that 7.7 percent of state prison inmates—convicted and incarcerated felony offenders—reported having been born in a foreign country. Foreign-born persons made up at least twice that percentage of the total state population, so the foreign-born appeared to be considerably underrepresented in the state prison population. Most of the foreign-born inmates (83 percent) were committed from New York City.

The four types of offenses for which most prisoners were incarcerated were homicide, robbery, burglary, and drugs. Among the four, the foreign-born had higher-than-average rates for homicide and drugs, and lower-than-average rates for robbery and burglary. There is some agreement here with the Wickersham findings.

There is also some agreement with New York City findings. The data for the first nine months of 1986 show that the three felony categories in which immigrants made up the highest percentages of arrests were possession or sale of marijuana (44.0 percent), weapons possession (26.0 percent), and possession or sale of a controlled substance (23.4 percent). They were 19.3 percent of homicide arrests. At the other end of the spectrum, the foreign-born represented only 9.1 percent of robbery arrests and 9.8 percent of burglary arrests.[3] Each of these percentages may be low because of foreign-birth underreporting, but the ratio between them is probably valid.

THE COCAINE WARS

Perhaps the most notorious crimes involving New York's aliens in recent years have occurred in the underworld cocaine trade. In February 1981 Orlando Galvez, a Colombian national, and his wife and family were shot to death after their car was forced to a shoulder of the Grand

Central Parkway in Queens. No one has been arrested for the killings. The police found 140 pounds of cocaine in the Galvez home, as well as a cache of weapons and several hundred thousand dollars in cash. They concluded that the massacre was an organized crime "hit," perhaps retribution for a broken cocaine trafficking contract.

Detective Mike Connors has been a member of the New York Drug Enforcement Task Force in Queens since 1982. The task force is a combined federal-state-city effort. Since the late 1970s the task force has found itself focusing increasingly on Colombians because of their prominence in the drug trade. "If it's coke-related," says Detective Connors, "it's mostly Colombians." The narcotics task force works hand in hand with the Queens Detective Task Force responsible for homicides because many homicides are drug-related.

Local and federal investigators agree that the immensely lucrative international cocaine trade is tightly controlled by about a dozen Colombian crime families. The term "family" is used literally; members of these crime rings often are related by blood or marriage.

The cocaine underworld is probably better understood as imported crime than as immigrant crime. Investigators say it is directed from the Colombian city of Medellin. Its principal organizers use counterfeit identification papers to travel to and from the United States, and they rarely make extended stays. Most of the profits derived from cocaine importation are believed to return to Colombia or to end up in numbered accounts in the world's banking havens.

This "remote control" operating style is quite different from the usual U.S. pattern of domestically controlled organized crime. One ramification is that the cocaine underworld seems to rely less on "local help" recruited from the immigrant population than, for example, did the rum-running gangs of the Prohibition era.

THE MARIELITOS

Crimes committed by Cuban Mariel entrants have received particular attention from policy makers, police, and the press. In 1980, shortly after the Cuban Mariel boatlift, an off-duty New York Housing Authority police lieutenant was shot to death during a tavern holdup in the Bronx. Two Cuban-born suspects, recent arrivals in the boatlift, were arrested and confessed to the crime.

Shortly afterward Lt. John Decker, who was head of the Bronx area detectives at the time, set up a three-man unit to investigate Mariel crime. According to Lieutenant Decker, intelligence gathered during the homicide investigation exposed the existence of large numbers of Marielitos "with a potential for violence."

There is considerable evidence that the Mariel entrants were at high risk of criminal activity. Of about 10,000 Mariel entrants believed to be living in New York City, about 90 percent were single males in their twenties and thirties, according to a 1983 survey by NYANA, a resettlement agency that includes Cuban entrants among its clientele. NYANA found that 60 percent of its Marielito clients suffered from mental disorder, alcoholism, or drug abuse. Many Marielitos were petty criminals in Cuba who had been brutalized by long periods of incarceration in primitive and violent Cuban prisons.

Law enforcement authorities from Los Angeles to New Jersey assert that the Mariel entrants are a disproportionately large crime problem.[4] Lieutenant Decker estimates that in 1983, New York City police arrested 200 Marielitos a month. Data from the Police Department's Crime Analysis Unit show that 734 self-reported Cuban-born suspects were arrested during the first three months of 1984. That figure included Marielitos and other Cuban-born persons, who together accounted for 1.2 percent of the city's arrests. Cuban-born persons made up under 1 percent of the city's population, so they were somewhat overrepresented in the arrest population. Furthermore, they made up 10 percent of all immigrant arrests, so they did appear to have been much more prone to criminal activity than other immigrant groups.

By 1984 the peak of Mariel criminal activity had apparently passed. By the end of 1983, Lieutenant Decker says, his Mariel unit had "broken the back" of the criminally inclined Marielito group. Many Marielitos had been arrested, incarcerated or deported, or had moved elsewhere. The Mariel task force no longer was needed, though a filing system on known Mariel criminals is still maintained.

It is not clear that New York's Marielitos were prone to more violent crime than the rest of the criminal population. About 32 percent of the Cubans arrested during the first quarter of 1984 were charged with the serious street crimes known in police work as "index" crimes: felonious assault, murder and manslaughter, rape, arson, felony larceny, robbery, burglary, and auto theft. During the same period 41 percent of all arrests in New York were for index crimes. In other words, arrested Cubans were less likely than the average defendant to have been arrested for a violent crime.

ORGANIZED CRIME

The difference between street crime and organized crime is sometimes hard to define. Violence and the threat of violence are employed in both, but organized crime may be more readily viewed as a business. Charles Silberman writes that organized crime "has customers rather than victims; it is in the business of supplying goods and services—narcotics, gambling, credit, prostitution, protection against business competitors or trade unions—that people willingly buy despite their illegality."[5] Organized crime enterprises may be among the first businesses formed in immigrant communities, regardless of nationality or point in time.

Chinese youth gangs, the so-called Russian "Mafia," Rastafarian smoke shops—all are part of a historical pattern in immigrant neighborhoods. "Organized crime as we know it in the United States," writes Francis Ianni, "requires an underclass of minority status ethnics to be operative."[6] Organized crime offers one route out of the ghetto.

Organized crime can meet other immigrant needs. Police and prosecutors in Brooklyn, for example, report that a brisk traffic in fraudulent identification papers flourishes in the borough's large Afro-Caribbean community, with its great number of undocumented aliens. Some criminally minded Dominicans have made it easier for immigrants to call friends and relatives at home on illegally manufactured "blue boxes" that duplicate long-distance switching signals while bypassing billing equipment. In some parts of Washington Heights, one police officer said, "there is a blue box for every pay phone around. You pay $10 or $15, and you get to talk to everyone in the home village for as long as you want."

POLICE AND IMMIGRANTS: BREAKING DOWN BARRIERS

Many immigrants retain a suspicion of police carried over from homelands where police were representatives of repressive authority. The Soviet Jewish refugees who have settled in the Brighton Beach neighborhood of Brooklyn are an example. Soviet Jews do not call the police when there is local trouble. "We never get called to fights at any of their social clubs," says Officer Billy Selwyn, a community relations officer assigned to the 60th Precinct in Brighton Beach. "And we still have incidents where people get shot, and when the police arrive, they can't find anyone who will say anything."

The Police Department has made various attempts to break down this reticence. Perhaps the most important was the assignment in 1981 of Officer Stephen Hrehus to a foot patrol beat along Brighton Beach Avenue. Hrehus grew up on the Lower East Side of Manhattan in a home where Russian and Polish were spoken. "For me," Hrehus says, "the language, the jokes, the music are all familiar. It's like going home. The people here don't even think of speaking to me in English any more."

"What do I do all day?" Hrehus asks rhetorically. "Community service. Answer questions. 'How do I get rid of my tenant?' 'How do I get heat in my apartment?' 'Where do I get an abortion?' " It is difficult to measure police-community relations, but Hrehus gives it a try. "When

I came here, on a scale of 1 to 10, I would say it was minus 2. Now it's about plus 6."

The increasing use of patrol cars instead of foot patrols had an unintended effect on police work: it distanced the local cop from the people on his beat. Now police are trying to bridge that distance. Hrehus' approach to policing a new immigrant community is at once old-fashioned and modern.

The department made a similar effort in Chinatown in 1975, after several demonstrations protesting alleged police brutality and indifference. A staff of civilian translators was assigned to a veteran Chinese-American police officer, and they were given an office in a Chinatown precinct house on Elizabeth Street. The "Chinatown Project" is now run by civilians.

Problems faced by another group of Asian immigrants—Korean greengrocers—prompted Deputy Commissioner Holliday set up the New Immigrants Unit in early 1985. The precipitating event was a bitter conflict between Korean merchants owning shops on or near 125th Street in Harlem, and angry black residents of the neighborhood. Black protesters, resentful of the Koreans as nonresident business owners, picketed the stores during 1984 and urged Harlem residents to drive the Koreans out of business with an economic boycott. At least one of these demonstrations turned violent, police say, and a Korean woman had to be hospitalized after she was assaulted in her store.

Neighborhood political leaders, staff of the Mayor's Office, and police community affairs staff urged merchants and boycotters to the negotiating table; and a tentative settlement, which included the merchants' agreement to employ some local teenagers, was reached. The incident demonstrated to the police the need for a unit especially attuned to the city's new immigrant communities.

Det. Philip Serpico, now retired, was project coordinator of the multiethnic New Immigrants Unit in its early stages. "Many of the new immigrants come here with the impression that the police are oppressive," he said, "because of their experience with the police in their homelands." Serpico believed that the unit's primary task was to develop immigrants' trust in the police. He directed community affairs and crime prevention officers throughout the city to establish contact with immigrant community leaders and to recruit new immigrants as auxiliary police.

Sgt. William Spooner has been supervisor of the unit since its inception. He emphasizes the need to bridge the language gap between non-English-speaking New Yorkers and the police. The unit is considering a "911"-type system of emergency phone numbers for foreign-language speakers. It plans to make an instructional videotape, for use in police precincts, to sensitize police officers to cultural "do's and don'ts" in various immigrant communities. Another set of tapes, in various languages, will be made to inform immigrant groups of police services.

The unit is expanding its public school program, in which officers make presentations in ESL classes. The program currently operates in Washington Heights, a heavily Hispanic area, and in multiethnic central Brooklyn.

Immigrant issues have gained new attention at the New York Police Academy, where instructors in 1984 revised and expanded the curriculum on the city's ethnic composition. Course material on the black community now includes West Indian immigrant culture and history. Material on the Hispanic community includes Dominican and Colombian history. There are new course units on Indians, Pakistanis, Russian Jews, Koreans, Greeks, and Filipinos.

Sgt. Pete Pinero summarized the problem that these new materials were designed to address: "Many cadets seem to lack a historical perspective on the founding and development of New York City. They can see why their own [ethnic] group came here, but they don't realize other groups might have come for the same reasons."

THE THREAT OF DEPORTATION

Immigrants' unease about the police has as much to do with the INS as it does with the police themselves. Theoretically speaking, undocumented aliens are subject to deportation at any time, and they try to avoid the attention of the police so as to avoid the attention of the INS. Not all arrests come to INS attention, but aliens don't know that, or don't want to bank on it. They dread the risk of exposure.

Legal aliens also have reason to fear the INS if they get into trouble with the law. A legal alien convicted of a crime of "moral turpitude" can be deported. These crimes are not defined in the law, but they are commonly understood to include murder, assault with a deadly weapon, rape, larceny, burglary, embezzlement, and tax fraud. The law also mandates deportation for crimes connected with drugs, prostitution, and unauthorized possession of a weapon.

The law requires that convicted aliens complete their sentences before deportation proceedings begin. Sometimes a newly released convict finds an INS investigator waiting at the prison gates. The INS is much more likely to devote investigative resources to an alien in prison, who can easily be apprehended, than to a repeat offender who is still at large. It does not have the manpower to deal with every convicted alien, much less every arrested alien or every alien suspected of significant criminal activity. (INS enforcement priorities are discussed in Chapter 15.)

At INS request the Police Department tries to supply it with same-day alien arrest information, but the reporting procedure is not routinely followed, and the INS receives notice of only a fraction of arrests. Because the INS is so short-staffed, it has not asked the Police Department for fuller arrest data.

The Police Department and the INS do not work at cross purposes, but neither do they work fully in concert. They function essentially as independent organizations, each with its own enforcement priorities.

NOTES

1. Robert Ernst, *Immigrant Life in New York City 1825–1863* (New York: Octagon Books, 1949), p. 57.
2. *U.S. News and World Report*, January 16, 1984, p. 27.
3. These data were taken from On-Line Booking System statistics and may differ from official Uniform Crime Report statistics because different hierarchies of charges are used in the two systems when there are multiple charges. Only the highest charge is recorded.
4. "Cuban Refugee Crime Troubles Police Across U.S.," *New York Times*, March 31, 1985, p. 30.
5. Charles Silberman, *Criminal Violence, Criminal Justice* (New York: Random House, 1978), p. 98.
6. Francis Ianni, *Black Mafia* (New York: Simon & Schuster, 1974), p. 326.

15 The Immigration and Naturalization Service

Modern management theory and techniques are trying to make their way into the hard-pressed federal bureaucracy that is the INS. It is a matter of sink or swim. The surge of immigration, both legal and illegal, in the 1970s and early 1980s multiplied the demands on an agency that is consistently overstretched and underfunded. Now, with passage of the Immigration Reform and Control Act of 1986, the demands on the INS are even greater than before. Will the President and the Congress provide financial support for the job they have asked the INS to do? In the answer to that question lies the future of the INS.

The new law asks the INS to run an "amnesty" program that may potentially affect millions of aliens throughout the country; it asks the INS to educate employers to new provisions that make it illegal for employers to hire aliens who lack work authorization; and it asks the INS to enforce a system of penalties against employers who violate the new regulations.

In addition to its new tasks, the INS opens America's door, or closes it, to millions of would-be immigrants, refugees, asylees, tourists, foreign students, and temporary workers each year. Its mandate encompasses service functions—granting authorizations to live, work, or visit in the United States; and enforcement functions—rejecting or ejecting aliens with no legal claim to be here, and prosecuting organized efforts to evade the immigration law.

The INS is part of the nation's chief law enforcement agency, the Department of Justice, where, in attention and budget, it consistently takes a back seat to more prestigious offices such as the Office of the Attorney General, the FBI, and the Drug Enforcement Administration.

When Leonel Castillo, President Carter's appointee as commissioner of the INS, resigned in 1979, his position went unfilled until 1981, largely because no one would accept an appointment to what was seen as a difficult and unrewarding job. Morale and efficiency plummeted during the leaderless period. It may be that the new immigration law offers the INS a new lease on life in that it has drawn national attention, and at least some additional resources, to the agency.

When Alan Nelson became commissioner in 1981, he brought with him the professional management concepts of a large company, Pacific Telephone of California, of which he had been general counsel, and a commitment to complete the computerization that had been planned during Castillo's tenure.

These concepts and commitments translate into policy in the local district offices. Charles Sava, director of the New York district since 1981, has made a personal mission of his INS mandate; he wants to make the New York district office, at 26 Federal Plaza in lower Manhattan, the showplace of the INS. He has his work cut out for him.

THE NEW YORK DISTRICT

The New York district office is the largest and most active of the 38 in the country. It encompasses the city's five boroughs, Long Island, Westchester, and Rockland, Dutchess, Orange, Putnam, Sullivan, and Ulster counties. Even before the amnesty program was created, the district received more than 300,000 applications for immigration benefits annually (22 percent of the national total). (With 790 employees, however, it had less than 7 per cent of the total INS staff of 11,650.) It admitted more than 3 million new aliens annually through John F. Kennedy Airport and the Seaport entry sites, and another 3 million returning residents. It fielded a million inquiries a year. It negotiated with employers who hired undocumented aliens, it raided workplaces when employers refused to cooperate, and it investigated and prosecuted immigration fraud, document counterfeiting, and smuggling of aliens into the United States. It did and does detain presumptively deportable aliens in its detention center at 201 Varick St. in Manhattan, and it arranges voluntary departures and deportations.

Today's game plan is the same in many ways, different in some important ways, and simply *more* in all ways. Three entirely new and separate offices have been established to run the amnesty program, with their own staffs and operating procedures. The employer compliance program has grown more complex and more persuasive now that the INS comes armed with penalties against employers who hire unauthorized aliens. The rest of the tasks continue without abatement.

It is enforcement functions that the public most often associates with the INS. The sight of INS agents racing through restaurant kitchens to apprehend unauthorized aliens has been a familiar television image. INS service functions have been less well publicized.

THE SERVICE FUNCTIONS

In INS terminology, to provide service is to admit visa-holding aliens to the United States, and to act on applications from aliens and citizens already in the country for a wide variety of status changes and permissions. The State Department, through its consulates overseas, is responsible for issuing visas to foreign citizens who want to enter the United States as residents, temporary workers, students, or visitors. Once entry is granted, the INS is responsible for all subsequent actions. Not all of the agency's clients are foreign citizens; many are U.S. citizens seeking actions on behalf of relatives or prospective employees.

A request for INS service might come from a Chinese immigrant who wants to become an American citizen, a Colombian national who has married an American citizen and wants to become a permanent resident alien, an American citizen who wants to petition for the admission of a sister in Italy, an American businessman who wants to employ a Japanese efficiency expert, an Afghan dissident who is seeking asylum, or an American couple who want to adopt an Amerasian orphan. Other requests come from tourists who want to extend their stay, foreign students who want work permits, visiting artists seeking permission to perform, and aliens seeking replacement of lost immigration documents.

In a sample month—July 1985—the New York district office received about 31,000 applications, of which about 8,300 were petitions for the admission of close relatives, 7,400 were applications for naturalization, 3,600 for extensions of temporary stay, 3,500 for replacement of missing alien registration cards, 2,000 for reentry permits that would allow permanent resident aliens to return to the United States after traveling abroad, 2,000 for adjustment of status to permanent resident alien, 1,400 requests for temporary workers and intracompany transfers from abroad, and the rest an assortment of similar requests.

The INS is infamous for its delays in service. In the recent past it has taken months, even years, for action on some kinds of applications. Throughout the country the agency is eliminating some delays through a combination of strategies. It sends relatively routine applications and petitions that do not require personal interviews to high-volume remote adjudicating centers. (New York applications go to St. Albans, Vermont.) Those applications may consequently take longer to process, but "remoting" them frees INS examiners to deal with higher-priority applications, especially those for permanent residence and citizenship—the procedures with meaning for the greatest number of aliens who wish to become permanent members of American society.

Adjudications and naturalizations are among the responsibilities of the Examinations Branch. In New York, Examinations was reorganized in 1984 to improve its service output. Supervisory positions were added, and half the work force was reassigned in order to generate interest in the task at hand: eliminating the backlog in permanent residence and naturalization applications.

Naturalization is a two-step process and therefore is doubly subject to delay. First, the applicant waits for a date on which he or she will be tested for knowledge of the English language and American civics, and screened for other citizenship prerequisites, such as five years' residence in the United States (three years for spouses of citizens) and "good moral character." If an applicant passes these tests, he or she must wait for completion of the naturalization proceedings and for the ceremony itself. The ceremony is conducted by a U.S. district court judge or, in some locations, a state court judge.

In 1986 the district's goals for naturalization were to schedule the screening interview within four months of application, and to complete the naturalization proceedings within four months of the interview. In late 1986 the interview goal was being met in 75 percent of cases, and the goal for completion was generally being met in the Manhattan office but not in Brooklyn. (The INS runs an office in Brooklyn for naturalizations only, since two-thirds of the district's naturalization work comes from Brooklyn, Queens, and Long Island.) At the Brooklyn office, approved applicants often waited eight months for completion of the proceedings. The delays were due in part to backlogs of higher-priority cases on the court calendars. One solution under discussion was to make naturalization an administrative rather than a judicial proceeding, so that applicants would not have to wait until a judge had time to conduct the naturalization ceremony.

The district's goal for permanent residence applications was to schedule all interviews within 65 days of application, to decide as many cases as possible on the day of interview, and to complete all pending actions within an additional 30 days. In late 1986 the interview goal was being met in all cases. Half the applicants received decisions on the interview date. The rest waited for varying periods, depending upon the reason for the delay. Ultimately two-thirds of permanent residence applications were approved.

CAUSES AND CONSEQUENCES OF DELAY

Some delays result from the monumental task of maintaining 2.3 million active case files. There are 3,000 actions in and out of the file room each day. A million and a half more files, presumed inactive but not always so, are stored in a depot in Bayonne, New Jersey. It can be time-consuming to locate and retrieve a file, whether it is in Manhattan or Bayonne.

File delays should be solved in large part by computerization. The INS has committed itself to computerizing throughout the country by 1988. A central index will carry basic data on each applicant, with reference to computer subsystems where information on case status is available; and a file-tracking system will make it possible to locate a file electronically rather than manually. By the fall of 1985, all files had been bar-coded, and by 1986 the tracking system hardware had been installed. The central index and its subsystems were scheduled for gradual installation over the next two years.

Other delays result from the necessity to investigate applications that are incomplete or possibly fraudulent. A consulate abroad may have to be contacted for the evidence that led to its granting a visa. A marriage may have to be investigated to determine if it was merely a business arrangement to qualify an alien for permanent resident status.

Nationwide, and in New York in particular, INS officials have been concerned about the high incidence of "marriages of convenience." New York's marriage fraud rate is said to be 34 per cent, compared to 7 or 8 percent nationwide. Most unsuccessful permanent residence applications in New York are denied because of marriage fraud. To cut down on the problem, Congress passed and the President signed a new law giving only "conditional" status to any spouse or spouse's child who becomes a permanent resident through marriage to a U.S. citizen or permanent resident alien. The condition will be removed two years afterwards if the couple can demonstrate that the marriage still stands and is genuine.

Delays are a boon to some applicants and a serious inconvenience to others. For undocumented aliens with weak claims for permanent residence, delays buy more time in the United States, time during which they may be able to strengthen their cases by developing new qualifications. An alien may marry a U.S. citizen. A relative may become a permanent resident and petition for the applicant's legal admission. Or a visa application made long ago at home may finally be approved.

Aliens and their lawyers are not always blameless for delays. Lawyers may prolong a case by inundating the INS with paperwork or by continually asking for extensions at hearings. Or they may file frivolous asylum applications for their clients, knowing that even a frivolous case must have its day in court.

Delays also bring problems for applicants. While an application is under adjudication, it is inadvisable for an alien to move to another state, since transferring a case to another district will only bring further delays. Changing jobs may be impossible if an application is based on a specific job. Traveling outside the country, even to deal with family emergencies, requires extra paperwork to assure readmittance. Applicants in need of public assistance or health care may have difficulty getting it, and they may jeopardize their applications if they do.

Delays encourage violations of the law. For example, permanent resident aliens are required to carry their alien registration cards at all times. Because it can take seven months to obtain a duplicate if the original is lost or stolen, aliens often leave their cards at home. If the INS raids an alien's work place, and the alien is not carrying the card, he or she may be arrested for not having proof of status.

In New York the sheer volume of cases impedes INS efforts to reduce delays. In 1983 the agency adopted a nationwide procedure called "one-step," in which permanent residence interviews were held on the day of application. In New York one-step had to be abandoned because aliens camped outside the building at night in order to ensure inclusion in the next day's one-step quota.

New York district INS officials are determined not to let their new responsibilities impede their efforts to run their regular operations on schedule. Separating the amnesty program from the daily operations should help toward that end, but it seems unlikely that additional delays can be prevented entirely.

ENFORCEMENT FUNCTIONS

The New York district's enforcement activities differ in some respects from those of the much-publicized Border Patrol, the main task of which is to prevent aliens from making unauthorized entry at the Mexican and Canadian borders.

Preventing illegal entries is one of the functions of the New York district office—the Inspections Unit, a part of the Examinations Branch, monitors all alien entries at Kennedy Airport and the Seaport—but it is not the district's only or main enforcement function. Most of the New York district's aliens enter legally. Some later become "illegal" when their tourist or student visas expire.

There are so many undocumented aliens that it would be impossible for the INS to find and apprehend them all. The agency's current management strategy is to concentrate on a specific set of enforcement issues:

- *Employer compliance.* Until passage of the Simpson-Rodino Act, it was illegal for unauthorized aliens to work, but it was not illegal for employers to hire them. The INS had no weapons to use against employers of unauthorized aliens, other than raids and detention of their employees. In general, the INS attempted to achieve employers' voluntary compliance and so to reduce unauthorized work.

The new law provides the INS with weapons in the form of fines and even imprisonment for employers who persist in employing aliens who lack work authorization. Still, the numbers of employers and employees are so large that the INS cannot and does not expect to prosecute every case. Again, the INS intends to rely on employer compliance, and it views its main role as educating employers about the new law and its requirements, and assisting them in finding substitutes for workers whom they may have to let go. These educational efforts will be punctuated by some prosecutions, of course, as the earlier compliance program was punctuated by raids.

- *Immigration fraud.* The INS investigates aliens and their collaborators who attempt to obtain immigration benefits through fraud—for example, arranging a marriage of convenience in order to obtain permanent resident status. The agency is particularly interested in those cases where third parties such as lawyers or government officials are implicated.
- *Entitlement fraud.* It has been one of the Reagan administration's priorities to identify and prosecute aliens who obtain public benefits by making false representations of their immigration status. Investigations of entitlement fraud are initiated by other government agencies that submit questionable applicants' names to the INS for verification of status. The New York district reports that in fiscal 1985 (October 1984–September 1985) it saved $4.3 million in public benefits that ineligible aliens would have received had the INS not ascertained that their claims were illegitimate.
- *Counterfeiting and selling immigration documents.*
- *Smuggling unauthorized aliens into the United States.* The New York district concentrates on alien-smuggling activities at Kennedy Airport, but it also cooperates in investigations that originate in districts on the Canadian and Mexican borders when smugglers have "drop" sites in the New York area. Smuggling at the airport can take the form of providing an alien with counterfeit documents, bribing an airline security guard to release detained aliens whose papers are not in order, or providing an alien with a disguise to help him or her evade airport authorities.

It makes good management sense for the INS to pick its shots carefully. The immigration system cannot handle more cases. The 225-bed detention center is almost always filled. More than 500 cases are assigned to each of 16 trial attorneys. The immigration courts, with eight judges and a law clerk, are stretched to capacity.

No one denies that the INS is overstretched, but some do argue its enforcement priorities. In July 1985 Sen. Alfonse D'Amato (R.-N.Y.) asked the GAO to conduct a study of INS enforcement activities against aliens who might be deportable on the basis of convictions for street crimes (as opposed to fraudulent immigration schemes) and had not yet been imprisoned. The GAO found that only about 16 percent of INS investigative time was spent on criminal aliens, and about three-quarters of that time was spent on aliens who were already in prison.[1] In comparison, 49 percent of time was spent on fraudulent immigration schemes and 30 percent on employer compliance.

Subsequently, the New York district INS joined state and city correctional officials in pilot projects to deport aliens convicted of drug-related felonies. The state pilot began in 1986 and the city pilot in 1987.

When INS agents conduct a raid, they usually cannot detain more than 25 people because of overcrowding in the detention center. They usually detain those with least "equity" (the fewest ties), who are the greatest absconsion risks. The rest are given summonses to appear at immigration hearings. Absconsions are common, however, even among those who are viewed as most likely to appear. If all aliens receiving summonses did appear, it would be difficult to fit them into the hearings schedule.

Many hearings are eliminated by offering aliens the option of making a voluntary departure from the country, by which they forgo a hearing, pay their own way home, and avoid deportation. Choosing voluntary departure often works to an alien's advantage. He or she is immediately eligible to apply for a new visa, whereas a deportee must wait one year or five, depending on the technicalities of the case.

Voluntary departure is offered not just in unauthorized employment cases but in many others, and it is used extensively. In fiscal 1985, 800 aliens were deported from the New York district, and about 12,000 left the country under voluntary departure.

The overcrowding problems in the detention center and in the immigration courts have grown increasingly severe in recent years as aliens and their advocates have gained sophistication in their rights and opportunities for redress under immigration law. Today's cases often require longer investigations and litigation. The average length of stay at the detention center has doubled, from 10 days to 20; although the large majority of detainees are released in less than a month, an increasingly large proportion remain longer, some as long as a year and a half or two years.

The most difficult and time-consuming cases on the INS litigation schedule involve aliens who are seeking political asylum. Asylum cases and their appeals can stretch out for years. The policies and procedures behind today's asylum actions are the focus of bitter controversy. The INS and the State Department hold that most of today's asylum seekers are fleeing depressed economic conditions, not threats of persecution. Critics of the system contend that asylum decisions are more likely to be based on foreign policy and immigration policy goals than on legally specified or humanitarian considerations. Like refugee status, asylum tends to be granted to persons in flight from governments with which the United States is not friendly. It is much easier for eastern Europeans, for example, to obtain asylum than it is for Haitians or Salvadorans.

Critics also contend that the INS improperly fails to distinguish between asylum seekers and other undocumented aliens whose need for sanctuary is less desperate. Asylum seekers, they say, are prosecuted with excessive vigor in order to discourage other unauthorized migrants.

The strength of feeling aroused by the asylum debate further strains the tense working relationship between immigrant advocates and the INS. As a solution some observers suggest the formal involvement of the U.N. high commissioner for refugees, or establishment of an asylum adjudications board that would be independent of the INS.

In 1985 Afghans were the largest group of asylum seekers attempting to enter the country at New York, and they made up the largest nationality group at the Varick St. detention center, where about 30 to 35 were detained at any given time. Afghans were particularly easy for the INS to apprehend because they arrived at the airport without valid passports or visas. Because they were apprehended before official "entry" into the United States, they did not acquire the legal rights of aliens who manage to reach the interior, and they were subject to detention without the possibility of bail.

Afghan political asylum seekers and their advocates made concerted efforts to influence the INS policies and procedures that were resulting in detention and deportation. Afghans at Varick St. undertook two hunger strikes in 1985 to protest what they viewed as unjust incarceration and violations of their human rights. The strikers eventually resumed eating, and no serious health problems developed. As a result of the pressure applied both politically and legally by the Afghans and their attorneys, federal authorities paroled 33 Afghans in January 1986; that is, the government released them from detention and agreed not to deport them unless conditions improved in their homeland. The action covered only the 33 Afghans in detention at that moment, and more recent Afghan arrivals have been detained, as they continue to be in other parts of the country. Federal policy on Afghan asylum seekers continues to be widely debated and widely unresolved.

Excluding the asylum seekers, the detention center population tends to be made up largely of aliens with criminal records who are fighting deportation proceedings, according to INS officials. On a sample day in June 1986, the largest number—69 out of 215—were Mariel Cubans, most of them recently released from New York State prisons, where they had served sentences for crimes committed after their arrival in the United States. Their convictions exposed them to deportation proceedings, and they were picked up by INS agents on their prison release dates. Before 1985 such Marielito convicts had been held in an INS detention center near Atlanta, but when the Atlanta center became filled to capacity, New York's Marielitos remained in custody in New York.

After the Mariel Cubans, the largest numbers in the detention center on the sample day were Dominicans (21), Jamaicans (18), and Colombians (16). Mexicans, Trinidadians, Afghans, Nigerians, Iranians, and Haitians were between nine and five in number, in descending order. Numbers smaller than five made up the balance.

Security is a constant problem at Varick St., a facility that was not intended to house a criminal population, nor to house detainees for long periods of time. The General Accounting Office reports that there were 15 escapes from the facility or from escorted detail between April 1984 and August 1986, and an additional 15 attempted or suspected escapes.[2] Several riots and near-riots required the INS to mobilize additional personnel to supplement the guard force.

The trial attorneys who prosecute cases and the immigration court judges who hear them are one and two steps removed, respectively, from the district office operations. The trial attorneys report not to the district director but to the regional counsel in Burlington, Vermont. The largest part of their work time, perhaps 70 percent, is spent in prosecuting exclusion and deportation cases, some of them political asylum seekers but many others involving immigration fraud or criminal records. The trial attorneys also undertake actions to rescind permanent resident status, and to deny or rescind naturalizations. Again, the cases most often are based on immigration fraud or criminal records. Finally, the trial attorneys respond to appeals from unsuccessful applicants for immigration benefits. The majority of the appellants are persons in the United States who have petitioned unsuccessfully for the admission of relatives abroad.

Immigration judges were INS employees until 1982, when Congress gave them independent status within the Department of Justice in order to separate the judicial from the prosecutorial functions. The judges still have strong ties to the INS—seven out of eight came up through INS ranks—but the newest judge, appointed in 1984, was formerly with the Legal Aid Society.

SERVICE VS. ENFORCEMENT

In theory, service and enforcement are complementary functions, not competing ones; control of immigration law violations can be viewed as a protection for the legal immigration system. INS officials do not see service and enforcement as separate. They view enforcement as granting immigration benefits to those who are entitled under the law, and denying benefits to those whom the law excludes.

Still, many observers feel that the INS has difficulty striking a balance between service and enforcement, in part because the enforcement mandate often appears to be stronger, and in part because the agency is too poorly funded to do either job well.

Figure 15.1
INS New York District, 1985 Organization Chart

(Staff: 766*)

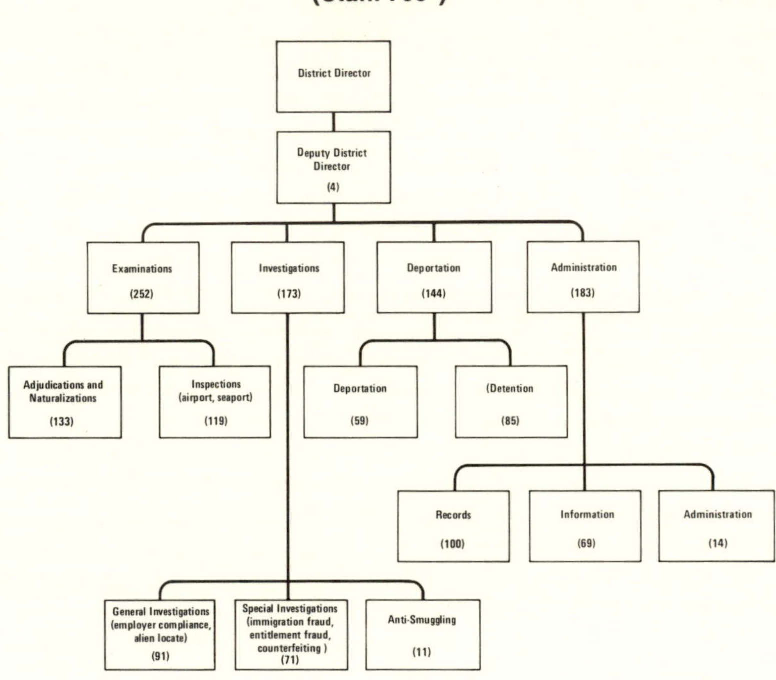

**The figures in parentheses represent approved staff lines. The total shown here does not include the Trial Attorneys staff of 24 which reports not to the New York district director but to the regional counsel in Vermont.*

The agency's location within the Department of Justice shows that enforcement, in the narrower sense, is its primary mandate. Staff deployment patterns suggest the same thing (see Figure 15.1). In 1985 twice as many staff members were assigned to enforcement functions as to service functions (assuming that Adjudications and Naturalizations is a service function, and that Inspections is half service and half enforcement).

The INS was not always part of the Justice Department. When it was created in 1891, it was part of the Treasury Department. In 1903 it went to Commerce and Labor, where it remained until its transfer to Justice in 1940. For the first half of its history, it was part of U.S. economic policy, not enforcement policy. There is an implicit message now that it is more important to apprehend immigration law violators than to incorporate law-abiding aliens into the U.S. economy.

The agency's ability to provide service is sometimes compromised by its coexistent enforcement mandate. Aliens whose applications for change of status are denied may subsequently be viewed as violators of the law; if so, Adjudications officers are supposed to report them to Investigations officers. The risk discourages some aliens from trying to change or legalize their status. Some immigration lawyers conjecture that substantial numbers of the city's undocumented aliens might have successfully applied for legal status even under the old immigration law but remained in illegal status because of misinformation, ignorance, or fear of the INS.

Government officials and immigration advocates generally agreed that the amnesty program could not be effective if amnesty applicants were subject to possible deportation. Consequently, the Simpson-Rodino Act was written to bar the use of application information for enforcement purposes. Furthermore, the INS has set up legalization offices that are separate from its daily operations; and non-governmental agencies are being used to screen prospective applicants so the most obviously unqualified are not made known to any part of the INS.

Many observers believe that underfunding impedes the agency's performance in all areas. They say the INS lacks the money to hire enough staff, attract good staff, and install its computers without drawing money away from other parts of the operation. New York's district director, Charles Sava, does not agree that underfunding can be blamed for INS management problems, at least not exclusively. He contends that more can be done with the resources that are available, and that is what he has attempted to demonstrate in New York by specifying management objectives and reorganizing staff.

WORKING LIFE AT 26 FEDERAL PLAZA

The problems at the INS create anger and frustration for staff and clients alike. Each "side" lacks sympathy for the other. Aliens and their advocates have little appreciation for the agency's problems—the enormous work loads, complex and inconsistent immigration laws, and the difficulty of working with application materials that are often incomplete, illegible, or fraudulent. Agency staff are numbed to the obstacles encountered by their clients—the impediments to getting information (a phone call to the information line can go unanswered for days, and information on the status of applications is rarely made available), the long delays, and the unpredictability of outcomes. Staff and clients literally do not talk the same language; interpreters are scarce.

The INS occupies parts of 12 floors at 26 Federal Plaza. Every morning a long line forms in the lobby as applicants wait to receive an appointment number, instructions or a form. By early afternoon all appointment slots are filled, and a sign tells that day's unlucky appointment seekers to come back tomorrow. Instructions and forms are available all day, but they do not generate the lines.

On other floors, petitioners sit quietly and anxiously in waiting rooms, or they huddle with their attorneys in the hallways, anticipating the decisions that will change their lives.

Because of the complexities of today's immigration law, and the difficulties in obtaining information from the INS, a legal service network has grown up to represent aliens in their immigration cases. Private lawyers, nonprofit agencies, congressional aides, and self-taught community members are the mainstays of the network. Their work was discussed in Chapter 8.

WHAT THE INS DOES AND DOES NOT KNOW ABOUT IMMIGRATION

In the late 1970s the INS asked the Committee on National Statistics of the National Research Council to assess the need for a review of federal immigration statistics. The committee found that such a review was needed, and in 1982 the Research Council began work on an evaluation of the adequacy of the nation's immigration statistics.

In 1985 the council released its report. It found that the nation's immigration policy was being made almost entirely without benefit of the kinds of information and analysis that were needed. The report said:

> It is not just a question of timeliness or quality, issues that may be resolved by the INS's enthusiastic pursuit of electronic sophistication, but also a conceptual failure to understand what data are for, and what data can do for the Service and the nation. The INS and other government agencies produce masses of data, if not always timely and not always accurate, about immigrants, refugees, and the foreign-born, but the data are not what we need to answer the fundamental policy issues of the day.[3]

Policy makers may need answers to such questions as the following: How many Iranian students are in the United States? Do aliens pay more in taxes and Social Security contributions than they use in social services? How many tourists and foreign students enter the country each year, and how many leave? How do the foreign-born fit into the American job market? The INS could never answer all these questions alone, but it could answer some of them; and it could provide data that would add immeasurably to the likelihood that someone else could answer the others.

The INS Washington office is responsible for aggregation and dissemination of immigration data. It attempts to produce an annual report and a statistical yearbook each year, but it is several years behind its publication schedule. The 1983 statistical yearbook was published in 1985.

The data in the yearbook were in some instances tantalizingly incomplete. It was possible, for example, to determine the number of Jamaican immigrants who planned to make their home in New York State in 1983, but not the number of Dominican immigrants—this in spite of the fact that Dominicans were probably the largest group to enter New York in 1983, if trends discerned in the 1980 census continued.

The National Research Council report specified that the INS alone could not provide adequate immigration statistics for policy making. Other federal, state, and local agencies would have to participate in a coordinated effort. In addition, the council proposed that the INS track a sample of immigrants for five years after entry to record the process of social and economic integration. The authors summed up thus:

> Immigration is an important and emotional area of public policy, yet as we have seen in this report the statistics on which informed debate and policy formation are based are woefully inadequate. Two of the major reasons for this inadequacy have been a lack of interest in or commitment to the production of relevant, high-quality statistics by the agencies having contact with aliens, and the failure of any one agency to take the lead in fostering a governmentwide coordinated system for collecting, processing, and analyzing the necessary data. This leadership role belongs by right to the INS as the agency primarily concerned with immigration policy and progress.[4]

The INS was sufficiently interested in the study's findings to hire one of its three editors, Robert Warren, as acting chief of statistical analysis in the Washington, D.C. office. Warren had been a Census Bureau demographer.

The amnesty program provides yet one more opportunity for useful data collection and analysis. If it eliminates applicants' names to protect their confidentiality, the INS can produce a data base for its own use and for the use of outside agencies. Data collected at amnesty intake will probably tell us more about undocumented aliens in the United States than we have been able to learn from all other sources put together. It is too good an opportunity to waste.

NOTES

1. *Criminal Aliens: INS' Investigative Efforts in the New York City Area*, GAO/GGD–86–58BR (Washington, D.C.: U.S. General Accounting Office,), p. 3.
2. *Criminal Aliens: INS' Detention and Deportation Activities in the New York City*

Area (GAO/GGD–87–19BR), Washington, D.C.: U.S. General Accounting Office, December 1986, pp. 1–2.

3. Daniel B. Levine, Kenneth Hill, and Robert Warren, eds., *Immigration Statistics: A Story of Neglect* (Washington, D.C.: National Academy Press, 1985), p. 2.

4. Ibid., p. 141.

PART IV

For the Record

16 Costs and Revenues

A study of New York's immigrants would be incomplete without an exploration of their fiscal impact on the city. Fiscal impact is a complex phenomenon that defies precise measurement. It is difficult to identify or establish measures for all the ways in which immigrants represent a cost in city services or a contribution in city revenues, and it is even more difficult to obtain hard data on costs and contributions.

City Planning analysts selected several significant measures that generally are chosen by economists who analyze fiscal impact. On the cost side City Planning looked at the three predominant social service areas: education, health care, and public assistance. On the revenue side they looked at city income tax and city sales tax.

No attempt was made to "balance" these costs and revenues, since there can be no true balance at the city level. Immigrants, like most other U.S. residents, pay most of their taxes to the federal government, but their social service costs are borne, in New York State, largely by the state and local governments. In this analysis of New York City, immigrants' costs and contributions were evaluated separately. Their share of the city's total tax revenues and social service costs was measured against their share of the city's households, which was 28 percent. On the whole, immigrants appeared to make slightly less than proportionate use of social services, and to contribute slightly less than their proportionate share of city sales and income taxes.

The slightly below-average tax contribution was largely a function of immigrants' lower-than-average incomes and of New York's progressive income tax structure. Although their tax share was not strictly proportionate, it was their "fair share" under the tax laws.

From this analysis there appeared to be no evidence that immigrants pose an overall fiscal problem to New York City. This finding will be discussed after a review of studies made in other jurisdictions.

REVIEW OF OTHER STUDIES

Few efforts have been made to measure immigrants' fiscal impact in the United States. Four studies are often cited in this context: Julian L. Simon's federal-level study of immigrants' social service costs and tax contributions[1]; Sidney Weintraub and Gilberto Cardenas' study of undocumented aliens in the state of Texas[2]; Thomas Muller and Thomas J. Espenshade's study of Mexican aliens, both legal and undocumented, in the state of California[3]; and David North's federal-level comparison of costs and revenues generated by the main subsets of the alien population—permanent resident aliens, refugees, and undocumented aliens.[4]

Most of these researchers constructed balance sheets comparing immigrants' costs in public services with their tax contributions. They all commented on the paucity of data on immigrants in general and on undocumented aliens in particular, leading to conclusions that would have to be considered speculative. The estimates of taxes paid were generally based on income data. Which taxes were analyzed depended on the level of analysis, federal, state, or local. In assessing costs all four studies focused on public assistance, health care, and education.

The researchers reached different conclusions about immigrants' cost/revenue ratio depending on which immigrants they were studying and at what jurisdictional level. They all agreed, however, that immigrants made their heaviest demand on the educational system, because they tend to arrive during their childbearing years.

Studying immigrants at the national level, Julian Simon concluded that immigrant families paid an average of $1,400 more in taxes and Social Security contributions than they used in social services each year. The main reason for the positive ratio was immigrants' lower-than-average use of Social Security and Medicare benefits, owing to their relative youth.

Simon found that immigrants' income, and therefore taxes paid, reached native levels within five years of entry. Despite high education costs, recently arrived immigrants made less use of social services than the native-born, reaching parity with natives after an average of 16 years.

Simon used income and public service utilization data obtained from a 1976 U.S. Census Bureau survey of 156,000 households, of which 15,000 were headed by immigrants. Although the study was intended to include both legal and undocumented immigrants, Simon conceded that undocumented aliens probably were underrepresented in the sample.

Weintraub and Cardenas analyzed the impact of undocumented aliens at the state and local levels in Texas. They found a positive fiscal impact at the state level and a negative impact at the local level. They attributed the difference to the fact that most services used by undocumented aliens were funded at the local level, but most taxes went to the state, either directly or in the form of federal taxes returned in grants. The costs they measured were in health care, public assistance, education, and criminal justice. They calculated income, sales, and excise taxes.

Weintraub and Cardenas noted that property taxes, a major source of revenue for local governments, were excluded from their analysis because they could not find a reliable method for estimating undocumented aliens' property tax contributions. They noted many other possibilities for error, based largely on the inadequacy of their data sources. Their data were obtained primarily from interviews with service agency staff, agency studies, and interviews with 868 undocumented aliens. Among other problems, they doubted the representativeness of their alien sample because half had been identified by agencies.

As part of a study of Mexican immigrants in California, Thomas Muller and Thomas J. Espenshade developed a cost/revenue balance sheet showing that Mexican immigrants' costs were greater than their contributions at both the state and local levels. The balance was least favorable at the state level, largely because the California state government bears 80 percent of the cost of education, compared, for example, with 49 percent in Texas. Mexican immigrants' large family size, and the cost of education, could not be offset by the taxes they paid, in part because of California's progressive tax structure, which requires less tax from low-income families.

Muller and Espenshade's study focused on recent Mexican immigration to California, including both documented and undocumented aliens. Since they relied primarily on census data for their fiscal analysis, the preponderance of their sample was probably documented aliens. They found that governmental outlays for education and health care were above-average for Mexican families, but the outlay for public assistance programs was below-average.

Over and above the fiscal analysis, Muller and Espenshade looked at Mexican immigrants' larger impact on the state and local economies, using such measures as wage and income levels, creation or elimination of jobs, and unemployment trends. They concluded that Mexicans had a positive effect on the local economy (of Los Angeles, the primary study area) but mixed effects on the state level.

David North compared the cost/revenue ratios of native-borns and the three main alien subgroups: permanent resident aliens, refugees, and undocumented aliens. He found that undocumented aliens had a more favorable cost/revenue ratio than average; permanent resident aliens, an average ratio; and refugees, a less-favorable-than-average ratio. North commented that his data were most complete for refugees, "skimpy" for permanent resident aliens, and least complete for undocumented aliens.

THE NEW YORK CITY ANALYSIS

As indicated earlier, this analysis of New York City's immigrant revenues dealt only with city taxes, although immigrants pay taxes to the state and federal governments, some of which return to the city in grants of various kinds.

The city tax analysis was limited to income and sales taxes, which in 1980 accounted for about 30 percent of the city's tax revenues. These were the only taxes for which it was possible to make estimates based on the national origin of the taxpayer; the 1980 census gave income and household information from which it was possible to construct tax returns for immigrant-headed and native-headed households. There was no comparable way to obtain information on business and property taxes paid by the foreign-born.

This analysis addressed the same social service areas as most of the studies cited earlier: education, health care, and public assistance. Education was divided into public schools and higher education; health care, into Medicaid and municipal hospital services. The costs computed were only those paid by the city; state and federal shares of service budgets were not included. In 1984 these services cost the city about $4.45 billion, according to the New York City Office of Management and Budget (OMB), about 37.7 percent of city tax levy funds for that year.

Time is a factor in analyzing immigrant costs and contributions, as Julian Simon showed in his study. Immigrants' service use, and their fiscal contributions, change over time. These differences are significant because New York City's immigrant population consists largely of two age clusters:

- Elderly immigrants, many of whom arrived in the United States before the restrictive immigration laws of the 1920s were enacted.
- The new wave of younger immigrants, who arrived in the United States after the immigration law liberalization of 1965, many of whom are in their prime working and childbearing years.

Each of these groups is a high user of some services and a low user of others. It is possible to calculate "average" immigrant service use, but the average is an artifact, skewed by the large remnant of the century's early immigrants. In 1980, 23 percent of census-recorded immigrants were elderly, compared with 10.4 percent of the native-born population.

The scarcity of hard data was as much a problem in estimating immigrant costs as it was in estimating revenues. In most cases, service agencies do not collect information on their clients' country of birth, or they do not record it in easily retrievable fashion. The main source of data for the cost analysis, as for the tax analysis, was the 1980 census, which provided direct information on immigrants' public assistance and public school use. Information on health care did not appear in the census; other, indirect, sources were used, so the health care estimates have much less certainty.

In comparisons of the immigrant and native populations, the units of measure were immigrant-headed and native-headed households—households whose self-identified heads were foreign- or native-born. Not all members of foreign-headed households are foreign-born, as has been shown before, but their costs are counted as "immigrant" costs because they are members of immigrant-headed households. This becomes especially significant in public education, where more than half the "immigrant" cost is for native-born children living in immigrant-headed households.

Household heads were considered to be immigrants if they were born outside the United States, regardless of whether they were naturalized citizens, permanent resident aliens, undocumented aliens, or any other immigrant classification.

TAX CONTRIBUTIONS

Immigrant-headed households accounted for 28 percent of the city's households in 1980. These households contributed about 24 percent of the city's income taxes in 1979 (the year for which income information was sought on the 1980 census questionnaire) and about 27 percent of the city's sales taxes (see Table 16.1).

In 1979 average immigrant-headed household income was $12,783, compared with $14,325 for native-headed households. Newer arrivals (1975–80) accounted for 47 percent of the immigrant households' city income tax liability, although they made up only 44 percent of the immigrant household population. That finding was somewhat surprising because immigrants' income and tax payments tend to increase over time as the newcomers work their way up the job ladder. The data show that the pre–1965 arrivals did have more taxpayers in the middle and upper tax brackets, but they also had more people with low tax liability because of the nature of their incomes—for instance, Social Security and

Table 16.1

Estimated New York City Income and Sales Tax Payments, 1979

	Total Households		Native-Headed Households		Immigrant-Headed Households	
	Number	Percent	Number	Percent	Number	Percent
Households	2,792,420	100.0	2,011,420	72.0	781,000	28.0
Aggregate taxable income of persons 16+ (million $)	$32,143.7	100.0	$23,975.2	74.6	$8,168.5	25.4
Aggregate income tax payments (million $)	$685.9	100.0	$520.6	75.9	$165.3	24.1
Aggregate sales tax payments (million $)	$511.8	100.0	$372.7	72.8	$139.1	27.2

Sources: 1980 U.S. Census Public Use Microdata File;
1979 New York State Department of Taxation and Finance Personal Income Analysis.

pensions. The older group, then, was a mix of low-tax payers in retirement and active workers with above-average incomes.

REVENUE METHODOLOGY

The method used to estimate city income and sales taxes was like the preparation of an individual tax return. In effect, tax estimates were prepared for every household in the 1980 census microdata sample, using average exemptions, deductions, and nontaxable income for each income level as reported by the New York State Department of Taxation and Finance in its 1979 Personal Income Analysis.

This method produced an estimate that was remarkably close to the actual sum of city income taxes paid in 1979; the estimate was only 5 percent below the actual sum collected. The close correspondence suggests that the method was valid. The city sales tax was computed on the basis of total household income, using the 1979 IRS optional sales tax table for New York City. The estimate may be low because it did not include major purchases like cars, for which the IRS permits an additional sales tax deduction to be made. There was no way to estimate these purchases by the nativity of the taxpayer.

If it had been possible to factor in major purchases, the estimate derived by City Planning as the total sales tax paid by all New York City households in 1979 ($512 million) would have come closer to the $585 million estimate made by the city's OMB for the period March 1979–February 1980. A total of $1.016 billion in city sales taxes was collected during that period, of which OMB estimated that 57.6 percent ($585 million) was collected from resident consumers, and the rest from businesses and visitors.

ESTIMATING COSTS

This analysis focused on New York City's five largest social service programs. In descending order of cost to the city (for services to the entire city population, immigrants and natives combined), the five programs were public education, Medicaid, municipal hospital services, public assistance, and higher education (see Figure 16.1). The immigrant population appeared to use the following:

- A little less than its 28 percent proportionate share of public education among the immigrant population as a whole, but post–1965 arrivals used more than their share
- Much less than its share of public assistance
- Much more than its share of higher education
- A little more than its share of Medicaid and municipal hospital services.

Figure 16.1
Use of Selected New York City Social Programs by Foreign- and Native-Headed Households, Fiscal 1984

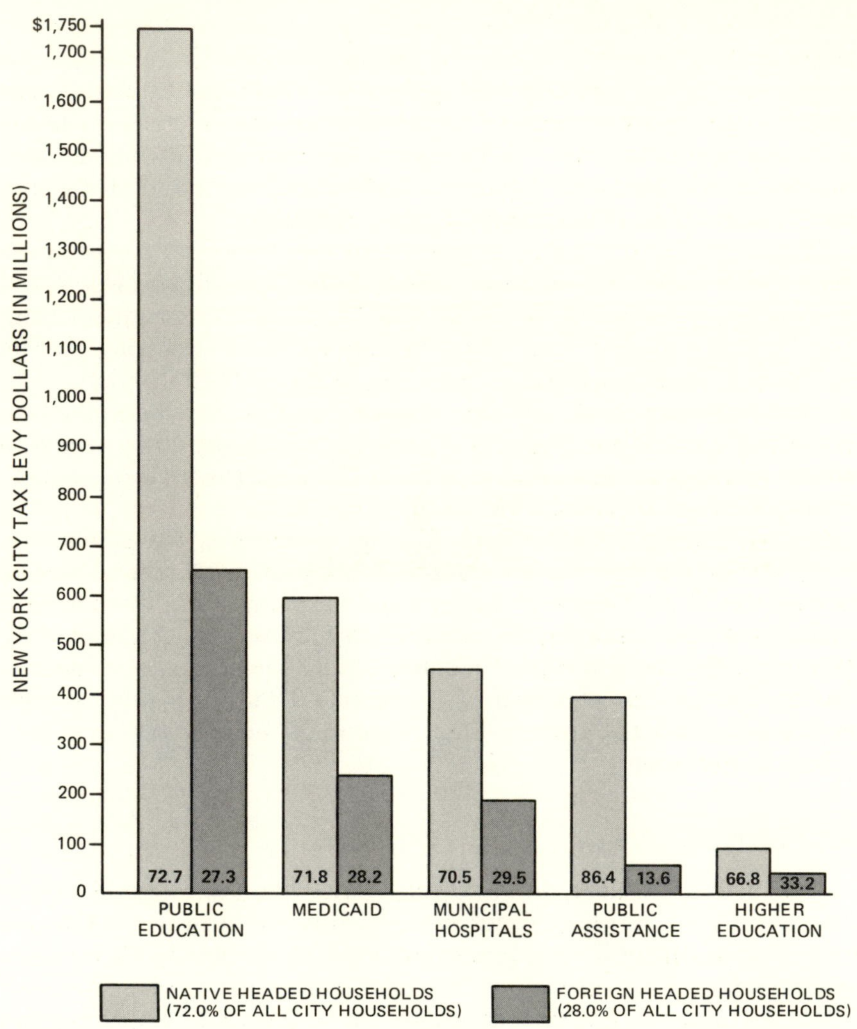

Public Assistance

In 1979 immigrant heads of household received much less than their proportionate share of the public assistance income reported by New York City heads of household in the 1980 U.S. census. Although immigrants were 28 percent of the city's heads of household, they received 13.6 percent of public assistance income.

This analysis excluded heads of household age 65 and over because most income assistance recipients in that age group were enrolled in the Supplemental Security Income (SSI) program, which is funded entirely by the federal government. By restricting the analysis to heads of household between the ages of 15 and 64, it was possible to concentrate on public assistance programs to which New York City makes dollar contributions, such as AFDC, to which the city contributes 25 percent, and Home Relief, to which the city contributes 50 percent.

If immigrants accounted for 13.6 percent of the city's public assistance expenditures in 1980, and if their public assistance use patterns remained the same through 1984, then it can be estimated that they used $62.1 million of the $456.9 million spent by the city on public assistance in fiscal 1984.

Health Care

Immigrants appear to cost the city just over their proportionate share of both Medicaid and municipal hospital expenditures. In 1984 this meant that immigrants used about $232.4 million of the city's $824.1 million in Medicaid costs, and $189.6 million of the city's $642.1 million subsidy to HHC for its Medicaid costs and unreimbursed patient care.

The 1980 census provided no information on health care, and data on immigrants' use of medical services were generally unavailable from service providers. Consequently, all health care cost estimates for immigrants must be considered tentative. It was possible, however, to identify factors that distinguish immigrants' health care use patterns from those of the native-born.[5]

Immigrants were found to be high users of some medical services and low users of others. They were low users of the Medicaid program for persons enrolled on public assistance, because they were low users of public assistance. In 1984 Medicaid for persons on public assistance made up almost 40 percent of the $1.5 billion in city health care costs under discussion here, so immigrants' low participation rate in this category was a substantial offset to the services of which they were higher-than-average users.

Hospital costs for uninsured patients constituted nearly 27 percent of the city medical costs discussed here. Immigrants were overrepresented in this category, which consisted of patients who were unable to pay the full cost of their care because they lacked personal funds, insurance, or Medicaid. The 1983 study commissioned by HHC found that 34.7 percent of uninsured patients who were admitted to the hospital during the study period were foreign-born. Using that percentage, immigrants are estimated to have accounted for $135.4 million of the city's $390.2 million subsidy to HHC for unreimbursed patient care in 1984. It is likely that most of the uninsured foreign-born were post–1965 immigrants, since earlier immigrants were likely to have jobs that provided insurance or to have reached the age of Medicare eligibility.

Medical services that were used primarily by the elderly, such as chronic care and home care services, constituted the city's second largest Medicaid expenditure and the third largest health care cost (22 percent) to the city as a whole. Since immigrants were overrepresented among the elderly, they were probably overrepresented among these Medicaid users, if they used these services at the same rate as the native-born elderly. Immigrants made up 40 percent of the city's elderly in 1980.

Education

Education is the area in which immigrants have their greatest impact on city expenditures. Precollege education is available to every child, and the city pays more than half the cost. Public school education meets a primary need of one of the large immigrant age clusters—young families with school-aged children.

In 1980 the children of immigrant-headed households made up 27.3 percent of the city's public school population, just under their proportionate share. More than half the children in these households were born in the United States, but their costs are ascribed here as immigrant costs because their parent or parents were immigrants.

About three-quarters of the immigrant children (20.5 percent of the entire public school population) were the children of post–1965 immigrants, although post–1965 households were only 12.3 percent of the city's household population. Overall, then, immigrants were not overrepresented in the public school population, but post–1965 immigrant families were considerably overrepresented.

The city's share of Board of Education expenses for 1984 was $2.4 billion, according to OMB. Immigrant children accounted for an estimated $652 million of the total (27.2 percent). Of the $652 million, children from post–1965 immigrant households accounted for an estimated $489.5 million.

Immigrants attend institutions of higher learning at the same rate as the native-born, but they are much more likely to attend publicly funded institutions. Consequently they represent a disproportionately large share of the city's higher education costs. But higher education is the least expensive to the city of the five social services analyzed in this chapter.

The City University's costs for 1984 were about $701.6 million, of which the city contributed $139.4 million, mainly for the support of the community colleges. Tuition and state funding paid the balance of the CUNY budget.

No data were available on the entire CUNY population by country of origin, nor on community college students. The 1980 census, however, provided information on foreign-born students who enrolled in publicly funded institutions of higher learning. City Planning analysts found that 33.2 percent of persons enrolled in the first two years of publicly funded colleges were foreign-born. Immigrants therefore represented $46.3 million of the city's higher education costs. Of the immigrant students an estimated two-thirds were from post–1965 households, which means they accounted for 22.2 percent of the city's higher education costs ($30.9 million).

THE EFFECTS OF SIMPSON-RODINO

The new immigration law undoubtedly will have some fiscal impact on the city, but how much or what kind is impossible to predict. It will depend upon such factors as the number of aliens who are legalized under the amnesty program, the use they make of publicly funded human service programs, the level of reimbursement to which the city is entitled under the federal reimbursement formula, and the amount of money that is available to the cities and states after the federal government takes its self-apportioned share of the $1 billion reimbursement available annually for the first four years of the amnesty program. It will behoove the city to record its costs fully and accurately so as to qualify for the maximum possible reimbursement.

NOTES

1. Julian L. Simon, *How Do Immigrants Affect Us Economically?* (Washington, D.C.: Center for Immigration Policy and Refugee Assistance, Georgetown University, 1985).
2. Sidney Weintraub and Gilberto Cardenas, *The Use of Public Services by Undocumented Aliens in Texas* (Austin: University of Texas Press, 1984).
3. Thomas Muller and Thomas J. Espenshade, *The Fourth Wave: California's Newest Immigrants* (Washington, D.C.: The Urban Institute Press, 1985).
4. David North, "Impact of Legal, Illegal and Refugee Migrations on U.S. Social Service Programs," in Mary M. Kritz, ed., *U.S. Immigration and Refugee Policy: Global and Domestic Issues* (Lexington, Mass.: Lexington Books, 1983).
5. Sources for the health care calculations in this chapter were Diane L. Baillargeon, *Medicaid Data Report, 1983 Year-End Summary* and *July–December 1983* (New York: New York City Human Resources Administration, 1984); *Message of the Mayor: The City of New York Executive Budget, Fiscal Year 1985* (New York: New York City Office of Management and Budget, 1985); unpublished data obtained from the Office of Management and Budget; and Eugene P. Ericksen, Andrea M. Vayda, and William S. Borden, *A Survey of Undocumented Aliens in Health and Hospitals Corporation Facilities, New York City, 1983* (Princeton: Mathematica Policy Research, 1983).

17 Ethnic Media

Foreign-language newspapers and broadcasts serve immigrants as an introduction to the United States, as a buffer against the culture shock that inevitably accompanies a move to a new country, and as a lasting connection with the homeland. They supply entertainment, news of the new country and the old, and information on goods and services available in the new land. Ethnic media are able to reach newcomers who have little or no knowledge of English, as well as long-established immigrants with English competencies ranging from nonexistent to fluent.

Foreign-language readers can find on New York City's newsstands more than 100 ethnic newspapers in some 30 languages (see Table 17.1), not counting such international dailies as *Le Monde* (Paris), *Die Welt* (Bonn), *Corriere della Sera* (Milan), and the *Jerusalem Post*. New York's diplomatic, academic, and business communities add to the immigrant demand for foreign-language press.

Many of New York's radio stations and some of its television stations carry foreign-language programs—a particular boon for immigrants who do not read well in their native language.

NEWSPAPERS

Foreign-language newspapers have been published in New York for more than 150 years; the oldest on the stands today is *France Amérique*, which began publication under another name in 1827. The *New Yorker Staats-Zeitung und Herold* dates from 1834; *Il Progresso*, from 1880; the *Jewish Forward*, from 1897; *Al-Hoda*, from 1898; and *Novoye Russkoye Slovo*, from 1910.

Table 17.1

New York City Ethnic Press 1986

Ethnic Group	Name	Place Published	Language	Frequency	Circulation
Arabic	Al-Ahram	London	Arabic	daily	*
	Al-Hoda	New York	Arabic	monthly	10,000
	Asharqal Awst	London	Arabic	daily	*
Armenian	Armenian Mirror Spectator	Watertown, MA	English	weekly	5,000
	Armenian Reporter	New York	English	weekly	5,000
	Baikar Armenian Weekly	Watertown, MA	Armenian	weekly	5,000
Chinese	Centre Daily News	New York	Chinese	daily	60,000
	China Daily News	New York	Chinese	daily	10,000
	China Times	New York	Chinese	weekly	30,000
	China Tribune	New York	Chinese	daily	10,000
	Hong Kong Entertainment	San Francisco	Chinese	daily	*
	International Daily News	Los Angeles	Chinese	daily	*
	Ming Pao News	Hong Kong	Chinese	daily	*
	Peimei News	New York	Chinese	daily	20,000
	People's Daily	Peking	Chinese	daily	*
	Sing Pao News	San Francisco	Chinese	daily	*
	Sing Tao Jih Pao	New York	Chinese	daily	30,000
	Sino Daily News Express	New York	Chinese	daily	30,000
	The New York China Voice	New York	Chinese	weekly	30,000
	United Journal	New York	Chinese	daily	20,000
	World Journal	New York	Chinese	daily	90,000
Estonian	Vaba Eesti Sona	New York	Estonian	weekly	6,000
Filipino	Philippine News	Jersey City	English	daily	*
	The Filipino Reporter	New York	English	weekly	10,000
French	France Amérique	New Rochelle, NY	French	weekly	30,000
	Le Monde	Paris	French	daily	*

Table 17.1

New York City Ethnic Press 1986

Ethnic Group	Name	Place Published	Language	Frequency	Circulation
German	New Yorker Staats-Zeitung und Herold	New York	German	weekly	25,000
Greek	Campana	New York	Greek	semiweekly	9,000
	Ellenika Nea	New York	Greek	weekly	5,400
	Ethnikos Kerix	New York	Greek	daily	40,000
	Greek American	New York	English	weekly	1,500
	Hellenic Times	New York	English	weekly	15,000
	Hellenikos Tachydromos (Hellenic Post)	New York	Greek/English	daily	5,000
	National Herald	New York	Greek	daily	45,000
	Orthodox Observer	New York	Greek/English	weekly	130,000
	Proini	New York	Greek	daily	35,000
Haitian	Haiti Demain	Haiti	French	weekly	*
	Haiti Observateur	New York	French/English	weekly	40,000
	Haiti Progres	New York	French	weekly	75,000
	La Voix d'Haiti	Haiti	French/English	weekly	*
Hispanic/General	El Diario/La Prensa	New York	Spanish	daily	109,000
	El Especial	Union City, NJ	Spanish	weekly	85,000
	El Mundo	San Juan	Spanish	daily	*
	El Nuevo Dia	San Juan	Spanish	daily	*
	El Tiempo	New York	Spanish	weekly	50,000
	Impacto	New York	Spanish/English	weekly	72,000
	La Voz Hispana	New York	Spanish/English	weekly	64,000
	Noticias del Mundo	New York	Spanish	daily	56,000

Table 17.1
New York City Ethnic Press 1986

Ethnic Group	Name	Place Published	Language	Frequency	Circulation
Hispanic/Argentine	Clarin	Argentina	Spanish	daily	*
Hispanic/Colombian	El Colombiano	Colombia	Spanish	daily	*
	El Espectador	Colombia	Spanish	daily	*
	El Estadio	Colombia	Spanish	daily	*
	El Occidente	Colombia	Spanish	daily	*
	El Pais	Colombia	Spanish	daily	*
Hispanic/Cuban	Diario Las Americas	Miami	Spanish	daily	*
Hispanic/Dominican	El Caribe	Dominican Rep.	Spanish	daily	*
	El Nacional de Ahora	Dominican Rep.	Spanish	daily	*
	El Sol	Dominican Rep.	Spanish	daily	*
	Hoy	Dominican Rep.	Spanish	daily	*
	La Noticia	Dominican Rep.	Spanish	daily	*
	Listin Diario	Dominican Rep.	Spanish	daily	*
	Ultima Hora	Dominican Rep.	Spanish	daily	*
Hispanic/Ecuadorian	El Comercio	Ecuador	Spanish	weekly	*
	El Universo	Ecuador	Spanish	weekly	*
Hispanic/Puerto Rican	El Vocero de Puerto Rico	San Juan	Spanish	daily	*
Hispanic/ Uruguayan	El Pais	Uruguay	Spanish	weekly	*
Hungarian	Amerikai Magyar Szo	New York	Hungarian	weekly	1,800
	Amerikai Nepszava	Cleveland, OH	Hungarian	weekly	45,000
Indian	India Abroad	New York	English	weekly	60,000
	News India	New York	English	weekly	15,000
Irish	Irish Echo	New York	English	weekly	3,300
	The Irish Advocate	New York	English	weekly	18,000
	The Irish People	New York	English	weekly	15,000

Table 17.1

New York City Ethnic Press 1986

Ethnic Group	Name	Place Published	Language	Frequency	Circulation
Italian	Il Progresso Italo-Americano	Emerson, NJ	Italian	daily	75,000
Japanese	New York Nichibei	New York	Japanese	weekly	1,500
	OCS News (Overseas Courier Service)	New York	Japanese	biweekly	17,000
Jewish	Algemeiner Journal	New York	Yiddish	weekly	*
	Aufbau	New York	German	weekly	31,000
	Der Yid	New York	Yiddish	weekly	7,300
	Freiheit	New York	Yiddish	weekly	6,100
	Hadoar	New York	Hebrew	weekly	5,100
	Israel Shelanu	New York	Hebrew	weekly	*
	Jewish Forward	New York	Yiddish/English	weekly	22,000
	Jewish Journal	New York	English	weekly	*
	Jewish Week	New York	English	weekly	85,000
	Jewish World	New York	English	weekly	45,000
	Morning Freiheit	New York	Yiddish	daily	7,000
	The Jewish Press	New York	English	weekly	175,000
Korean	Cho Sun Daily	New York	Korean	daily	11,000
	Korea Central Daily News	New York	Korean	daily	5,000
	Korea News	New York	Korean	daily	15,000
	Korean-American Journal	New York	Korean	weekly	5,000
	Sae Gai Times	New York	Korean	biweekly	6,000
	The Korean Herald	New York	Korean	daily	10,000
	Tong A Daily	New York	Korean	daily	25,000

Table 17.1

New York City Ethnic Press 1986

Ethnic Group	Name	Place Published	Language	Frequency	Circulation
Latvian	Laiks	New York	Latvian	semiweekly	10,000
Lithuanian	Darbininkas	New York	Lithuanian	weekly	4,000
	Laisve	New York	Lithuanian	biweekly	1,500
	Tevyne	New York	Lithuanian	monthly	4,500
Norwegian	Nordisk Tidende	New York	Norwegian/ English	weekly	6,000
Polish	Gwiazda Polarna	Stevens Point, WI	Polish	weekly	*
	Nowy Dziennik	New York	Polish	daily	7,000
	Panorama	Chicago	Polish	weekly	*
Portuguese	Luso Americano	Newark	Portuguese	weekly	15,000
Russian	Novoye Russkoye Slovo	New York	Russian	daily	50,000
	Russky Golos	New York	Russian	weekly	2,600
Swedish	Norden	New York	Swedish/ English	weekly	1,000
	Nordstjernan-Svea	New York	Swedish/ English	weekly	3,500
Swiss	Swiss American Review	New York	German/ English/ French/Italian/ Romansche	weekly	4,000

Table 17.1

New York City Ethnic Press 1986

Ethnic Group	Name	Place Published	Language	Frequency	Circulation
Turkish	Hurriyet	New York	Turkish	daily	6,000
Ukrainian	America Ukrainian Catholic Daily	Philadelphia	Ukrainian/ English	daily	*
	Narodna Volya	Scranton, PA	Ukrainian	weekly	*
	Nationalna Tribuna	New York	Ukrainian	weekly	6,000
	Svoboda	Jersey City	Ukrainian	daily	13,000
	The Ukrainian Weekly	Jersey City	Ukrainian	weekly	7,000
West Indian	The New York Carib News	New York	English	weekly	62,000

Source: Editor and Publisher: International Yearbook 1986 (New York: Editor and Publisher, 1986); 1986 Media Encyclopedia (Chicago: National Research Bureau, 1985); Wynar, R. Lubomyr and Wynar, T. Anna, Encyclopedic Directory of Ethnic Newspapers in the United States (Littleton, CO: Libraries Unlimited Inc., 1976); 1986 IMS Directory of Publications (Fort Washington, PA: IMS Press, 1986); visits to selected newsstands; telephone conversations with newspaper staff members.

Despite the market pressures that drive major English-language dailies out of business, the foreign-language press survives and proliferates. In 1986, four English-language dailies were published in New York—and eight Chinese dailies. Changes in the city's ethnic mix are reflected in the assortment of papers on sale at a given time, and in circulation figures and frequency of publication. Some of today's dailies, such as *Novoye Russkoye Slovo*, used to be weeklies, and some of today's weeklies, such as the *Jewish Forward*, used to be dailies.

Foreign-language papers thrive because they provide a slant that can't be found in the English-language press. On one randomly selected day (July 16, 1986), for example, the *New York Times* front page carried stories on U.S. troops being sent to Bolivia to assist in cocaine raids; congressional support for economic sanctions against South Africa; a case of false billing by a military contractor; and a robot's-eye view of the sunken *Titanic*. In contrast, *El Diario/La Prensa* (commonly known as *El Diario*) devoted its front page to a series of rapes in Brooklyn; Basque separatists' responsibility for a bombing in Madrid; a proposed immigration law amendment intended to stop "exploitation" of undocumented aliens; and the shooting, in Puerto Rico, of a politician's nephew. The Chinese-language *Centre Daily News* ran front-page stories on Asian and Hispanic demonstrations in Los Angeles against a proposed law making English the city's official language; a typhoon in Canton that killed 200 people and injured 2,000; the Taiwan baseball team's victory over the Chinese team in world competition in Taiwan; and a federal judge's ruling that undocumented aliens were entitled to Medicaid benefits. The *Times* and *El Diario* had carried the Medicaid story the day before, the *Times* on the first page of its second section and *El Diario* on page 5.

Display advertising in the *Centre Daily News* was a virtual guide to Chinatown, listing Chinese-owned food stores, legal services, restaurants, and Chinese and other Asian banks and investment companies. The *News* carried no advertising from outside the Chinese community.

The sample day was a Wednesday—supermarket advertising day—and *El Diario* carried many pages of food ads from large chains including Key Foods, Red Apple, Met, and Dunkin' Donuts. Other ads in *El Diario* were about evenly divided between Hispanic-owned and non-Hispanic-owned businesses; there were ads for moving companies, entertainment, English lessons, medical services, and furniture stores.

In 1986 there were more Chinese newspapers published in New York than any other language group. Of 13 Chinese dailies, 8 were published locally, as were both of two weeklies. In 1965 there were half as many. The city's first Chinese newspaper, *China Daily News*, was founded in 1940. Many others began to publish, or expanded, in the 1970s, as the Chinese population grew.

Spanish-language newspapers reach Puerto Ricans as well as foreign-

Figure 17.1
New York's Ethnic Newspapers Include These Published in Greek, Russian, Spanish, Haitian, Ukrainian, Chinese, and Korean

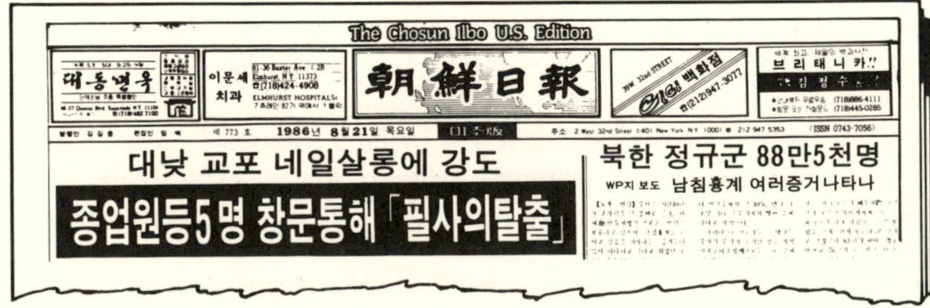

born Hispanics from many nations, giving them the largest potential readership of any language group in the city. Four dailies serving the general Spanish-speaking population can be found on local newsstands, two of them published in New York and two in San Juan, as can four weeklies, all published in the greater metropolitan area. In addition, New York's Hispanics read many newspapers originating in their home countries and sold in neighborhoods with concentrations of immigrants from one particular country. Five papers published in Colombia, for example, can be found on some newsstands in Jackson Heights, and seven from the Dominican Republic in Corona. Table 17.1 almost certainly does not include all papers originating abroad (nor all papers originating in the United States) because only some, strategically located newsstands were visited.

The largest of the locally published dailies serving the general Spanish-language community is also the largest ethnic newspaper in New York: *El Diario* claims a circulation of about 110,000, which edges out the largest Chinese daily by about 20,000. (Most circulation figures in this chapter were obtained from the newspapers themselves and are unaudited.)

El Diario's full name attests to its being the product of a merger in 1963 of *La Prensa*, founded in 1913, and *El Diario de Nueva York*, founded in 1948. The Gannett chain acquired *El Diario* in 1982, intending to make it "the first Hispanic national newspaper."

Also widely read in the Hispanic community is *Noticias del Mundo*, commonly shortened to *Del Mundo*, which began publication in 1980 under the ownership of the Unification Church. It claims a daily circulation of 56,000.

RADIO

Foreign-language radio is an attractive means of communicating with ethnic groups because it can reach immigrants who have little or no knowledge of English, and immigrants who are illiterate in their native language and therefore are unable to read ethnic newspapers. Furthermore, ethnic groups that cannot support a locally published newspaper may be able to afford to buy air time.

Spanish-language programs predominate in New York's ethnic radio programming. Four commercial stations—WSKQ-AM, WKDM-AM, WADO-AM, and WJIT-AM—carry only Spanish-language programming, 24 hours a day. Like much of ethnic radio, their programs consist largely of local and international news, music, religious programs, and talk shows. Sports programs and immigration forums are often heard on other stations.

Ethnic groups can buy time from two commercial stations most of whose programming is ethnic: WEVD-FM and WNWK-FM. WEVD was founded in 1927 by the *Jewish* (then *Jewish Daily*) *Forward* to provide educational and cultural programs for Jewish immigrants. (Its call letters are for Eugene V. Debs, the well-known Socialist presidential candidate who died a year before the station's founding.) WEVD now carries Italian, Portuguese, Albanian, Hebrew, Yiddish, Greek, Irish, Russian, and Turkish programs.

WNWK-FM was founded in the 1960s as WHBI; it changed its call letters in 1985. WNWK offers ethnic programming in 35 languages representing 40 countries, according to station officials. It broadcasts from Newark but serves the entire metropolitan area. Language groups for which there is no local newspaper, such as Bulgarian and Malayalam (an Asian Indian language), can be heard on WNWK. So can Hispanic subgroups like Argentines, Chileans, Dominicans, Ecuadorians, and Peruvians.

Greeks and Italians are the largest buyers of WNWK air time, with 44 and 25 hours a week, respectively. Smaller amounts of time are bought by Armenians, Russians, Norwegians, Irish, Jews, Jamaicans, Poles, Haitians, Croatians, Hungarians, and Hispanics.

Some other commercial stations broadcast small amounts of ethnic programming, but none equal to the hours broadcast by WEVD and WNWK.

Four university radio stations broadcast ethnic programs. WKCR-FM from Columbia University devotes 18 hours a day to ethnic broadcasts, largely of traditional ethnic music. Students run the shows. WFUV-FM of Fordham devotes 17 hours a day to ethnic talk shows and music programs, also run by students. WNYE-FM at Medgar Evers College offers 19 hours a week to ethnic groups for their own broadcasts. WSOU-FM from Seton Hall University in New Jersey sells 23 hours a week for ethnic programming.

If ethnic groups or their members can put together the money and talent for a demanding business venture, they can acquire a cable station. Such cable programs can be heard by anyone who buys a special radio from the cable service, for about $140. Sinocast is a cable service that broadcasts in Chinese 24 hours a day. Radio ICN (Italian Communication Network) and Radio Uno broadcast in Italian 24 hours a day. Radio Uno cable service is made available by WNWK apart from its regular Italian programming.

TELEVISION

Of the media discussed in this chapter, television has the most limited reach into the foreign-language community, partly because of broadcasting costs and partly because of the geographic limitations of cable TV. Thirteen channels in the New York metropolitan area (see Table

Table 17.2
Ethnic Television Programming
1986

Station	Channel	Type of Station	Ethnic Groups Served	Hours per eek
WNET	13	VHF	French Hispanic Russian Greek German Italian	From 0.5 to 2 for each group, 6 to 9 months per year
WNYE	25	UHF	Korean Chinese Hispanic	5 3.5 2
WNYC	31	UHF	Italian Japanese Chinese	16 12 8
WXTV	41	UHF	Hispanic	168
WNJU	47	UHF	Hispanic Asian Indian Japanese Greek Korean Yugoslav	75 5.5 5 4 1.5 0.5
C.S. Television	15, 16, or 3	pay UHF	Chinese	128
ITV	63	pay UHF	Asian Indian	34
Group W Cable	C	cable	Hispanic Irish Jewish	6 1 0.5
	D	cable	Hispanic Asian Indian Irish Jewish	7 1 1 0.5
	J	pay cable	Hispanic	6.5
Galavision (subsidiary of Group W Cable)	E	pay cable	Hispanic	92
CUNY Television	A or 14	cable	Hispanic French German Italian	2 1 1 1
Manhattan Cable (WMHT)	M	cable	Chinese	20

Source: New York City Department of City Planning.

17.2) carry ethnic programs for the relatively small total of 620 hours a week, broadcast to 13 ethnic groups in 12 languages. The predominant language is Spanish, with 360 hours (58 percent) of the total. Chinese is second with 160 hours (26 percent). Other ethnic groups served, in descending order of hours, are Indians, Italians, Japanese, Koreans, Greeks, French, Irish, Germans, Russians, Jews, and Yugoslavs.

Like other television stations, those with foreign-language programs carry news, movies, soap operas, dramatic series, variety shows, children's shows, music, sports, and religious programs.

The major commercial VHF channels carry no foreign-language programming. The public VHF station, WNET (Channel 13), does carry a few hours. Since 1984 WNET has broadcast programs in Italian, French, Russian, and Spanish; in the fall of 1986 it added German and Greek programs to its schedule.

Most ethnic programs are carried on one of six cable channels and six UHF channels. Two in each group are by paid subscription. The stations with the largest numbers of hours of ethnic programming are WXTV, which broadcasts in Spanish 24 hours a day, 7 days a week; C.S. Television, which broadcasts 128 hours in Chinese; and Galavision, with 92 hours in Spanish. Most of the cable channels go only to parts of Manhattan, except for Galavision, which also goes to Brooklyn and Queens. The quality of UHF reception varies according to the strength of each station's transmitter, the size of the viewer's antenna, and distance from the transmission site.

18 Inventory of Academic Studies

New York City tends to be ignored in immigration research. Investigators often look at national and international events rather than local ones, or their attention is drawn to immigration phenomena in other parts of the country. But immigration in New York is qualitatively different from immigration in Los Angeles or Miami, and information about New York's experience must be collected if the city is to be represented fairly in setting national immigration policy. Fortunately, since 1980 some research specific to New York City has been conducted.

The greater part of this research is being done in the city's universities. Several major universities have established centers for immigration studies, and many faculty members are doing individual research on the subject. Moreover, various nonacademic institutions, such as labor unions and ethnic associations, are investigating aspects of immigration that touch their specific interests.

Foundation support can encourage city-specific research. Some foundations are making grants for local studies, though most funding for immigration studies is national in focus. Local studies have recently been funded by, among others, the Ford, Rockefeller, Revson, Tinker, New World, and Spencer foundations, the New York Council on the Humanities, and the New York Community Trust; the last of these provided financial support for this book.

In sheer quantity, research on Caribbean and Hispanic immigrants dominates the local immigration research field. Asian immigration is the subject of only a few studies. In part this discrepancy is due to the numbers of Caribbeans and Hispanics in New York; at 60 percent of the new immigrants, they far outnumber the Asians, with only 18 percent.

But the difference is due as well to practical considerations: it is easier for potential researchers to learn Spanish than Chinese, and it is cheaper and quicker to do fieldwork in Santo Domingo than in Seoul. Many non-Hispanics are doing research on Hispanic immigration, but by and large only researchers of Asian stock are doing research on Asians.

Earlier immigration research concentrated on immigrants' social impact; today it concentrates on labor market impact. Columbia University and New York University predominate in labor market studies on immigrants. Columbia's Conservation of Human Resources center is known for its studies of immigrants in the garment, restaurant, and construction trades. NYU is producing work on a variety of economic topics, ranging from the capital and labor relationship between New York and the Caribbean, to Dominicans' participation in the city's garment trade.

This chapter presents an inventory of research in which New York City is the primary focus. Many researchers in this listing are doing work on national and international migration topics, but only their local work is listed here. The inventory is divided into sections on research institutions, nonacademic institutions, and individual researchers. Each entry describes the research focus and lists publications on local immigration topics.

RESEARCH INSTITUTIONS

Institution

Center for Migration Studies (CMS)

Research Focus

The center was founded in 1964 to publish *International Migration Review (IMR)*, a technical journal in migration studies that the center's director, Lydio Tomasi, had begun while teaching at the College of Staten Island, CUNY. Today, the center is involved in a wide range of migration endeavors. In addition to IMR, it publishes a magazine, *Migration World*, (formerly *World Migration Today*); conducts national and international conferences; sponsors research; publishes books and papers on migration and ethnic group relations; and maintains a research library and archives at 209 Flagg Place, Staten Island.

Historically the center has had particular interest in Italian migration and the development of the Catholic Church in New York. CMS frequently conducts research with the local dioceses. The Brooklyn Diocese, with the Community Development Agency of Brooklyn, commissioned a CMS study of housing (see Papademetriou, 1983). CMS has conducted a study with the Newark Diocese on unapprehended illegals in the New York-New Jersey metropolitan area. The study, based on long interviews with 200 aliens, was published in 1986.

Publications

Chaney, Elsa M., and Constance R. Sutton, eds. *Caribbean Life in New York City: Sociocultural Dimensions*. New York: CMS, 1985.

Keely, Charles, Patricia J. Elwell, Austin T. Fragomen, Jr., and Silvano Tomasi. *Profiles on Undocumented Aliens in New York City: Haitians and Dominicans*. New York: CMS, 1978.

Papademetriou, Demetrios G. *New Immigrants to Brooklyn and Queens: Policy Implications, Especially with Regard to Housing*. New York: CMS, 1983.

Papademetriou, Demetrios G., and Nicholas DiMarzio. *Undocumented Aliens in the New York Metropolitan Area*. New York: CMS, 1986.

Tomasi, Lydio F. *Italian Americans: New Perspectives on Italian Immigration and Ethnicity*. New York: CMS, 1985. (Includes New York immigrants.)

Tomasi, Silvano M. *Piety and Power: The Role of Italian Parishes in the New York Metropolitan Area, 1880–1930*. New York: CMS, 1975.

Tricario, Donald. *The Italians of Greenwich Village*. New York: CMS, 1984.

Institution

Columbia University

Unit

Center for Social Sciences (CSS)
Immigration Research Program

Research Focus

The program focuses on the way immigrants settle into communities. Headed by anthropologist Josh DeWind, the program began operations in 1981 with a grant to develop a model for studying Hispanic immigrants. The first use of the model was in a national bilingualism study; DeWind's portion examined how bilingualism in New York increased the participation of Hispanic parents in the schools.

Three projects are currently under way. In "Commercial Revitalization in Manhattan Valley," DeWind is observing a group of Dominicans and Puerto Ricans as they form a merchants' association. "The Formation of Haitian Ethnic Associations in New York" will examine the way non-Haitian organizations influence Haitian immigrants in organizing themselves. "Immigrants and Self-Help in New York City" will produce two separate studies on how community organizations integrate immigrants into politics, and how churches integrate immigrants into community life.

Publications

DeWind, Josh. *The Organizing of Parents to Support Bilingual Education*. New York: CSS, Columbia University, 1983.

———. *Undocumented Workers and the Labor Market: The Impact of Employers*. New York: CSS, Columbia University, 1983.

Georges, Eugenia. *Conflict and Cooperation: Dominican Immigrants and Their Neighbors*. New York: CSS, Columbia University, 1985.

Schiller, Nina Glick, Marie Lucie Brutus, and Josh DeWind. *"Right Here on Flatbush Avenue": The Development of Multiple Organizational Identities among Haitian Immigrants*. New York: CSS, Columbia University, 1985.

Institution

Columbia University

Unit

Conservation of Human Resources (CHR)
The Project on Newcomers to New York City

Research Focus

Conservation of Human Resources was founded during World War II to study personnel issues for the armed forces. Headed by Eli Ginzberg, of the Columbia Business School, it continues to study human resource issues from an employment and economic perspective. The Project on Newcomers, begun in 1980, is known for its labor market studies, which look at immigrants as they adapt to the New York economy, and as they do or do not compete with native workers. Principal researchers have been Thomas Bailey and Marcia Freedman. (For other labor market studies, see individual listings for Roger Waldinger and Saskia Sassen-Koob.)

Publications

Bailey, Thomas. *The Effects of Immigrants on the Employment of Blacks and Youth and on the Level of Wages in the New York Restaurant Industry, 1950–1981*. New York; CHR, Columbia University, 1983.

———. "Immigrants in the Restaurant Industry," *Industrial Relations*, Vol. 24, No. 5, Spring 1985, pp. 205–221.

———. "The Influence of Legal Status on the Labor Market Impact of Immigration," *International Migration Review*, Vol. XIX, No. 2, Summer 1985, pp. 220–238.

———. *Immigrants and Native Workers: Contrasts and Competition*. Boulder, Colo.: Westview Press, 1987.

Freedman, Marcia. "The Labor Market for Immigrants in New York City." *New York Affairs* no. 4 (1983): pp. 94–111.

Freedman, Marcia, and Josef Korazim. "Self-Employment and the Decision to Emigrate: Israelis in New York City." Paper presented at the Conference on Israelis in New York, City University of New York, November 13, 1983.

Gallo, Carmenza. *The Construction Industry in New York City: Immigrants and Black Entrepreneurs*. Working Paper. New York: Conservation of Human Resources. Columbia University, 1983.

Institution

Fordham University

Unit

Hispanic Research Center

Research Focus

The center is funded by the National Institute of Mental Health to conduct research on Hispanics. Its primary focus is Puerto Ricans, but the senior research associate, Douglas Gurak, does research on Dominican and Colombian immigrants as well. In 1981 he directed a research team that interviewed more than 900 immigrants, gathering information on their occupational and marital history, fertility, mental health status, and all moves since age 15. This data base represents an important resource; no other survey in the city has reached as many immigrants or asked as broad a range of questions.

Gurak and Mary Kritz, an associate director of the Rockefeller Foundation, have published one paper from this material and have three others in progress: an analysis of the role of the family in adaptation; an examination of socioeconomic mobility; and an epidemiological study of anxiety levels in relationship to migration and acculturation. The data are available to other researchers.

Publications

Gurak, Douglas T., with Mary M. Kritz. "Dominican and Colombian Women in New York City." *Migration Today* 10, no. 3/4 (1982) pp. 15–21.

Institution

New York University

Unit

Center for Latin American and Caribbean Studies (CLACS)
New York Research Program in Inter-American Affairs

Research Focus

The NYU program has established a reputation for being lively and prolific by funding short fellowships and following an aggressive publishing schedule. In addition to its master's program in Latin American studies, the center founded a postgraduate fellowship program in 1981 with grants for six-month fellowships on Latin American migration to New York. With a change in funding in 1984, the center will sponsor longer projects, but it plans to maintain its emphasis on contemporary migration issues in New York. The project director is Christopher Mitchell.

Publications

Balmori, Diana. *Hispanic Immigrants in the Construction Industry: New York City, 1960–1980*. New York: CLACS, 1983.

Castro, Mary Garcia. *'Mary' and 'Eve's' Social Reproduction in the 'Big Apple': Colombian Voices*. New York: CLACS, 1982.

DeWind, Josh. *Caribbean Immigrants and Housing in New York City*. New York: CLACS, 1981.

Fagen, Patricia Weiss. *Applying for Political Asylum in New York: Law, Policy and Administrative Practice*. New York: CLACS, 1984.

Foner, Nancy. *Jamaican Migrants: A Comparative Analysis of the New York and London Experience*. New York: CLACS, 1983.

Fox, Geoffrey. *Organizing the New Immigrants: The Hispanic Trade Unionists' Perspective*. New York: CLACS, 1983.

———. *Hispanic Organizers and Business Agents in the New York Apparel Industries*. New York: CLACS, 1984.

George, Eugenia. *New Immigrants and the Political Process: Dominicans in New York*. New York: CLACS, 1984.

Marshall, Adriana. *Immigration in a Surplus-Worker Labor Market: The Case of New York City*. New York: CLACS, 1984.

Pessar, Patricia R. *Kinship Relations of Production in the Migration Process: The Case of Dominican Emigration to the United States*. New York: CLACS, 1982.

Sassen-Koob, Saskia. *Exporting Capital and Importing Labor: The Role of Caribbean Migration to New York City*. New York: CLACS, 1981.

Institution

Queens College, CUNY

Unit

Continuing Education Division
Ethnic Studies Project

Research Focus

The new immigration has made Queens the most ethnically diverse borough in the city. In 1978 a group of professors at Queens College received funding from the State Assembly to found an institute to study newcomers to Queens. Between 1980 and 1982 researchers completed several pieces of work on major immigrant groups, including Colombians, Greeks, Indians, Israelis, Italians, and Koreans. They studied socioeconomic factors, levels of community involvement, ethnic identity, and problems with discrimination. The project has since shifted away from conducting its own research, and it now sponsors visiting scholars from foreign universities who are interested in Queens migration issues. It also directs the college's overseas studies program and maintains the Jewish Heritage Collection at the Central Queens Library. The director is Elayne P. Bernstein.

Publications

Cohen, Steven M. *A Social Profile of the Ethnic Groups of Queens: Preliminary Findings from a Sample Survey*. New York: Queens College, 1981.

Grant, Geraldine. *Six Immigrant Groups in Queens: A Pilot Study*. New York: Queens College, 1980.

———. *New Immigrants and Ethnicity: A Preliminary Research Report on Immigrants in Queens*. New York: Queens College, 1981.

Shokeid, Moshe. "The People of the Song: An Anthropologist's View of Israeli Culture in New York." Paper presented at Conference on Israelis, New York, City University of New York, November 13, 1983.

INDIVIDUAL RESEARCHERS

Name

Grant, Geraldine

Affiliation

Department of Social Science
Fiorello H. LaGuardia Community College, CUNY

Research Focus

Grant is an anthropologist interested in family structures and their relationship to the migration process. Using data from New York immigrants, she is currently working on a comparison of Colombians, representing new immigration, and Italians, representing an older, continuing migration.

Publications

Grant, Geraldine. "Immigrant Family Stability: Some Preliminary Thoughts." *Journal of Children in Contemporary Society; special issue on immigrant families*, Spring 1983, pp. 27–37.

———. "Looking for a Home: International Migrants in Multiple Political Fields." Paper presented to the Annual Meetings of the American Anthropological Association, Chicago, 1983. (Based on Queens data.)

Grant, Geraldine, and Judith Herbstein. "Immigrant Mobility: Upward, Downward or Outward?" Paper presented to the Annual Meeting of the Society for Applied Anthropology, San Diego, 1983. (Based on Queens data.)

Name

Kessner, Thomas, and Betty Boyd Caroli

Affiliation
Department of History
Kingsborough Community College, CUNY

Research Focus
Kessner and Caroli currently are working on nonimmigration topics, but their book, *Today's Immigrants*, stands as one of the best descriptions of the daily lives of new immigrants in New York. The stories of individual immigrants are used to tell the immigration history of national groups coming to New York, including Indochinese, Koreans, West Indians, Russians, Chinese, and Italians. The book vividly depicts the way changes in U.S. immigration law, and political and economic events around the world, combined to produce the new wave of immigration.

Publications
Kessner, Thomas, and Betty Boyd Caroli. *Today's Immigrants: Their Stories*. New York: Oxford University Press, 1981.

Name
Kim, Illsoo

Affiliation
Department of Sociology
Drew University, Madison, NJ

Research Focus
The evolving middle class among Asian immigrants, and Asian enterprises in the New York metropolitan area.

Publications
Kim, Illsoo. "The Big Apple Goes Bananas Over Korean Fruit Stands," *Asia*, September/October 1981, pp. 30–32, 50–51.
———. *New Urban Immigrants: The Korean Community in New York*: Princeton: Princeton University Press, 1981.
———. "Organizational Patterns of Korean-American Methodist Churches: Denominationalism and Personal Community." In Russell E. Richey and Kenneth E. Rowe, eds., *Rethinking Methodist History*, Nashville: Abingdon Press, 1985. (Discusses New York churches.)

Name
Kuo, Chia-ling

Affiliation
Department of Anthropology
Hunter College, CUNY

Research Focus
Social networks in Chinese communities.

Publications
Kuo, Chia-ling. *Social and Political Change in New York's Chinatown: The Role of the Voluntary Associations*. New York: Praeger, 1977.
———. *Political Leadership and Immigrants in American Chinatowns*. Forthcoming from Schenkman Publishers.

Name
Mann, Evelyn S., and Joseph J. Salvo

Affiliation
Population Division
New York City Department of City Planning

Research Focus

Mann and Salvo are, respectively, director and deputy director of the Population Division, which produces New York census data analyses, including those used in this book. The paper cited is an independent study they did on socioeconomic differences among Hispanic groups in New York. It focuses on economic status and its relationship to family composition and labor force participation. It compares Puerto Ricans with non-Puerto Rican Hispanics (excluding Mexicans and Cubans), and examines differences between Dominicans and Colombians.

Publications

Mann, Evelyn S., and Joseph J. Salvo. "Characteristics of New Hispanic Immigrants to New York City: A Comparison of Puerto Rican and Non-Puerto Rican Hispanics." Paper presented at the Annual Meeting of the Population Association of America, Minneapolis, May 3, 1984.

Name
Ryan, Angela Shen

Affiliation
Hunter College School of Social Work

Research Focus

The psychosocial needs of Asian-Americans.

Publications

Ryan, Angela Shen. *New York City's Asian-Americans: Their Distribution, Needs and Patterns of Service Utilization.* Chicago: Pacific-Asian-American Mental Health Research Center, 1981.

Name
Sassen-Koob, Saskia

Affiliation
Department of Urban Planning
Columbia University

Research Focus

Sassen-Koob's research generally has an international context, examining the impact on migration of economic development in sending nations and labor markets in the receiving nations. But much of her information is gathered in New York, and the city frequently figures as a case study of her economic theories.

Publications

Sassen-Koob, Saskia. "Formal and Informal Associations: Dominicans and Colombians in New York," *International Migration Review*, 13:2, Spring 1979, pp. 314–332.

———. "Immigrant and Refugee Women in New York City." Paper presented at the 8th Annual Women's Conference, New York, Barnard College, April 1984.

———. "New York City's Informal Sector." Paper presented at the International Symposium on the Informal Sector, Baltimore, Johns Hopkins University, June 1984.
———. "Changing Composition and Labor Market Distribution of Hispanics in New York City, 1960–1980," in *Hispanics in the U.S. Economy*, Marta Tienda and Jorge Borjas, eds. New York: Academic Press, 1985, pp. 299–322.
———. "New York City: Economic Restructuring and Immigration," *Development and Change*, Vol. 17, 1986, pp. 85–119.

Name
Sung, Betty Lee

Affiliation
Department of Asian Studies
The City College of New York, CUNY

Research Focus
Chinese immigration, employment, and acculturation.

Publications
Sung, Betty Lee. *Mountain of Gold*. New York: Macmillan, 1967. (New York material.)
———. *Survey of Chinese American Manpower and Employment*. New York: Praeger, 1976. (New York material.)
———. *Gangs in New York's Chinatown*. Washington, D.C.: Department of Health, Education and Welfare, 1977.
———. *Chinese Population in Lower Manhattan, 1978*. Washington, D.C.: Department of Labor, 1978.
———. *Transplanted Chinese Children*. Washington, D.C.: Department of Health, Education and Welfare, 1979. (New York material.)
———. "Chinese Immigration." In D. L. Cuddy, ed., *Contemporary American Immigrants*. New York: Twayne, 1981. (Includes New York material.)

Name
Tobier, Emanuel

Affiliation
Graduate School of Public Administration
New York University

Research Focus
Tobier's main interest is urban economics and municipal policy making. His chapter on immigration in *Setting Municipal Priorities* (an annual state-of-the-city evaluation of New York) is a widely read discussion of the effects of immigrants on New York.

Publications
Tobier, Emanuel. "The Orientals." *NYU Education Quarterly* 11, no. 4 (Summer 1980): 24–28.
———. "Foreign Immigration." In Charles Brecher and Raymond Horton, eds., *Setting Municipal Priorities*, 1983. New York: New York University Press, 1983.

Name
Waldinger, Roger

Affiliation
Department of Sociology
The City College of New York, CUNY

Research Focus
The role of immigrants in the labor market and the development of immigrant businesses.

Publications

Waldinger, Roger. "Immigrants and Enterprise in New York City," *Kaleidoscope: Current Research and Scholarly Activity at CCNY*, Vol. 1, No. 2 (Fall 1984), pp. 12–22.

———. "Immigrant Enterprise and the Structure of the Labor Market." In *New Approaches to Economic Life*, Brian Roberts, ed., Manchester, England: University of Manchester Press, 1985. (Based on New York City data.)

———. "Immigrants and Industrial Change: A Case Study of the New York Apparel Industry." In *Hispanics in the U.S. Economy*, Marta Tienda and Jorge Borjas, eds., New York: Academic Press, 1985.

———. *Through the Eye of the Needle: Immigrants and Enterpise in New York's Garment Trade*, New York: NYU Press, 1986.

NONACADEMIC ORGANIZATIONS

Organization
The Archdiocese of New York

Research Focus
In 1979 the archdiocese commissioned a study of its Hispanic constituency, now estimated at 40 percent of its urban membership. The goal was to define the religious beliefs of Hispanics and to describe their cultural presence in the city.

Volume I of the published study presents the results of 1,200 interviews covering religious, economic, and sociological issues. Volume II contains a series of papers on Hispanic Catholicism, the socioeconomic and cultural characteristics of the various Hispanic nationalities, Hispanic family structure and acculturation, and the history of the hierarchy's response to Hispanics.

The Church did a short follow-up study on Hispanic youth in 1982. It covered religious and moral beliefs, including attitudes toward birth control, abortion, and drug use. It was based on 515 questionnaires completed by Hispanics between the ages of 14 and 17 in Catholic schools and youth groups.

Publications

Church-Related Youth in New York: An Exploratory Study. New York: Office of Pastoral Research, Archdiocese of New York, 1983.

Hispanics in New York: Religious, Cultural and Social Experience, 2 vols. New York: Office of Pastoral Research, Archdiocese of New York, 1983.

Organization
Church World Service (CWS)

Research Focus
The CWS Immigration and Refugee Program coordinates refugee resettlement by Protestant congregations throughout the United States, including New York. In 1983 the

organization commissioned a private research firm to evaluate the self-sufficiency of client refugees who had arrived since 1980, and the role of sponsors in helping refugees adjust. Questionnaires were sent to a randomly selected sample of 4,500 sponsors and refugees, and the study was based on responses from 1,600 sponsors and 500 refugees.

Publications

Making It on Their Own: From Refugee Sponsorship to Self-Sufficiency. New York: Calculogic Corporation, 1983.

Organization

The Community Council of Greater New York

Research Focus

The Community Council, a research center for human service issues, studied the role of ethnic associations in meeting the needs of new immigrants. The study examines the associations' historical roles, current goals and structure, perception of their constituents' needs, role in acculturation and preservation of ethnic identity, services provided, and interaction with the formal service structure.

Publications

Jenkins, Shirley, Mignon Sauber, and Eva Friedlander, *Ethnic Associations and Services to New Immigrants in New York City.* New York: Community Council of Greater New York, 1985.

Organization

The Hellenic-American Neighborhood Action Committee (HANAC)

Research Focus

HANAC undertook a study in 1979 to determine whether the needs of post–1965 Greek immigrants were being met by the Greek community's established social service system, whose primary service population had become U.S.-born Greek-Americans. The new immigrants—in need of assistance with English, job skills, and acculturation—were becoming a marginal, isolated group within the larger Greek community. To develop programs for them, HANAC interviewed 500 "new" and "old" Greek immigrants, assessing the socioeconomic status and needs of each group.

Publications

The Needs of the Growing Greek-American Community in the City of New York. New York: HANAC, 1984.

Organization

The International Ladies' Garment Workers Union (ILGWU) Local 23–25 and the New York Skirt and Sportswear Association

Research Focus

Local 23–25 of the ILGWU represents more than 20,000 garment workers in New York's Chinatown, where shop owners and workers are almost exclusively newly arrived Chinese immigrants. In 1981 the union and an association of garment manufacturers commissioned a study of the Chinatown garment industry to analyze its past growth and to assess obstacles to its continuing development. A private research firm was retained to analyze changes in the industry and to make recommendations for ensuring continued prosperity.

Publications

Abeles, Schwartz, Haeckel & Silverblatt, Inc., *The Chinatown Garment Industry Study*. New York: Abeles, Schwartz, Haeckel & Silverblatt, 1983.

Organization

New York City Health and Hospitals Corporation (HHC)

Research Focus

The Health and Hospitals Corporation, which administers the municipal hospitals, in 1982 commissioned a research firm to calculate the cost of providing inpatient medical care to undocumented aliens who had no health insurance. Researchers interviewed 89 hospitalized aliens who were probably or positively undocumented, gathering medical, employment, and immigration data.

Publications

Erickson, Eugene P., Andrea M. Boyda, and William S. Borden. *A Survey of Undocumented Aliens in Health and Hospitals Corporation Facilities*, New York City, 1983. Princeton: Mathematica Policy Research, 1983.

19 Conclusions and Recommendations

Immigrants constitute so large and important a component of New York City's population that to analyze their "impact" on the city seems almost as artificial as it would be to analyze the impact of New York City's children, firefighters, or housewives. Do we honestly believe that there could be a New York City without its immigrants, its young people, or its hopes for the future?

Immigrants made up almost a quarter of the city's population in 1980, according to U.S. census figures. At current rates of migration and immigration, they will account for nearly 28 percent of the population by 1990. By 2000 the figure may reach 32 percent.

Because the 1980 census figures did not include all foreign-born persons, neither do these projections. If substantial numbers of documented or undocumented aliens went uncounted in 1980, then the foreign-born made up well over a quarter of the city's population at that time, and they will constitute well over a third in 2000.

The city's native population is aging; birth rates are low, and lives are longer. Without the regular infusion of migrants and immigrants, today's young workers would be carrying an intolerable burden in supporting the dependent elderly. Newcomers of working age regenerate the labor force and offer their Social Security and tax payments among their many contributions to those who came before.

Immigrants' role in regenerating the labor force inevitably leads to the question of whether documented or undocumented workers deprive native-born Americans of opportunities to work, or depress wages in industries where immigrants make up a large portion of the work force. Despite the fact that the immigration debate of recent years has focused on the question of whether immigrants take jobs from the native-born, there have been few studies of the question nationwide, and none that can be considered sufficiently conclusive to inform national policy decisions. Researchers who have looked at this question in New York City have found no evidence of pervasive job displacement but some evidence of wage depression in industries with large foreign-born labor pools. More study of these issues is needed nationwide and in New York.

Even without further study, however, it is clear that immigrants bear little responsibility for the employment problems of American's minority underclass, a charge on which immigrants are often called to account. Immigrants' steady success in making their way into the U.S. economic mainstream is always a painful reminder that a portion of the native-born are unable to do so. Immigrants, in New York at any rate, do not seem to cause employment problems for native-born minorities, but they do call attention to these problems through their greater success. The "problem" of immigration in the United States can probably best be solved by tending to the problems of the native underclass; the needs of the native minorities must be served. U.S. minorities must be helped to achieve the motivation and the skills that so many immigrants bring with them to the United States.

Besides job displacement, another common fear among Americans is that immigrants use far more in public services than they pay in taxes. Although the current state of data on immigrants does not permit definitive conclusions, the City Planning analysis of these issues suggests that immigrants use less than their proportionate share of city-funded social services except higher education. They appear to pay slightly less than their proportionate tax share because their average income is slightly lower than that of the native-born. There is no evidence to substantiate the fear that immigrants are a drain on the public coffers.

Furthermore, it would be impossible to quantify the larger social and economic benefits that immigrants contribute to U.S. society in the cultural richness they bring to business and the arts, in their tendency to draw tourism and foreign investment, in the energy and seriousness of purpose they bring to their new "careers" as Americans. These benefits cannot be measured, but they ought to be recognized and acknowledged.

IMMIGRATION STATISTICS

The dearth of reliable data on immigrants and their participation in the U.S. economy poses an obstacle to responsible policy formulation at the local and national levels. The U.S. census is the single richest source of data on immigrants, but even the census cannot tell policy makers all they need to know about immigrants. Such issues as labor market impact and the use of public services are beyond the scope of the census. It will take special studies to illuminate them.

Still, the Census Bureau can do more to furnish the country with immigration data. In 1990 it can make an even greater effort than it did in 1980 to ensure that all immigrant households are counted by census takers. It can standardize its immigration-related questions from one decennial census to the next so that the data are comparable over time.

The INS also can play an important role in providing the nation with immigration statistics now that its computer system is being installed. In the past the INS has gathered and disseminated only those data that it needed for its own administrative purposes. In the future it should gather data with national policy needs in mind. Ultimately the INS bears the most natural and insistent responsibility for the accumulation of immigration data that can be used to develop responsible federal policy. *Immigration Statistics: A Story of Neglect*, the study commissioned by the INS and conducted by the National Research Council of the National Academy of Sciences, offers valuable suggestions on how the INS might shape its data collection program.

The National Research Council report calls for many other public and private agencies to participate in the data collection effort. Although the report focuses on federal agencies, it is clear that local agencies, including those of the New York City government, ought to be partners in the effort. For the most part, city agencies do not analyze their client population by such demographic characteristics as country of birth. The New York City Board of Education could tell us much more about its immigrant students—their academic strengths and weaknesses, their language needs, their need for cultural orientation. HHC could tell us more about the numbers of immigrants it serves, the health needs that bring them to municipal hospital facilities, and their ability to pay for service. HRA could tell us more about the numbers and ethnicities of foreign-born persons receiving public assistance and Medicaid. Only with data like these can the city be sure it is providing adequate service to the foreign-born, and that it is being adequately recompensed by higher levels of government.

The census undercount of 1980 was seriously detrimental to New York City because the city lost some potential federal aid. Everything must be done to avoid a recurrence in 1990. It is also essential that the city resist congressional efforts to eliminate undocumented aliens from official census counts. New York City is required by law to provide many kinds of services to the undocumented, and there is no reason why the city should be penalized financially for fulfilling its legal obligations.

SERVICE NEEDS

New York City has for so long enjoyed a harmonious and mutually beneficial relationship with its foreign-born that their changing needs and problems have sometimes gone unattended. Today's immigrants arrive in a city that is far different from the New York City of 1890 and 1910. Gone, for the most part, is the network of settlement houses and private charities that catered almost exclusively to newly arriving immigrants, cushioning the shock of arrival for participants in the great wave of immigration. Today government has become the chief caretaker of the needy, foreign-born and native-born alike. New York City's public agencies must reevaluate their responsibilities to immigrants in light of the legislative and social changes since the early 1960s. Today's U.S. residents are the inheritors of a new social contract in which government has assumed far greater responsibility for everyone.

The City of New York began such a reevaluation process in 1984 with the creation of the Office of Immigrant Affairs in the Department of City Planning. The office is a policy planning and service coordinating body. The next step must be to establish the responsibility for immigration planning within each city agency at the executive level. No agency can afford to be without a high-level immigrant service planning function.

It is an unfortunate but perhaps inevitable fact of government life that cooperation is often minimal among agencies at different jurisdictional levels. In immigration matters this means that city agencies do not communicate regularly with the New York district office of the INS, and vice versa. There is much to be gained from closer cooperation between the city and the INS. The City of New York is committed to providing immigrants with the highest level of service allowed by law, but it is not willing to provide public benefits to unentitled aliens, nor is it willing to shelter aliens who commit crimes. These goals are consistent with the goals of the INS. City agencies should work closely with the INS to ensure that lawbreaking aliens are subject to deportation proceedings and that immigrant applicants do not obtain public benefits through the use of fraudulent documents. Further, city agencies and the INS can cooperate on assisting applicants for public services and immigration benefits through the complexities of each system.

Government's assumption of responsibility for the needy serves immigrants well in some ways and not so well in others. It is often hard for large public or publicly funded bureaucratic organizations to provide the language services and culturally sensitive program planning that are needed to deliver services to a foreign-language-speaking population. The study of city language services undertaken in 1985 by the Office of Immigrant Affairs, and further developed in 1986 by the Mayor's Commission on Hispanic Concerns, is one step toward improved service. At this time small, private agencies with ethnic ties are likely to provide better orientation, mental health services, personal counseling, and immigration counseling.

Although service improvements take time, government can increase its assistance immediately by strengthening the city's ethnic associations, particularly the newer ones created by the immigrants of the last five or ten years. The city can lend its strength through such activities as funding and technical assistance.

LEGISLATIVE COMPLEXITIES

Immigration law and social service law have become so complex, and their interactions so ambiguous, that it is a wonder any alien can make his or her way through either system. Legislators ought to strive for a uniform set of definitions in immigration law and social service law, so that a modicum of coordination can exist between the two systems.

On their own, social service laws, regulations, and guidelines need overhaul as they apply to immigrants because they are internally inconsistent and inequitable. In the current state of the laws and regulations, it is virtually impossible for local agencies to administer public assistance and Medicaid to immigrants in a uniformly reasonable way.

The problem of unauthorized immigration, which has absorbed national attention for so many years, is indeed a weighty issue that is worthy of attention. But there are other national immigration issues that deserve rethinking and reform. The entitlements system is one of them. New York City performed a valuable service in challenging the Medicaid regulations that denied Medicaid to some classes of aliens despite the fact that the Medicaid statute made no exclusions based on alien status. It is unacceptable for federal agencies to limit alien entitlements through usurpation of congressional responsibility.

The city's involvement in the Medicaid suit is a good sign. New York has not been using its political muscle as the nation's premier immigrant city. The city belongs in the thick of immigration policy making. Its comfort with its immigrant population should not deter it from assuming the national role that it is both entitled and obligated to assume.

THE NEW IMMIGRATION LAW

The Immigration Reform and Control Act of 1986 was signed into law shortly before this book went to press. In the clamor and excitement of the early months, a few important principles stood out. It is to New York City's advantage for the amnesty program to work well for many. The city is best off when its residents can live as full members of the body politic, not as members of a frightened underground. From a strictly financial standpoint, the city is better off when it can claim reimbursement for services that it already provides.

A successful amnesty program is dependent upon the good will and cooperation of the INS, the city government, and many private and religious organizations that will have roles to play in advising, screening, and signing people on for legal U.S. residence. Openness and a willingness to work at it until it's right are essential from all the interested parties.

It is now the law of the land that employers cannot hire workers who lack the necessary authorization. The INS cannot enforce this law; no single agency could possibly enforce a law that affects so many. Voluntary employer compliance is required to make this law work. The law deserves to be followed, in part because it is the law, and in part because Americans need to know for sure if immigrants are hurting our economy or any members of our native workforce. If Americans follow the law, and the law hurts more than it helps, the law can be changed.

SUMMARY OF RECOMMENDATIONS

- New York City should assume leadership in immigration data gathering, policy formulation, and coordination of nationwide service and planning activities.
- The question of whether immigrants take jobs from or depress wages for the native-born, particularly native-born minorities, requires further study in New York and throughout the nation. So does the question of whether immigrants make disproportionate use of public services, and whether they cost more than they contribute to U.S. society. No rational U.S. immigration policy can be made in the absence of such information.
- The fact that some segments of the native minority population are less successful economically than the average immigrant should be addressed by strengthening native minorities rather than by weakening immigrants.
- The U.S. Census Bureau and the INS should improve the mechanisms by which they count immigrants arriving and living in the United States, and should make that information available to policy makers. The INS should design its data collection system to better serve the data needs of policy makers.
- New York City should cooperate in the data collection effort by analyzing the use that immigrants make of its public services, especially those provided by the HRA, Board of Education, HHC, DOH, Department of Mental Health, Mental Retardation and Alcoholism Services, and the criminal justice agencies. Data should be kept on clients' country of birth, among other demographic indicators. Client confidentiality can, and should, be protected in data gathering.
- Each city agency that serves large numbers of immigrants should establish an immigrant service planning function at the executive level. These functions should be coordinated by the Office of Immigrant Affairs.

- Coordination should be improved among all agencies, public and private, at all jurisdictional levels, to ensure that immigration policy and service are consistent and adequate, yet not duplicative. It is particularly important for New York City and the district office of the INS to establish a consistent working relationship.
- City agencies should work closely with the INS to ensure that lawbreaking aliens are subject to deportation procedures and that immigrant applicants do not obtain public benefits through the use of fraudulent documents.
- The city should coordinate and strengthen its language services to clients who are not proficient in English.
- The city should strengthen local ethnic associations by providing them with as much funding and technical assistance as possible.
- State and federal legislators should strive for a uniform set of definitions in immigration law and social service law in order to promote consistency and fairness within and between the two systems. Social service laws should be rewritten to eliminate the inconsistencies and inequities that exist from program to program.
- Governmental and nongovernmental agencies at all levels should work for a full and fair amnesty program as prescribed under the Simpson-Rodino Act.
- Employers should voluntarily comply with the hiring provisions of the law because it is the law. In so doing, they will be making a fair test of this question: do we or don't we want our immigrant workers as much as they want us?

20 Epilogue: A Paean to the Lady

The secret of U.S. immigration is that this nation has never had to welcome the world's "tired and poor." In the last hundred years, like the hundred years before it, the Lady of the Harbor has drawn new Americans who were anything but tired and poor—of spirit, if not of material possessions. The world's wealth continues to make its way to the vicinity of New York Harbor, though other ports of entry have come increasingly to claim their share of the world's living resources.

New York is a world-class city. Its great harbor, its rivers, its bracing climate, and its sturdy bedrock all have contributed to making it what it is, but the most important ingredient has been its various inhabitants. The throbbing intensity of city life is what draws people to it—visitors, new residents, investors. Everyone wants to be where the action is. And what action! Theater, opera, dance, publishing, high finance, small businesses, universities, restaurants, department stores, hairdressers, couturiers, jewelers—you name it, New York has it, and in an abundance and quality that are hard to find anywhere else in the world. The streets may not be paved with gold—not for everyone—but they lead nonetheless to unimagined opportunities. This is the place. And immigrants have made it what it is—constantly changing, constantly seeking the new way, sweaty and disheveled, cool and impeccable, scrambling for a buck, gambling for a million, willing to try anything once.

Glossary

Adjustment of Status: An INS procedure that permits aliens to obtain permanent resident status, without leaving the United States. To be distinguished from "change of status," which permits aliens to make any other alteration in visa classification, such as from visitor to student.

Afro-Caribbean: Pertaining to the cultures of the Caribbean that show a marked African influence.

Aid to Families with Dependent Children (AFDC): The nation's largest public assistance program, funded by the federal, state, and city governments. Serves children under 18 whose parents are dead, incapacitated, absent, or unemployed, and who meet financial need criteria.

Alien: A person present in the United States who is not a U.S. citizen.

Amnesty: In immigration terminology, a time-limited legalization program for undocumented aliens who have lived in the United States since 1981.

Asian: Pertaining to or coming from the nations of the Asian continent and Pacific islands, excluding the Soviet Union, Australia, and New Zealand.

Aspira Consent Decree: A 1974 out-of-court settlement in *Aspira* v. *Board of Education of the City of New York*, in which the board agreed to provide bilingual education programs for all Spanish-speaking or Spanish-surnamed public school pupils with English-language deficiencies.

Asylum: A status granted by the INS to aliens in this country who cannot return to their home country because of likely persecution based on race, religion, nationality, or social or political ties. Asylum differs from refugee status in that asylum applicants are already on U.S. soil.

Bilingual Education: A school program in which the major academic subjects are taught in a foreign-language speaker's native language until he or she is proficient in English. ESL is taught as well.

Caribbean: Pertaining to the islands of the Caribbean Sea and to those bordering countries, such as Panama and Guyana, that share a cultural heritage with the islands.

Change of Status: An INS procedure that permits an alien to change from one temporary visa classification to another.

Citizen: A person entitled to all rights conferred by U.S. law, based on birth in the United States or of U.S. citizen parents. Also, an immigrant who has been naturalized as a citizen.

Conditional Permanent Resident: An alien who has achieved legal permanent residence through marriage to a U.S. citizen or permanent resident alien. The condition can be removed in two years if the couple can demonstrate that the marriage was and is still legitimate. A definition created by the Marriage Fraud Amendments of 1986.

Country of First Asylum: The first country to which a refugee flees after leaving his or her native land, and from which he or she must apply for refugee status in the ultimate country of residence.

Deportation: A civil proceeding in which the immigration authorities evict an alien from the United States.

Eastern Hemisphere: In immigration law before 1977, the nations of Europe, Asia, Africa, and Australia.

Emigrant: A person who leaves his or her country of birth to reside in another country.

English as a Second Language (ESL): A form of instruction in which foreign-language speakers learn the English language in classes taught in English.

Entrant: An immigrant classification established by President Carter for about 139,000 Cubans and Haitians who made an unauthorized entry into the United States in 1980 in a massive boatlift to Florida.

Entry Without Inspection (EWI): The act of entering the United States without making one's presence known to immigration authorities; one form of illegal immigration.

Exclusion: An immigration procedure by which an alien is denied formal entry into the United States.

Family Reunification: The act of reuniting persons overseas with their close relatives in the United States; an express goal of current U.S. immigration policy.

Foreign-Born: Born outside the territorial United States of noncitizen parents. Not applicable to Puerto Ricans, since Puerto Rico is part of the territorial United States.

Foreign National: A citizen of a foreign country who is present in the United States. The term is often used to refer to foreigners who are visiting the United States and do not intend to become permanent residents.

Green Card: Unofficial name for the identification card of a permanent resident alien. The card used to be green but is now blue and white; nevertheless, the old name is still used.

Guest Worker: A foreign national who is granted permission by the INS to work in the United States for a fixed period in order to fill a specific need for temporary workers.

Hart-Celler Act of 1965: Common name for the 1965 amendments to the Immigration and Nationality Act. Hart-Celler replaced the national origins quota system with a 20,000 per-country limit for the nations of the Eastern Hemisphere and a 120,000 total limit for the Western Hemisphere. It elaborated the preference system from four to seven tiers, and assigned priority chiefly on the basis of family ties and secondarily on the basis of needed job skills.

Head Tax: In the 1800s a fee exacted from each entering immigrant, first by the states, then by the federal government, to defray admissions and processing costs.

Hispanic: Pertaining to persons born in Spanish- and Portuguese-speaking countries, or who claim descent from such persons, or who carry Spanish or Portuguese surnames. The term is used here as virtually equivalent to "Latin American."

Home Relief: A public assistance program funded jointly by state and city; available to single adults who meet the financial criteria and to other persons not eligible for SSI or AFDC.

Illegal Alien: See *Undocumented Alien*.

Immigrant: In INS terminology, an alien admitted to the United States as a potential or actual permanent resident; a person who has the right to become a citizen in time. Used colloquially and often in this book to refer to all aliens, legal or illegal, who are living in the United States for any extended period of time.

Immigration and Nationality Act: The current immigration law. Established by the McCarran-Walter Act of 1952, substantially amended by the Hart-Celler Act of 1965, and further modified by the Simpson-Rodino Act of 1986.

Immigration and Naturalization Service (INS): The federal agency that administers immigration law, located in New York City at 26 Federal Plaza, Manhattan. A section of the U.S. Department of Justice.

The Immigration Reform and Control Act of 1986: See *Simpson-Rodino Act*.

Job Displacement: The replacement of one group of workers by another. The phrase arises in the immigration context as a question of whether immigrants take jobs from native workers by their willingness to work for longer hours at lower pay.

Johnson-Reed Act of 1924: The first comprehensive legislative statement of U.S. immigration policy. It established quotas for every country outside the Western Hemisphere, limiting new immigrants to a percentage of each ancestry group already living in the United States. It set a total ceiling of 150,000 immigrants per year, and prohibited Asian immigration. Known officially as the Permanent National Origins Quota Act.

Labor Certification: A statement by the U.S. Department of Labor that the job skill possessed by an alien is needed in the United States. Required for anyone whose application to enter the United States is based on a job skill.

Latin American: Pertaining to or coming from the Hispanic nations of the Western Hemisphere, including those of North, Central, and South America, and of the Caribbean.

Lau Decision: A 1974 U.S. Supreme Court ruling, in the case of *Lau* v. *Nichols*, on behalf of Chinese children with limited English-language proficiency in San Francisco public schools. The Court ruled that the Board of Education must take steps to ensure adequate education for all Chinese speakers with English-language deficiencies.

Legal Alien: Any foreign citizen with a valid visa who is visiting, studying, working, or living in this country.

Legal Permanent Resident: See *Permanent Resident Alien*.

Marielitos: A term used for the 125,000 Cubans who sailed from the port of Mariel, Cuba, to the Florida Keys in a massive boatlift in 1980, after having been given permission by Castro to leave Cuba. See also *Entrant*.

McCarran-Walter Act of 1952: The first major change in U.S. immigration law since 1924, McCarran-Walter retained the national origins quota system but established a four-tier preference system within the quotas to assign individual visas on the basis of needed job skills or family ties. It repealed prohibition of Asian immigration, although the numbers of Asian immigrants stayed low because of the national origins quotas. Enacted at the height of the McCarthy era, the act included many anti-Communist screening and deportation procedures. Officially called the Immigration and Nationality Act, it is the cornerstone of today's law.

Medicaid: An entitlement program, funded by federal, state, and city governments, that pays medical expenses of the poor.

Migrant: A person who moves from one region of the United States to another. A Puerto Rican who moves from Puerto Rico to New York is a migrant, not an immigrant, since he or she is moving within the territorial United States. Foreign-born persons who settle in one part of the country and subsequently move to another are generally called "secondary migrants."

National Origins Quotas: The fixed numbers of immigrants from each nation that were permitted to enter the United States annually, as stipulated by U.S. immigration laws from 1921 to 1965. Each nation's quota was based on a percentage of that ancestry group already living in the United States. For example, since 42 percent of Americans were of British ancestry in the year selected as the base year, 42 percent of all visas were reserved for immigrants from Great Britain.

Native-Born: Born in the United States, regardless of parents' alienage.

Naturalization: The process of becoming a citizen. Applicant must be at least 18 years old, a lawful permanent resident with at least five years of continuous residence in the United States (three years for spouses of U.S. citizens), of "good moral character," able to read and write English, with an understanding of U.S. history and government.

New Immigrants: Traditionally the most recent arrivals; in this book, immigrants who arrived in this country after 1965, when the Hart-Celler Act became law.

Nonimmigrant: In INS terminology, an alien who is authorized to be in the United

States only temporarily and for a specific purpose. Nonimmigrants include visitors for business or pleasure, foreign government officials, students, and temporary workers.

Parolee: An alien who is allowed to enter the United States under emergency conditions, for a limited period of time. A parolee is required to leave the country when the conditions supporting his or her parole cease to exist.

Permanent National Origins Quota Act: See *Johnson-Reed Act*.

Permanent Resident Alien: A legal immigrant authorized to work and live in the United States, and eventually to apply for citizenship. A "green card" holder.

Preference System: A system introduced into immigration law in 1952 that set priorities on immigrant admissions based on job skills and family ties. Since 1965 there have been seven preference categories, four relating to relatives and two to employment. The seventh, unspecified, was not used between 1978 and 1987.

PRUCOL: Commonly used acronym for aliens "permanently residing in the United States under color of law" and therefore eligible for certain public benefits. Social service laws often fail to define which types of aliens are to be viewed as PRUCOL, thereby creating confusion and conflict over aliens' entitlements.

Quota: In current INS terminology, the number of permanent resident aliens from each nation who may be admitted to the United States each year. At present no country is permitted to send more than 20,000 immigrants.

Refugee: A person who flees his or her country and cannot return because of likely persecution based on race, religion, nationality, or social or political ties. Differs from an asylee in that the application for refugee status is made in a country of first asylum and not in the country of final destination.

Refugee/Entrant Assistant Program (REAP): A federally funded program administered by the New York State Department of Social Services that makes grants to local agencies serving refugees and entrants. The program goals are to facilitate adjustment to life in the United States and to promote employment.

Registry: A process by which an alien who has lived in the United States for many years can apply for legal permanent resident status. The Simpson-Rodino Act changes the registry cutoff date from June 30, 1948, to January 1, 1972.

Resettlement Services: Assistance provided to refugees and entrants in their first months of U.S. residence. The federal government provides funds to voluntary and private agencies that participate in the work of resettlement.

Service Providers: Public and private agencies funded by the New York State DSS to assist refugees and entrants in achieving self-sufficiency. Services include vocational training, ESL, and counseling.

Simpson-Mazzoli Bill: An immigration bill that died in the 1984 Congressional session. Its main features—a limited amnesty for undocumented aliens, and sanctions against employers for knowingly hiring undocumented aliens—became part of the Simpson-Rodino Act.

Simpson-Rodino Act of 1986: A set of amendments to the immigration law that attempts to limit illegal immigration by limiting job opportunities for undocumented aliens. It does so by making it illegal for employers to hire undocumented workers. As a humane counterbalance, it grants the opportunity for legal status to aliens who have lived in the United States in undocumented status since before January 1, 1982.

Sponsor: In social service law, a person or organization that assists an applicant for admission to the United States by signing an affidavit of financial support. Such an affidavit is sometimes required by immigration authorities if an applicant seems likely otherwise to become a public charge.

Supplemental Security Income (SSI) Program: A federally funded income maintenance program for the poor elderly and handicapped.

Targeted Assistance Program: A federally funded program administered by the New York City HRA to enhance the employability of refugees and entrants who are at risk of welfare dependency.

Temporary Resident Alien: An alien authorized to live and work in the United States for 18 months under the first stage of the amnesty program established by the Simpson-Rodino Act. Temporary legal residents must become permanent legal residents at the end of that time or lose their legal status.

Undocumented Alien: A foreign national who entered the United States without authorization, or who entered legally but remains beyond his or her visa expiration date.

Visa: A document signifying permission from the State Department to enter the United States.

Visa Overstayer: An alien who entered the country legally on a temporary visa but became illegal by staying beyond the visa's expiration date.

Visitor: A foreign national who is in the country temporarily on business or for pleasure.

Volag: See next entry.

Voluntary Agency (Volag): A nongovernmental agency funded by the Department of State to provide intensive resettlement assistance to refugees and entrants for their first 90 days in the United States. Volags receive a grant for each refugee or entrant resettled.

Wage Depression: In discussion of immigrant employment issues, the tendency for wages to fall when an influx of workers willing to work for low wages enters an industry or locality. Immigrants are sometimes charged with depressing the wages of native-born workers in the same industries.

Western Hemisphere: In immigration law before 1977, the nations of North and South America, including Central America and the Caribbean.

West Indian: Pertaining to the islands of the Caribbean Sea that were once called the British, French, and Dutch West Indies, whose populations are predominantly black and non-Hispanic. Not included are former Spanish possessions: Cuba, the Dominican Republic, and Puerto Rico.

Work Permit: An INS authorization for an alien to hold a job.

Acronyms

AFDC—Aid to Families with Dependent Children

DOH—Department of Health

DSS—Department of Social Services

ESL—English as a Second Language

GAO—U.S. General Accounting Office

HEW—U.S. Department of Health, Education and Welfare

HHC—Health and Hospitals Corporation

HHS—U.S. Department of Health and Human Services

HIAS—Hebrew Immigrant Aid Society

HRA—Human Resources Administration

ILGWU—International Ladies Garment Workers Union

INS—Immigration and Naturalization Service

IRC—International Rescue Committee

NYANA—New York Association for New Americans

OIA—Office of Immigrant Affairs

ORR—Office of Refugee Resettlement

PRUCOL—"permanently residing in the United States under color of law"

REAP—Refugee/Entrant Assistance Program

SMSA—Standard Metropolitan Statistical Area
SSI—Supplemental Security Income
USCC—U.S. Catholic Conference
Volag—voluntary agency

Bibliography

Abeles, Schwartz, Haeckel & Silverblatt, Inc. *The Chinatown Garment Industry Study: An Overview*. New York: Local 23–25, International Ladies Garmet Workers Union and the New York Skirt and Sportswear Association, 1983.

Baillargeon, Diane L. *Medicaid Data Report, 1983 Year-End Summary* and *July–December 1983*. New York: New York City Human Resources Administration, 1984.

Bayor, Ronald. *Neighbors in Conflict*. Baltimore: Johns Hopkins University Press, 1978.

''Castro's 'Crime Bomb' Inside U.S.'' *U.S. News and World Report*, January 16, 1984, p. 27.

Crewdson, John. *The Tarnished Door*. New York: Times Books, 1983.

Criminal Aliens: INS' Detention and Deportation Activities in the New York City Area (GAO/GGD–87–19BR). Washington, D.C.: U.S. General Accounting Office, December 1986.

Criminal Aliens: INS' Investigative Efforts in the New York City Area (GAO/GGD–86–58BR). Washington, D.C.: U.S. General Accounting Office, March 1986.

''Cuban Refugee Crime Troubles Police Across U.S.,'' *New York Times*, March 31, 1985, p. 30.

Curvin, Robert and Bruce Porter. *Blackout Looting*. New York: Gardner Press, 1979.

de Leon, Dennis and Rosemarie Maldonado, *Report of the Mayor's Commission on Hispanic Concerns*. New York: Mayor's Commission on Hispanic Concerns, December 10, 1986.

Editor and Publisher: International Yearbook 1986. New York: Editor and Publisher, 1986.

Ericksen, Eugene P., Andrea M. Vayda, and William S. Borden. *A Survey of Undocumented Aliens in Health and Hospital Corporation Facilities, New York City, 1983*. Princeton: Mathematica Policy Research, 1983.

Fallows, James. ''Immigration: How It's Affecting Us.'' *Atlantic Monthly*, November 1983, pp. 45–106.

Farber, M. A. ''Million Illegal Aliens in Metropolitan Area.'' *New York Times*, December 29, 1974, pp. 1, 28.

Fitzpatrick, Joseph P. *Puerto Rican Americans: The Meaning of Migration to the Mainland.* Englewood Cliffs, NJ: Prentice-Hall, 1971.

Freedman, Marcia. "The Labor Market for Immigrants in New York City." *New York Affairs* 7, no. 4 (1983): 94–111.

Gallo, Carmenza. *The Construction Industry in New York City: Immigrants and Black Entrepreneurs.* Working paper. New York: Conservation of Human Resources, Columbia University, 1983.

Glazer, Nathan, ed. *Clamor at the Gates.* San Francisco: Institute for Contemporary Studies, 1985.

Glazer, Nathan, and Daniel Patrick Moynihan. *Beyond the Melting Pot.* Cambridge, MA: MIT Press, 1963.

Griffin, John I. "America's Gateway—Immigration Through the Port of New York, 1821–1975." *New York City Perspective* (Graduate Division of Baruch College, City University of New York) 3, no. 2 (April, 1976), pp. 1–7.

Handlin, Oscar. *The Uprooted.* Boston: Atlantic-Little, Brown, 1973.

Harrington, Michael. *The New American Poverty.* New York: Holt, Rinehart and Winston, 1984.

Hendricks, Glenn. *The Dominican Diaspora.* New York: Teachers College Press, 1974.

Hispanic Presence: Challenge and Commitment. Washington, D.C.: United States Catholic Conference, 1984.

Hispanics in New York: Religious, Cultural and Social Experiences. 2 vols. New York: Office of Pastoral Research, Archdiocese of New York, 1982.

Immigrant Entitlements Made (Relatively) Simple: A Pamphlet for Agency Workers. New York: Office of Immigrant Affairs, New York City Department of City Planning, 1985.

"Inventory of Languages Spoken at Manhattan Mental Health Services." New York: Department of Mental Health, Mental Retardation and Alcoholism Services, December 1986.

Jenkins, Shirley, Mignon Sauber, and Eva Friedlander. *Ethnic Associations and Services to New Immigrants in New York City.* New York: Community Council of Greater New York, 1985.

Kebede, Hailu, *Immigrant Services in New York City: An Agency Directory.* New York: Department of City Planning, Office of Immigrant Affairs, 1986.

Kessner, Thomas, and Betty Boyd Caroli. *Today's Immigrants: Their Stories.* New York: Oxford University Press, 1981.

Kleiman, Dena. "A Surge of Immigrants Alters New York's Face." *New York Times,* September 27, 1982, pp. A–1, B–4.

Levine, Daniel B., Kenneth Hill, and Robert Warren, eds. *Immigration Statistics: A Story of Neglect.* Washington, D.C.: National Academy Press, 1985.

Making It on Their Own: From Refugee Sponsorship to Self-Sufficiency. New York: Church World Service, 1983.

Maldwyn, Allen Jones. *American Immigration.* Chicago: University of Chicago Press, 1960.

Marshall, F. Ray. *Illegal Immigration: The Problem, the Solutions.* Washington, D.C.: Federation for Immigration Reform, 1982.

Marshall, Paule. *Brown Girl, Brownstones.* Old Westbury, N.Y.: Feminist Press, 1981.

Message of the Mayor: The City of New York Executive Budget, Fiscal Year 1985. New York: New York City Office of Management and Budget, 1985.

Muller, Thomas. ''Economic Development: Dealing with Contraction.'' *New York Affairs* 5, no. 2 (1978), pp. 23–36.

———. *The Fourth Wave: California's Newest Immigrants, A Summary*. Washington, D.C.: Urban Institute Press, 1984.

Muller, Thomas, and Thomas J. Espenshade. *The Fourth Wave: California's Newest Immigrants*. Washington, D.C.: Urban Institute Press, 1985.

1986 IMS Directory of Publications. Fort Washington, PA: IMS Press, 1986.

1986 Media Encyclopedia: Working Press of the Nation. Chicago: National Research Bureau, 1985.

North, David. ''Impact of Legal, Illegal and Refugee Migrations on U.S. Social Service Programs.'' In Mary M. Kritz, ed., *U.S. Immigration and Refugee Policy: Global and Domestic Issues*. Lexington, MA: Lexington Books, 1983.

Passel, Jeffrey S. ''Immigration to the United States.'' Speech delivered at symposium ''The New Immigrants,'' Southwestern University, Georgetown, Texas, June 25, 1985.

Passel, Jeffrey S., and Karen A. Woodrow. ''Geographic Distribution of Undocumented Immigrants: Estimates of Undocumented Aliens Counted in the 1980 U.S. Census by State.'' *International Migration Review* 18, no. 3 (Fall 1984): 642–75.

Poblete, Renato, and Thomas F. O'Dea. ''Anomie and the Quest for Community: The Formation of Sects Among Puerto Ricans in New York.'' *American Catholic Sociological Review*, Spring 1960, pp. 18–36.

Ravitch, Diane. *The Great School Wars*. New York: Basic Books, 1974.

Rosenwaike, Ira. *Population History of New York City*. Syracuse, NY: Syracuse University Press, 1972.

Schuck, Peter H. ''The Transformation of Immigration Law.'' *Columbia Law Review* 84, no. 1 (January 1984): 1–90.

Segal, Aaron. ''The Half-Open Door.'' *The Wilson Quarterly* 7, no. 1 (1983): pp. 116–129.

Simon, Julian L. *How Do Immigrants Affect Us Economically?* Washington, D.C.: Center for Immigration Policy and Refugee Assistance, Georgetown University, 1983.

———. *Nine Myths About Immigration*. Washington, D.C.: The Heritage Foundation, 1984.

Sowell, Thomas. *Ethnic America*. New York: Basic Books, 1981.

Standard Periodical Directory 1985–1986. New York: Oxbridge Communications, 1985.

Statistical Yearbook of the Immigration and Naturalization Service, 1981. Washington, D.C.: U.S. Department of Justice, 1981.

Stern, Robert L. ''Evolution of Hispanic Ministry in the New York Archdiocese.'' In *Hispanics in New York: Religious, Cultural and Social Experiences*. New York: Office of Pastoral Research, Archdiocese of New York, 1982.

Task Force Report: Refugee Resettlement and Neighborhood Impact. New York: Brooklyn Community Board 14 and the Flatbush Development Corporation, 1983.

Tobier, Emanuel. ''Foreign Immigration.'' In Charles Brecher and Raymond Horton, eds., *Setting Municipal Priorities*. New York: New York University Press, 1983.

Tomasi, Silvano. *Piety and Power: The Role of the Italian Parishes in the New York Metropolitan Area, 1880–1930*. New York: Center for Migration Studies, 1975.

U.S. Immigration Policy and the National Interest: The Final Report and Recommendations. Washington, D.C.: Select Commission on Immigration and Refugee Policy, 1981.

Waldinger, Roger. "Immigrants and Enterprise in New York City." *Kaleidoscope: Current Research and Scholarly Activity at CCNY* 1, no. 2 (Fall 1984), pp. 12–22.

Weintraub, Sidney, and Gilberto Cardenas. *The Use of Public Services by Undocumented Aliens in Texas*. Austin: University of Texas Press, 1984.

Wynar, Lubomyr R., and Anna T. Wynar. *Encyclopedic Directory of Ethnic Newspapers and Periodicals in the United States*. Littleton, CO: Libraries Unlimited, 1976.

Index

About the Author

ELIZABETH BOGEN is director of the Office of Immigrant Affairs in the New York City Department of City Planning. The office was established in July 1984, in part as a result of the research that went into this book.

Miss Bogen holds an A.B. degree in English literature from Bryn Mawr College and an M.S.W. from the Hunter College School of Social Work. Before she joined City Planning in 1982 as a social service planner, she held jobs in journalism, manpower rehabilitation, and clinical social work. All her grandparents were immigrants.